RapaLa®

Legendary Fishing Lures

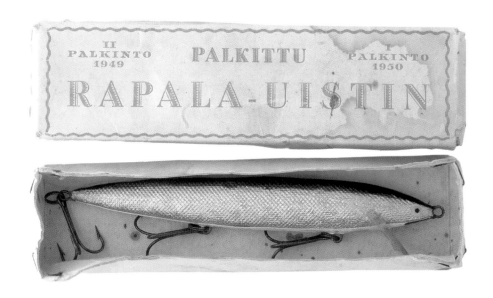

John E. Mitchell

Research by
Sirpa Glad-Staf

Dedication

This book is dedicated to the life and work of Lauri Rapala (1905–74), and to the members of the Rapala family who have worked or still continue to work in the Rapala group of companies.

It is also dedicated to the employees of the Rapala group of companies, the worldwide network of Rapala distributors, and the many hundreds of fishermen around the world who have, in their own way, contributed to the establishment of Rapala as the leading lure manufacturer in the world today.

Preface

The line vibrated in time with the movements of the crudely carved lure as the man slowly rowed his boat along the reedy margins of Lake Päijänne. He knew that the predatory fish stayed in the shelter of the weed beds, silently waiting for smaller fish to swim by. His lure was designed to imitate those smaller fish, especially the sick or injured ones that swam with a slightly slower or lopsided action, for the man had carefully watched the way that predatory fish selected their prey.

Suddenly, the line stopped vibrating, and tightened. The man stopped rowing. He carefully lifted the line in his fingers, and he could feel the weight of a fish on the end. The fish fought for its life, but the man was a skilful fisherman, and he carefully brought the fish to the side of the boat, and lifted it aboard. The man looked at the fish. It was a pike; not big, about 6 lb. (2.7kg). The lure was firmly hooked in its mouth. The man smiled and killed the fish with a quick blow to the head. Now he had dinner for his family.

However, the smile lingered for a few minutes more. He had been experimenting with different-shaped lures for many months, and now, at last, he had one that worked. The man was Lauri Rapala, and the year was 1936. Lauri's success that day would give birth to the largest and most respected lure-manufacturing company in the world.

This is the story of Rapala; a story that moves from poverty to wealth, from failure to success, and from just one man to a multinational corporation with over 3,000 employees. It is the story of the largest and most respected lure manufacturer in the world, and how the efforts of a poor fisherman to feed his family spawned the international group of companies that we know today.

First published in Great Britain in 2005
by Rapala VMC Corporation.
© Copyright 2005, Rapala VMC Corporation.

Acknowledgements
Every member of staff of each company within the Rapala VMC Corporation has played their part in formulating the history of the company.

The following people have supported and advised the author during the creation of this book.

Bob Bussey: Bob ensured that the complete Normark Corporation photo archive was available, and worked so hard to provide the best quality images.

Jerry Calengor: A former President of Normark Corporation, whose recollections of events in the USA during the 1980s and 1990s were so helpful.

Roger Cannon: An Englishman who joined Normark in 1972, and who has managed Normark Inc. Canada for almost 30 years. Roger's recollections of the early days with Normark and Rapala were a tremendous source of information.

Sirpa Glad-Staf: An employee of the company for over 30 years, Sirpa was a continuous source of information. Her close relationships with the Rapala family made the compilation of information an easy matter. This book could not have been written without her constant help, advice and support.

Jorma Kasslin: Joined Rapala in 1989 as vice-president, and is now the group's chief executive officer. A tremendous source of information regarding the development of the Rapala group through the 1990s and beyond.

Ari Lappalainen: Thanks go to Ari of The Finnish Fishing Museum Association, for his research into the fishing history of Lake Päijänne, and the professional fisheries of central Finland.

Raymond G. Ostrom: Co-founder of Normark Corporation in the USA. Ray was responsible for the marketing and publicity of Rapala lures, which resulted in their fame.

Ensio Rapala: Third son of Lauri and Elma. Ensio had the foresight to keep detailed records of the early days of the fledgling Rapala company. His records provided vital reference material.

Esko Rapala: Fourth son of Lauri and Elma. Esko's attention to detail has made the writing of this book a pleasure.

Jarmo Rapala: Grandson of Lauri and Elma, and former president of the Rapala group of companies. Jarmo's honest and factual recollections of the company's history during his time as CEO proved to be extremely enlightening.

Risto Rapala: Eldest living son of Lauri and Elma. Risto's earliest recollections have proved to be invaluable.

Ronald W. Weber: Co-founder of Normark Corporation in the USA. It was Ron who discovered Rapala lures and had the foresight to envisage their potential. Without him it is likely that there would be no story to tell.

ISBN 0-9550133-0-5

Project Manager: J. Parker, Kite Associates Oxford UK

Design: Ian Winter Design, Oxford UK

Copyediting: Ilios Publishing, Oxford UK (www.iliospublishing.com)

Printed in China through World Print Ltd.

Contents

Foreword

The story of the Rapala company, its people and its lures demonstrates the love that the company has for its products, and for the sport that it has served for almost 70 years. Rapala was founded by a fisherman, and now, as one of the largest international fishing tackle companies in the world, it continues to be controlled by people who love fishing.

Indeed, this book could not have been researched and written by anyone other than a long-serving employee of the company who has learned to love the Rapala products just as much as Lauri Rapala did in the late 1930s. The dedication to detail displayed by Ensio Rapala, who supplied much of the archive material, Jarmo Rapala, who checked and corrected much of the text, Sirpa Glad-Staf, who carried out much of the research, and John Mitchell, who had the unenviable job of collating the material into an entertaining and educational book, is uncannily similar to that of Lauri Rapala and his sons when they started their small lure-manufacturing business just after the Second World War.

We at Rapala are proud of our history. We are proud that for 70 years we have led the way in lure design, and have maintained the high standards of quality set by our founder so many years ago. Now, as we celebrate the centenary of the birth of Lauri Rapala, we look forward with confidence to the future, and promise that we will continue to maintain his high standards as we work to bring anglers around the world new lures that will deliver memorable fishing experiences every time.

Jorma Kasslin
Chief Executive Officer
Rapala VMC Corporation

CHAPTER 1

The birth of a legend

1905–33

It is not fair to describe Finland at the turn of the twentieth century as backward; underdeveloped is probably a more accurate term. The reasons for this state of affairs are documented in Finnish history.

According to archaeological and natural-history findings, the Finns migrated from south-east Europe sometime around 8,000 years BC, and joined the already established Lappish community that occupied present northern Finland. These migrant tribes lived on fishing, hunting and gathering along the coastal areas of the Yoldia Sea and the Ancylus Lake, formed after the Ice Age as the early phases of the present Baltic Sea.

During the twelfth century the Roman Catholic Church (in Sweden) and the Greek Orthodox Church (in what is now Russia) vied for supremacy in the region. Sweden was the dominant power, and eventually ruled Finland for some 600 years. However, in 1323 a treaty was signed that stopped further Swedish expansion and ceded eastern Karelia[1] to Russia.

In 1714, when Sweden was busy fighting in Europe during the Spanish War of Succession, Russia invaded and occupied all of Finland. The war between Sweden and Russia, which became known as the Great Northern War, continued until 1721 when Sweden ceded south-eastern Finland to Russia. The military struggle over Finland continued with the War of 1741–43, when the Swedish army was soundly defeated and yet more Finnish territory was ceded to Russia.

Towards the end of the eighteenth century the Swedish-controlled area of Finland experienced some industrialisation and development. There was talk of possible self-government, but the Napoleonic Wars put an end to that. In a bizarre twist of fate Czar Alexander I of Russia exercised the second term of a protocol signed with Napoleon in 1807, and seized complete control of Finland from Sweden. Whilst Finland was now controlled by Russia, it was not occupied in the accepted sense. Czar Alexander wished to protect his north-west border, and his policy was to work with the Finns. In fact Russia provided Finland with considerable support during its final separation from Sweden. Finland was declared a Grand Duchy with the freedom to rule itself, and enjoyed a guarantee that Russia would uphold the Finnish constitutional laws.

- **Finland at the turn of the 20th century**
- **Finding work on the farm land**
- **A time of unrest**
- **'Rapala' by mistake**
- **Traditional fishing in Finland**
- **The start of the Rapala dynasty**

---

[1] A region in eastern Finland adjoining part of Russia.

The status quo remained for almost 100 years until Czar Nicholas II came to power in Russia at the turn of the twentieth century. His policy was to bring Finland in line with Russia, and to end its independence. The changes in Finland were severe and led to feelings of animosity towards Russia.

In October 1905, as a direct result of the First Russian Revolution, the Finnish press carried reports of Czar Nicholas's manifesto, which promised the people of the Russian Empire political and cultural reforms. Shortly after, a general strike took place in Finland that lasted for just one week. As a result of the strike, the basis of Finnish government was transformed. Proposals for wide-ranging reforms were submitted to the Russian government in St Petersburg. In July 1906 Czar Nicholas accepted almost all the proposals. The most significant proposal was for every Finn over the age of 24 to have the right to vote. The elections of 1906 were based on proportional representation, and were the first in Europe to be totally open. However, Finland remained under the control of Russia.

It was into this unstable political and social environment that Lauri Rapala was born on 27 November 1905.

Lauri's early years (1905–17)

Lauri's birth can best be described as an accident. He was born out of wedlock to Maria Eerikintytär. The surname is typically Scandinavian in form, in this case meaning 'daughter of Erik'. Lauri was born on an island in Lake Päijänne, the largest lake in central Finland and part of the Sysmä Parish, in the village of Rapala. Local records show that Maria had two other children at that time; Hilma Maria, born in 1888, and Kalle August, born in 1898. Kalle subsequently died in 1910 aged 12 years. Lauri did not recall these two children living with his mother and himself, and their personal stories are not known. As far as can be ascertained, Lauri never met his father, but his son Esko recalls Lauri telling him that his father was called Kalle Sten. Records show that Kalle Sten moved to eastern Finland, and the fact that his mother had christened her elder son Kalle lends this story some credence. Additionally, Lauri's elder sister also bore a son whom she christened Kalle. Lauri was an active child, and though times were hard, and Maria had to take on any available work (usually as a maid or domestic help) to feed Lauri and herself, she managed to raise a healthy, strong boy.

As a result of the 1905 general strike, public-minded volunteers throughout Finland formed groups called the Järjestyskaarti, or Orderly Guard. These groups, formed in an effort to maintain public order, can best be described as vigilante groups. However, it was not long before left-wing activists bent on revolutionary reform infiltrated them. The two factions differed so greatly in their beliefs and desires that it took little time for the Järjestyskaarti in Helsinki to divide into the Suojeluskaarti (or Protection Guard) and Red Guard factions. Suojeluskaarti groups were formed throughout Finland in an effort to protect the new political order. Many believe that the formation of the regional Suojeluskaarti organisations also resulted in the formation of rival Red Guard groups throughout rural Finland, where the benefits of the new reforms were less apparent.

The Social Democrats became the accepted representatives of the labour movement in Finland and won almost half of the seats in the election of 1907 – but the Russian government was soon to restrain the powers of the Finnish government. Finland was now restricted to dealing only with minor internal matters, and was permitted only to submit suggestions about more important matters to the Russian government. In Finland this period is known as 'the Years of Oppression'.

By 1910 the Finnish Senate had been populated with members appointed by the Russian government. It had virtually no powers and was totally controlled by St Petersburg. Finland was no longer independent, and no longer a Grand Duchy of Russia. It was just another part of the Russian Empire.

In 1914 Maria and Lauri moved to Asikkala, where Maria obtained work as a maid and net mender to a metal craftsman called Simolin who lived in Särkijärvi village. In this period it was common for families to move around on an almost annual basis to find work in more wealthy houses or farms. They were provided with free accommodation and food from the farm, and were paid a small wage.

It was at this time that a record was made in the Sysmä Parish register. People who did not already have a family name were required to adopt one for the purposes of registration. The clergyman made a mistake when entering Lauri's particulars and wrote the name of the village where Lauri was born in the space allocated for his surname. Instead of being registered as Lauri Saarinen (the adopted family name) he was registered as Lauri Rapala. Little did that

An aerial view of Rapalanniemi, the place of Lauri's birth.
(Hannu Vallas)

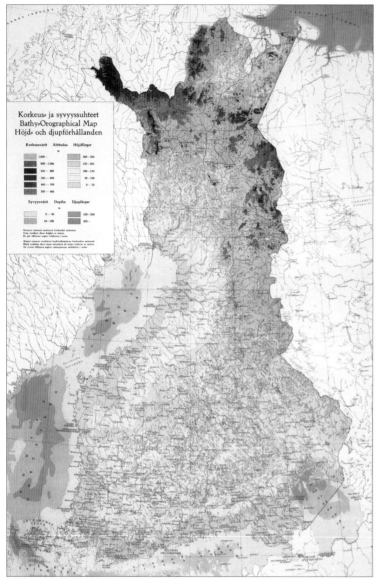

A map of Finland showing the international boundaries in 1928.
(Eero and Erkki Fredrikson)

clergyman know that he had single-handedly changed the course of fishing history forever, and had made an insignificant village in central Finland famous throughout the fishing world.

The outbreak of the First World War in 1914 resulted in many thousands of Russian soldiers being stationed in the south and west of Finland. The Russians believed that Germany would try to invade Russia through Finland. In Maria and Lauri's local town of Lahti there were about 8,000 Russian troops. The troops remained stationed throughout southern and central Finland until the start of the Russian Revolution.

In 1917 things were to change dramatically. The sailors of the Russian Baltic Fleet mutinied in March. The leaders of the mutinies quickly identified themselves with either extreme socialist or Bolshevik movements in Russia.

The Finns, never slow to take advantage of a situation, quickly secured a manifesto from the provisional Russian government to cancel the decrees that restricted Finnish self-rule, and to permit the Finnish government elected in 1916 to be formed. At the same time, the Finnish Senate that was controlled by Russian Prime Minister Stolypin's nominees was dissolved. However, Russian troops remained in Finland. Whilst the country had regained a measure of independence it was still occupied by Russian troops charged with stopping any German advance towards Russia through Finland.

The summer of 1917 witnessed unrest throughout Russia and Finland. In Finland, factories that had been busy manufacturing munitions and stores for the occupying Russian forces found themselves without orders. At the same time over 100,000 Finns who had been employed building Russian fortifications in Finland found themselves out of work. Outbreaks of violence erupted between unemployed Finns and Russian troops.

In June of 1917 Finland's Social Democratic Party drew up a resolution demanding full independence from Russia; this was presented to the government in St Petersburg the following month. The resolution did not meet with complete approval. Only the right to Finnish self-determination was agreed. However, the Social Democrats interpreted this as a signal to push for complete independence, and steered a bill through the Finnish parliament known as the 'Law of 18 July'. The Law granted the Finnish parliament all the powers previously retained by the Russian Emperor and the Russian Provisional Government.

The Riihelä family gathering the hay.
(Kalkkinen Area Village Association)

In July 1917 Lenin launched a failed coup attempt in St Petersburg. News of the coup's failure spread quickly throughout the Russian military depots in Finland. The already ill-disciplined troops became even more unruly. Lenin himself took sanctuary in Finland. The failure of the coup strengthened the hand of Alexander Kerensky, the Russian Minister for War. He was appointed Prime Minister of Russia and immediately repealed the 'Law of 18 July' and dissolved the Finnish parliament.

In October 1917 new elections to the Finnish parliament were arranged. The Russian Provisional Government was now under tremendous pressure, and was beginning to crumble. At the same time, the Soviets were increasing their hold over the Russian military. The Finnish non-socialists won a narrow victory. Then, at the end of October, Lenin's second uprising was successful, and the Russian Provisional Government fell.

A Finnish delegation was despatched to Petrograd (the new name for St Petersburg) to request independence for Finland from Lenin and the new Soviet government. Lenin immediately issued orders to withdraw over 60,000 Russian troops from Finland.

The rise of the Finnish Red Guards, who supported Lenin's theories of communism, caused deep concern to its rival organisation, the Suojeluskaarti. The latter also began a recruitment drive, and attempted to obtain arms and ammunition from whoever it could. Finland was on the brink of a civil war. Records show that serious fighting occurred between the Red Guards and the

*Ladies cutting flax whilst the
men prepare it.*
(Kalkkinen Area Village Association)

Suojeluskaarti in and around the village of Kalkkinen, which was very close to where Lauri and his mother lived. The Red Guards mounted armed patrols around the local villages in order to flush out their Suojeluskaarti enemies.

The period from 1905 to 1917, Lauri's childhood, was a time of continual change, political uncertainty and fermenting revolution. It is little wonder that the infrastructure of Finland suffered during those 12 years. The young boy was probably not aware of the political upheaval that seemed constantly to affect his homeland. The fact that Lauri and his mother lived in the countryside also insulated Lauri from the day-to-day problems of Finland, and he was too young to be affected by the perils of unemployment.

There was little formal schooling in Finnish rural areas during the early part of the twentieth century. The larger towns and villages had schools, but only children living within easy travelling distance were able to attend. It is possible that Lauri did receive a certain amount of formal education. Travelling teachers used to pay visits to the more remote villages and teach the children for a few weeks before moving on. The children would then have to wait several months for the teacher to return in order to continue their education. The church also arranged yearly parish meetings to teach both children and adults to read the bible; lessons were given in advance of the following year's meeting to improve reading skills. The priests were strict in their teaching and anyone failing to make good progress was disciplined with having to attend more lessons for the next meeting. Lauri attended these meetings from the age of 15.

Lauri was put to work as soon as he was old enough to contribute meaningfully to the upkeep and running of the Tommola farm where he lived in Särkijärvi. It is likely that he began work at the age of ten. Typical children's work included planting potatoes, caring for animals, picking fruit, and doing simple jobs around the house. Reading and writing were not considered essential; what mattered was that you could put in a full day's work on the farm.

An independent Finland

The Finnish Senate declared independence from Russia on 6 December 1917; however, formal recognition of independence was not forthcoming from Russia, nor any other European countries. Prime Minister P.E. Svinhufvud took another delegation to Petrograd and secured Lenin's recognition of independence, which would be effective from 31 December 1917. Britain and France were amongst the first countries to welcome Finnish independence when it was announced to the Finnish Senate on 7 January 1918. However, there was no move by Russia to withdraw its troops from Finland, and the Red Guard units were still creating tension in the south and south-east of the country. In mid January 1918 the Finnish parliament decided to form a national army with the aim of evicting Russian soldiers.

At this time one of the most famous men in Finnish history began to exert his influence – C.G.E. Mannerheim. Of Finno-Swedish extraction, he had served with distinction in the Russian cavalry, rising to the rank of lieutenant-general. However, due to his Finnish connections he was relieved of his command during the Revolution, and returned to Helsinki in December 1917. Mannerheim was asked to join a committee dedicated to the expulsion of the Russians. In mid January 1918 he took over the chairmanship of the committee, and almost immediately gained authority to form a national army initially based upon the Suojeluskaarti, which was soon to become known as the 'White Guard'.

On 26 January 1918 the Red Guards overthrew the Finnish senate in Helsinki. Some senators fled to Vaasa with Mannerheim; other senators together with Prime Minister Svinhufvud managed to reach Vaasa two months later, having escaped to Estonia and travelled through Germany. During this period, Mannerheim was able to use his powers of judgement to deal with the widespread civil disorder. There is no doubt that Mannerheim was a gifted tactician. The Russian soldiers who had threatened his headquarters at Vaasa were surrounded and disarmed, virtually without a shot being fired.

The fighting between the Red Guards and government troops was sporadic and widespread. Towards the end of February 1918 Red Guard troops attacked Sysmä, the village where Lauri Rapala's birth was registered. Government troops under the command of Major-General Löfström regained control of the town quite quickly, and continued driving south towards Lauri's nearest town of Lahti. However, they met stiff opposition from Red Guard forces at Heinola, a town situated a few kilometres east of Kalkkinen village, and having sustained heavy casualties they withdrew and formed a new 'front' just south of Mäntyharju between lakes Päijänne and Saimaa.

During the remainder of February and throughout March fighting was concentrated in the south of Finland and also in Karelia in south-eastern Finland. The government forces made small gains, but the major cities and towns were well defended by the Red Guards. Tampere was the first major city to fall to the government forces in early April. Helsinki followed in mid April when White Guard soldiers hiding in Helsinki attacked the remaining Red Guards from within the city.

Whilst Lauri and his mother were not directly involved in the war, they would have seen both Red Guard and government forces in the area of their home. The war was fought along roads and railway lines, the railways being of vital strategic importance because they were the only means of moving troops and equipment quickly from one area to another.

During the Karelian offensive Finnish troops surrounded a force of about 14,000 Red Guards at the southern end of Lake Päijänne close to the villages of Järvelä, Koski and the town of Lahti. Several days of heavy fighting followed as the Red Guards tried to break through the government force's cordon, but the majority had surrendered by the end of the first week of May. The Red Guards in south-western Finland were defeated by government troops at about the same time.

Mannerheim entered Helsinki on 16 May 1918 after just four months of fighting. He had both formed and led the Finnish government forces throughout the Finnish War of Independence. At last Finland was a free and independent country after hundreds of years of occupation. Pehr Svinhufvud, the former prime minister, was elected 'Regent'.

A logging crew on the Kalkkinen Canal.
(Kalkkinen Area Village Association)

Lauri's mother Maria Eerikintytär mending fishing nets.
(Rapala family archive)

The summer of 1918 was a hard one for the people of Finland. The country was on the verge of famine, and shipments of grain promised by both Britain and America had been delayed. The cause of this was Finland's apparent allegiance to Germany due to the great assistance afforded to the government troops by the German forces during the War of Independence.

Mannerheim was requested by the Finnish government to visit both Britain and France in an endeavour to secure recognition of Finland's independence, and to obtain the release of the grain shipments that were so vitally needed throughout Finland. His reception in both London and Paris in November was courteous, but both Britain and France had serious qualms about Finland's close association with Germany.

The end of the war on 11 November 1918 resulted in political changes in Finland. Prime Minister Juho Kusti Paasikivi resigned and Mannerheim was asked to replace Pehr Svinhufvud as Regent. A new coalition government was set up to deal with Finland's worsening financial and domestic crises. Mannerheim was now in a better position to deal with the British and the French governments, and he secured the release of grain shipments from Britain before leaving for Finland. He landed at Turku on 22 December 1918 as the new Regent.

The coalition government set about putting right the effects of the War of Independence. National and local industries, including the two major industries of forestry and farming, were re-established, and factories that had previously been concerned with the manufacture of armaments turned to the manufacture of machinery and machine parts to support Finland's growing industrial sector.

It was at last a time of peace for the Finnish people – and for Lauri Rapala and his mother too. They continued to work for farmers around Asikkala and the

Ladies cleaning fish.
(Lahti Regional Museum)

A Finnish boatman netting fish.
(Lahti Regional Museum)

neighbouring parish of Padasjoki for a considerable number of years. During the 1920s Lauri, in common with most Finnish men living in the 'Lake District' of Finland, had taken up fishing. He used traditional angling methods to fish for perch, roach and whitefish, or used a long-line or baits to catch pike or an occasional trout.

The history of fishing and its methods

Fishing was vital for the prehistoric people whose dwellings were located on the shores of the lakes and rivers of modern-day Finland. They extended their fishing trips to locations that gave the best catches in any given season. Slash-and-burn land occupation and long-ranging fishing and hunting trips were typical of the hunting and fishing era that extended to the Middle Ages. This way of life slowly spread permanent settlements into the areas of wilderness. Seasonal fishing in waters far away from home was typical of the population of the countryside during this period. As the settlements became permanent, fishing became vital for the livelihoods of the villages situated on the shores of lakes and rivers.

The seasonal nature of fishing in the Päijät-Häme region of Finland necessitated the preservation of the catches for consumption during periods when fishing was not possible or fish were seasonally scarce, and it continued thus until the end of the twentieth century. In prehistoric times, the drying of fish was the most important method of preservation, but at the end of the Middle Ages people began to salt the catches. Fish has always played a traditional part in food management, and its regular consumption has maintained its importance for rural households in particular.

Fishing became in part a profession in lakes Päijänne and Vesijärvi in the twentieth century when the catches began to bring money into the households. Prior to this, salmon and eel had had a commercial value, and vendace[2] and whitefish had been sold as salt fish in the markets of the larger towns and cities. The fish from lakes Vesijärvi and southern Päijänne were sold in Lahti, Heinola and Hämeenlinna from the end of the nineteenth century onwards. Overland and waterway transport routes made the trade in fresh fish possible.

Modern sport fishing began to flourish in Finland in the latter half of the nineteenth century. This was influenced by English river and stream fishing, as the earliest sport fishermen were travelling, upper-class English gentlemen. From the end of the nineteenth century, the rapids of Kalkkistenkoski in Asikkala were among the most famous sport fishing locations. The oldest fishing club in Finland and in the Nordic countries, Kalkkis Jakt och Fiskeklubben, has operated there since 1886.

---

[2] A freshwater whitefish, also found in Scotland and the English Lake District.

Ice fishing in Padasjoki.
(A. Th. Book)

Recreational fishing spread slowly to the wider populace, and also from the rivers and streams to the lakes and coastal regions. This development was probably caused by changes in society and increasing urbanisation. The pleasure of fishing had overtaken the need to do so.

The old, seasonal fishing methods concentrated on maximising the catch during the spawning and shoaling periods. Until the twentieth century, fishing was mainly divided into seasons of fishing in inshore waters and fishing in open waters, although the main methods of catching had been in use since prehistoric times. Archaeological finds in Finland have revealed the use of spears, hooks, different kinds of traps and fykes[3], nets and seines[4]. We know that hooks made of a combination of bone and wood were in use 5,000 years ago. Finland's first stone lures appeared in the Stone Age; the hook was attached to a stone lure honed in the shape of a fish. The oldest leaf-shaped lures were made of metal and were cast in a mould.

Fishing for salmonoids, white fish, eel and other species was carried out by building dams. Various kinds of traps and fyke nets were used in dam construction in fast water, and nets and seines were used in calm water. A crown fishery with dams and traps was built by the order of King Gustavus Vasa in the rapids of Vääksynkoski in Asikkala in the sixteenth century.

Seine-net fishing is still practised in the Päijät-Häme region of the country, as in other inland areas. Historically, it was practised by farmers as well as by professional fishermen. During the open-water season, seine netting for vendace and bream was most common on the large lakes, but the popular late autumn and early spring seine netting was also of importance until the

---

[3] A bag-net.
[4] A large fishing net with floats at the top and weights at the bottom, which hangs vertically in the water.

Lauri in army uniform in 1925.
(Rapala family archive)

nineteenth century. Seine nets were usually owned by several households, and knowledge of the best catching areas was based on local experience refined over the course of many years. At the beginning of the twentieth century, professional fishing on lakes Päijänne and Vesijärvi was carried out by seine netting and also by trap and hook, the last two especially popular among rural households of limited income.

Lauri in his twenties

Lauri was called up to do his military service on 11 September 1925, and he served in the Finnish army until 3 September 1926. He served as an infantry soldier and was stationed in the army barracks at Kouvola some 37 miles (60km) east of Lahti. When his service was over, he returned to live with his mother on the Tommola farm in Särkijärvi.

In 1927 a young lady came to work on the farm by the name of Elma Leppänen (1908–86). Elma was a little over two years younger than Lauri, and love blossomed between them. They were married on the Mattila farm on 29 September 1928, and moved to the Leppänen family home in the nearby village of Riihilahti.

The remains of Elma's family home.
(John Mitchell)

The only work available to the newlywed couple was for farmers and the more wealthy families, just like Lauri's mother had done. During the next few years they worked for a number of families on what was basically yearly contracts. Elma was a maid and Lauri was a farm worker, turning his hand to any jobs that needed to be done. Farm work took up most of his time in the summer, and any free time was taken up with fishing, which Lauri enjoyed. The fish he caught supplemented the usual diet of potato soup and pork stew. During the winter Lauri would be involved in forestry, felling trees, trimming branches and cutting firewood. Life was hard for both of them. Their accommodation was very basic, and their income so low that it was almost impossible to buy decent clothes to protect them from the harsh Finnish winters. The farmers paid them a minimal wage, plus farm produce in the form of food, firewood, and linen or wool to make clothes for themselves and their family. Elma was a skilled woman who could spin yarn and weave fabrics for sewing.

Elma Leppänen in a rowing boat on the Kalkkinen Rapids.
(Rapala family archive)

Although Lauri had received little or no formal education, Elma had attended the Riihilahti elementary school and was able to read and write well. Gradually she taught Lauri the basics of both, which would later prove to be so very important in their lives.

In 1929, whilst Lauri and Elma were still living in the Leppänen family home, their first son, Reino, was born. Reino would be the only one of Lauri and Elma's children who did not become involved in the Rapala lure business. Initially he did the same type of work as his father, but later entered the timber industry, floating logs on Lake Päijänne, and working on the tugs that towed the logs across the lake. In 1948 Reino began studying to become a technician, and moved to central Finland to work in machinery maintenance. During the early 1960s Reino spent some time working with his brothers in Riihilahti, but he did not feel comfortable in the business and returned to engineering. Reino died of a viral infection in January 1989 leaving his wife and three children Ari, Eeva and Arto.

In 1932 Lauri and Elma's second son, Risto, was born. Not long after this Lauri and his family left the Leppänen family home and moved to a cottage called Jeetteri in an area called Supittu, where they worked for another farmer for just one year. In 1933 they moved to the Murto farmhouse by the Kalkkinen Canal close to Riihilahti to work for yet another farmer. Moving from farm to farm to find work was common practice in Finland during the 1920s and 1930s. However, Lauri and Elma were getting tired of moving, and their lives were about to change.

Towards the end of 1933 Lauri and Elma made a significant decision. They decided that the way of life to which they had become accustomed was not for them. They did not want to spend the rest of their lives doing menial jobs for other people for a pitiful wage. They decided that the best course of action would be to find work for themselves, and live by their wits. Lauri had become a successful fisherman, and he could also turn his hand to farming and forestry

Elma Leppänen and her mother.
(Rapala family archive)

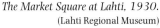

The Market Square at Lahti, 1930.
(Lahti Regional Museum)

Lyyranmäki cottage.
(Rapala family archive)

work. Elma had skills as well; she made brooms and brushes from plants such as crowberry and heather, and she made Christmas tree decorations from pine cones, which Lauri could sell on his fish stall in the nearby Lahti market.

Elma and Lauri moved back to Riihilahti. They rented a small wooden cottage on the Lyyranmäki (Hill of Lyyra) farm from Miina Lyyra. Miina was married to a neighbouring farmer, Santeri Tommola, for whom Lauri had occasionally worked over the years. The story goes that Miina Lyyra was an excellent masseuse, and that Santeri Tommola often used to visit her for a massage. Eventually Miina and Santeri married – from which point on Santeri presumably received his massages free of charge. Elma and Lauri could not afford to rent the whole cottage, and so they took just one room where the family lived, ate and slept. The other room was used by the farm for storage. It was in this cottage that Lauri, Elma and their growing family spent many years. They called their new home 'Kotikallio' – 'the bedrock of home'.

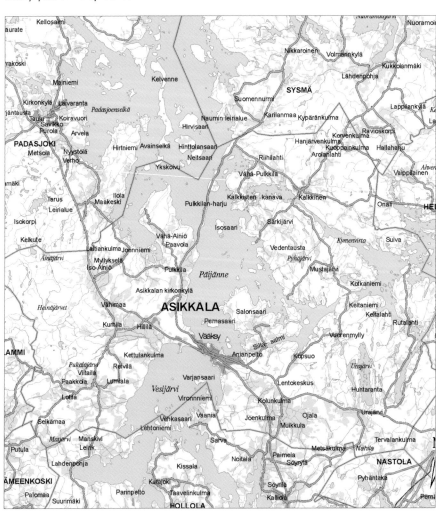

The Asikkala municipality area.
(Municipality of Asikkala)

Rapala lures

Their history, development, specifications and uses

If only lure fishing was as simple as casting a lure into the water and reeling it back again. In its simplest form, that is what lure fishing is about, but there is much more to lure fishing than mindlessly repetitive casting and retrieving.

Each lure in the Rapala range is designed for a specific purpose. There are floating and sinking lures that dive, there are others that have neutral buoyancy, and there are lures to be retrieved on the surface.

Each Rapala lure is ready to fish straight out of the box. It has been hand-tuned and tank-tested at the factory. It is the fisherman's skill that will get the lure to perform to the best of its ability.

In the *Lure profiles* at the end of each chapter, and the various appendices at the back of this book, we attempt to supply fishermen around the world with the necessary information to get the best from their Rapala lures. However, before moving on to the technical aspects of successful lure fishing, it is necessary to understand some of the basics.

Balance

In order to enjoy your day's fishing to the full, it is imperative that your tackle is properly balanced. The weight of the lure will generally dictate the diameter of the line and the power of the rod. A powerful rod fitted with high diameter line will not cast a light lure, like an Original 5cm. On the other hand don't expect a light, single-handed rod and small-diameter line to successfully handle a Countdown Magnum 22cm. Properly balanced tackle makes fishing a pleasure, and ensures that when a fish is hooked, the fisherman can play the fish to the bank or boat and enjoy the experience.

Local knowledge

Take your time to get to know a new water. Ask regular fishermen for information and visit the local tackle shops. Learn what fish are available. Do they move to different parts of the water at certain times of the year? Do other fish move into the water at different seasons? What species are the local bait-fish? The more information that you have, the more successful your fishing will become.

Be systematic

Search the water from the bottom to the top, and select lures for a good reason. Always think of what you are doing and what you want to try next. Always have a logical reason to make a change. Eliminate the guesswork and use logic instead. Look at the weather, the water colour and temperature, the wind direction and don't stay in one place too long if you are being unsuccessful.

Get in the fishing zone

The information in the pages at the end of each chapter will help you to select the lures suitable for your style of fishing. The important considerations are:

- Casting ability — Do you need to make long casts?
- Fishing depth — It's no good fishing above or below the fish.
- Action — Do the fish want a fast or slow action lure? Do they need to have the lure suspended in front of them?
- Lure size available — What is the size of the bait-fish in the water? What is the size of the predator that you are after?
- Lure colour — What is the colour of the bait-fish in the water? Is it necessary to use a brightly coloured lure in cloudy water or poor light conditions?
- The retrieve — Learn how each lure reacts to different styles of retrieve, then you can imitate bait-fish or stimulate a strike by antagonising a predator.

The delight of fishing, and of lure fishing in particular, is that regardless of how good a fisherman you become, you will never know it all. There is always something to learn, and the supplementary pages are packed full of information to help you.

If you do not find your particular Rapala lure mentioned in these pages, it will be due to the fact that the lure is no longer in production. The Risto Rap, Countdown Jointed and Fat Rap are amongst those lures recently removed from the product range. Their removal does not mean that they are unsuccessful, merely that production resources have been allocated to lures for which there is much greater demand. Tips and suggestions for similar lures can be adapted for use with unlisted lures with an equal chance of success.

The Original

The history of the Original

1936   The first Rapala lure is designed by Lauri Rapala. It is an 11cm floating model, and is developed over the years into the Original that we know today.

1938   The first original lures are commercially sold in Finland.

1945   Silver (S) and Gold (G) colours are made available.

1951   9cm model introduced.

1953   13cm model introduced.

1964   7cm model introduced.

1965   18cm model introduced. New Blue (B) colour launched.

1967   5cm model introduced.

1977   Perch (P) colour introduced.

1979   Rainbow Trout (RT) colour introduced.

1988   Minnow (MN) colour introduced.

1991   Trout (TR) colour introduced.

1992   Firetiger (FT) colour introduced.

1995   3cm model introduced.

1997   Clown (CLN) introduced.

1998   Red Clown (RCL) and Vampire (V) colours introduced.

1999   Redfin Shiner (RFSH) and Shiner (SH) colours introduced.

2000   Rapflash Holographic colours Blue Shad (HBSD) Emerald Shad (HESD) and Shad (HSD) introduced.

2001   Silver Minnow (SMN) and Fathead Minnow (FH) colours introduced.

2002   Fire Minnow (FMN) and Muddler (MD) colours introduced.

2003   New colours introduced:
         Golden Muddler (GMD)
         Bleeding Minnow (BLM)
         Redfin Spotted Minnow (RFSM)
         Silver Spotted Minnow (SSM)
         Blue Spotted Minnow (BSM).

2004   New colours introduced:
         Black Muddler (BMD)
         Brook Trout (BTR)
         Holographic Silver (HS)
         Purple Descent (PD).

Fishing the Original

Attach the Original floating lure with a Rapala knot. Cast or troll with a normal retrieve. A variation of this retrieve that is known to work is to run this lure just under the surface so that it bulges the water without breaking the surface. This necessitates a slow retrieve, and is most effective in the early morning or in the evening when the fish are in the shallows.

Remember, the further the lure is from the boat (up to a point approximately 50ft./15m to 100ft./30m maximum), the deeper the lure will run. Approximately 50ft. (15m) of mono will keep the lure running between 1–4ft. (0.3–1.3m).

Fishing the depths can be easily varied by the addition of weights, starting with a small BB-sized split shot, and working your way up to heavier weights to achieve your desired depth. Don't use too much weight, and place it at approximately 20in. (50cm) from the lure, in order not to impair the swimming action.

The bottom-walking technique is carried out with a three-way swivel rig and a suitable bell sinker or other suitable weight for fishing close to the bottom.

Tips from the pros

• The effects of wind crashing in on a spot linger even after the wind dies down. If a sustained wind blows in on a spot for a day or more, spend some time fishing that same area even on the day after the wind switches or lies down. Often the fish will remain in the area, and remain active.

• Here's a tip for catching fish on crank baits after a cold front: wait until afternoon, when the sun begins to warm the water. Move in shallow, and make casts with smaller lures such as the Original Rapala. Try twitching them slowly, jerking them three or four times and pausing or simply retrieving them steadily.

• Minnow baits like the Original Rapala can be fished super slow behind bottom bouncers through schools of fish you see on a depth finder. Rig up bottom bouncers for the anglers in your boat, choosing weights of about one ounce (28g) per 10ft. (3m) of depth. Run Original Rapalas on leads of 2–3ft. (30–60cm), and work through the fish very slowly. Try trolling them steadily, and see if the fish strike them. If not, try pumping your rod forward to make the bait rush ahead (don't overdo it), then stall out and let it pause in the water. Sometimes, this presentation does the trick when a steady presentation gets ignored. These baits look and 'feel' to the fish just like minnows.

• On major river systems, here's a crank bait trolling trick that can really catch a lot of fish: get out in the main channel, along what would seem to be a 'flat' stretch of uniform bottom. The constant current creates a series of small ridges on the riverbed. Many fish will hold on the down current, slack-water side of the ridges. Slow-troll an Original Rapala, weighted down to reach the bottom, and you can catch a variety of species of fish.

The Original

Code: F   Freshwater – Floating

Main features:

- The first Rapala lure (designed in 1936)
- Unweighted balsawood body
- Suitable for all kinds of predators
- The most popular Rapala lure ever
- Lifelike wounded minnow action
- Works well in lakes and rivers

Fishing tips:

- Floats when stationary, then dives when retrieved and swims near the surface
- Change the retrieve speed and move the rod tip to impart action
- Use additional weight for longer casting or trolling in deeper waters

Target predators:

Asp, perch, chub, trout, black bass, salmon, sea trout, zander (walleye), pike

Technical features:

Code	Body length	Weight	Treble hooks	Swimming depth
F-03	3cm / 1 1/4in.	2g / 1/16 oz.	Two No. 12	0.6–1.2m / 2–4ft.
F-05	5cm / 2in.	3g / 1/16 oz.	Two No. 10	0.9–1.5m / 3–5ft.
F-07	7cm / 2 3/4in.	4g / 1/8 oz.	Two No. 7	0.9–1.5m / 3–5ft.
F-09	9cm / 3 1/2in.	5g / 3/16 oz.	Two No. 7	0.9–1.5m / 3–5ft.
F-11	11cm / 4 3/8in.	6g / 3/16 oz.	Three No. 6	1.2–1.8m / 4–6ft.
F-13	13cm / 5 1/4in.	7g / 1/4 oz.	Three No. 5	1.2–1.8m / 4–6ft.
F-18	18cm / 7in.	21g / 11/16 oz.	Three No. 1	1.8–3.3m / 6–11ft.

CELEBRITY BITES

Larry Dahlberg on discovering Rapala

I met my first Rapala in Burnett Larsen's Hardware store in Grantsburg, Wisconsin. It was in the early sixties and I had just entered my teens. When I was 11, I'd landed a job as a fly-fishing guide on a local river where I got a daily wage of $14. So for a kid, I used up a lot of tackle and haunted the tiny tackle section of Burnett Larsen's Hardware on a weekly basis. The way I looked at it, a carpenter needs a hammer, saw and nails, a mechanic needs wrenches, screw drivers, nuts and bolts, and a fishing guide needs reel, rod and lures. Lots of lures.

I happened to be there the day the first Rapalas arrived. It was love at first sight. Instead of a plastic lure with a metal lip, crude hook hangers and a cartoon-like finish, this new lure actually looked like a real minnow. The workmanship and appearance made all the others look clumsy and childish.

I took the silver one from the box to examine it. It had the most realistic finish and the sharpest hooks I'd ever seen. I was suspicious of the plastic lip, and it felt so light. Would it run straight? Would I be able to cast it? This baby was oozing big fish and I had to have one. I'd troll it or add lead if I couldn't cast it. I bought it before Burnett even had a chance to put his price sticker on the box.

On the opening day of the season, my father and I spent an hour anchored at the mouth of a creek casting the old favourite lures in all the right places and catching nothing. I'd already located most of the snags and it felt pretty safe to tie on my new Rapala. I gave it a hard cast with my Mitchell 300, but it only traveled about 20ft. On the retrieve it only went a foot or so below the water, but when I pulled it beside the boat in the current it had a unique, nice, soft wiggle and flash.

I made lots of lures myself from scratch and was pretty good at tuning them, so I picked my new lure out of the water and toyed with the nose to see what effect I could have. Moving the knot up a touch made it roll out of control. Sliding the knot a little lower produced the sexiest wiggle I'd ever seen, with only a whisper of current against it.

After adding a shot and sinker 18in. ahead of the lure, I launched it spinning and twirling through the air. It landed slightly up inside the creek and close to the lower bank. After feeling the sinker hit bottom, I lifted the rod tip and walked the sinker without reeling so the lure swung out from the creek along the current seam and fell off the sandbar into the main river. As the lure swung and turned I felt a distinct tap. A small, but perfect walleye went on the stringer. Ten more casts in exactly the same place produced ten more fish exactly the same size. My dad was amazed. With his baitcasting reel, nylon line and traditional lures casting in exactly the same place, he had not caught a thing.

To cap it off, on the 'just one more cast' part of the trip, I hooked a fish that bolted for the middle of the river and peeled off so much line we had to pull anchor and follow it. We were sure it was a big musky and would bite through the mono any second. After about 20 minutes of coaxing, the largest walleye I had ever seen came to the surface. It was a 34in.-long monster with both of those needle-sharp trebles hooked in its dorsal fin! I'm not sure if it was trying to eat the lure or mate with it, but we ate it along with the others.

Since that day, I've had the opportunity to fish all over the world specifically looking for really big fish. I've carried Rapala lures with me everywhere and can honestly say a great deal of my success has been due to the fact I've taken them along. Without question Rapala makes the most consistently effective and most versatile lures that have ever been made. Period.

When you're travelling with Rapalas, the fish bite when you get there!

CHAPTER 2

Necessity – the mother of invention

1934–45

It is probably true to say that Lauri Rapala was not the hardest-working man you might have met in Finland in the 1930s. He enjoyed his fishing and he enjoyed the company of his friends. When not engaged in forestry or farming Lauri would take himself off in his rowing boat and search for fish. Sometimes he would stay with friends overnight, and continue fishing the next day, but he would always bring some fish home for his family or to sell at Lahti market.

Lauri used two methods to catch his prey: nets, and long-lines with up to a thousand hooks on each. Both the nets and long-lines were made of cotton treated with tar, in order to prevent them rotting. The nets were usually staked out overnight around weed beds or across stream mouths, and were then retrieved in the morning. Nothing went to waste. Good fish went to the market, the poorer fish were used to feed the family, and the worst were used as bait for the long-lines. The latter would be baited with whatever was available, including worms, portions of fish or live fish. With no motor on his boat, Lauri would row 30km (20 miles) each day weather permitting to set his long-lines and retrieve the ones laid earlier. If Lauri's fishing trips were successful he would catch the bus to Lahti, and sell his fish at the market.

Elma also had her part to play in Lauri's fishing expeditions. About 3km (2 miles) from their cottage was a small forest lake where small crucian carp[5] thrived. Lauri would make fish traps and bait them with flour paste, then lower them carefully into the lake. Three times a day Elma would check the traps and collect all the crucian carp in a bucket and carry them to a small pond near the cottage where Lauri had constructed a large keep-net. Elma would transfer the crucian carp to the keep-net ready for Lauri to use on his long-lines during his next fishing trip. Live crucian carp were without doubt the best bait, but collecting them was hard work.

Elma also wove rag rugs for Miina Lyyra, their landlady, in order to help pay the rent on the cottage. The completed rugs were kept in the storeroom of the cottage, the part that Lauri and Elma did not rent. Risto Rapala recounts the story that the roof of the cottage sprung a leak, and the rugs so lovingly woven by his mother became wet and gradually rotted away. It has never been clear if Miina Lyyra planned to use or sell the woven rugs, or whether she was happy to accept the rugs as part payment of the rent so that Elma would have a clear

- **The first Rapala lure**
- **Signs of a small business**
- **Unrest in Europe**
- **The Second World War**
- **The Rapala children are born**
- **Peace in 1945**

---

[5] *Carassius carassius*, a European cyprinid with an olive-green or reddish-brown back, paler sides, and bright reddish-bronze fins.

Ensio Rapala at the site of the original Lyyranmäki cottage.
(John Mitchell)

conscience about the rent being paid. Whatever the truth may be, Miina Lyyra was obviously a very understanding lady, and both Lauri and Elma no doubt owed her a debt of gratitude. In addition to keeping the family home, Elma found work in the fields of the local farms, and would also assist in milking cows or shearing sheep. In fact she would willingly take on any job that she was physically able to do.

Lauri and Elma's third son, Ensio, was born in the cottage in 1934. Lauri had to borrow a horse to ride to the local village to fetch the midwife to attend the birth. The translation of Ensio is 'the First' meaning the first son born in Lauri and Elma's new home. Ensio was a 'blue baby' and was very weak. He suffered from a congenital disease that reduced the flow of oxygen-rich blood to the lungs, and which gave his skin a blue tint. A neighbour's wife predicted, 'That child will not hear many cuckoos,' intimating that Ensio would not live for long. However, she would be proved wrong.

Sport fishing – and an idea is born

While Lauri was fishing in what can be described as a commercial way, sport fishing in Finland was already established. Records show that a company owned by Herman Renfors was producing spinners as early as 1871. There are also records of Heddon lures being imported from the USA in small numbers during the 1930s. Jim Heddon founded his lure company in Michigan USA in 1898, seven years before Lauri was born.

Lauri's wife Elma had two male cousins, Uuno and Urpo Laaksonen, who lived in Helsinki. Both young men enjoyed fishing, and would occasionally visit Lauri, Elma and their family. The cousins were sport anglers rather than commercial fishermen, and they certainly enjoyed fishing with lures. They would join Lauri on his trips, and their favourite methods of fishing used spinners, spoons or wobblers[6].

At some point during a fishing trip with Uuno and Urpo, Lauri's attention might have been drawn to one of their American wobblers. Perhaps Uuno and Urpo told him that it worked, but that it was far from perfect. It is possible that Lauri studied the lure and asked the cousins some questions about it, and perhaps asked them how easy it was to get hold of these new lures. We cannot be sure that events happened this way, but in later years Lauri told his son Ensio that an American lure, best described as 'a well-worn fish imitation' came into his possession and started him thinking about carving his own lures.

---

[6] Spinner: a bait that revolves when pulled through the water.
 Spoon: an artificial bait in the shape of the bowl of a spoon.
 Wobbler: a lure that wobbles and does not spin.

We can, however, be certain that a simple sport-fishing lure had captured Lauri's attention, and given him an idea. Using his years of experience and his knowledge of how fish behaved, he would improve its design – and would make a better living for himself and his family in the process. Lauri's new lure, he hoped, would be more productive than his traditional live bait, long-lining and netting techniques. The story of Rapala lures had begun.

Lauri had a couple of friends with whom he discussed the wobbler. One of these was the hermit Toivo Pylväläinen who lived on Koreakoivu (Beautiful Birch) Island in the middle of Lake Päijänne. Toivo was to become an influential friend of Lauri's over the years. The other friend was Akseli Soramäki, who lived on the island of Virmaila. Lauri would stay with these two when out on his fishing expeditions, and they would talk long into the night whilst carving and whittling new shapes for lures from locally available materials, such as cork and pine bark, experimenting with various shapes in the quest for the perfect specimen.

However, it was not until 1936 that Lauri managed to carve a rough-looking lure that produced an off-centre and enticing wobbling action. The story of Lauri's hunt for the correct action is well documented. He studied the habits of pike in the clear waters of Lake Päijänne, and noted that they would take a slower or off-balance bait-fish in preference to apparently more healthy fish. The lures carved by hand by Lauri and his friends were unlikely to travel in a perfectly straight line anyway, as they were all slightly off-centred, and the person carving the lure would incorporate his own ideas into the basic pattern.

The first successful Rapala lure.
(Rapala company archive)

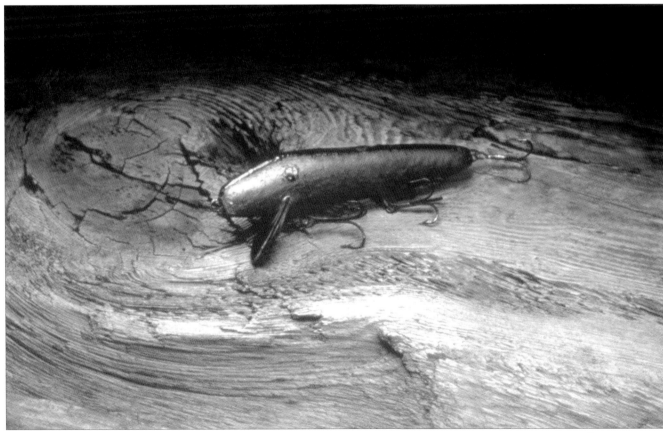

Lauri's first successful lure was made of cork, and thus was extremely buoyant. Its buoyancy necessitated the use of an oversized swimming lip to get the lure to dive. The lure was sealed with a varnish containing flecks of gold-coloured metal. A number of coats were applied in order to seal the cork and achieve a reflective gold finish. The lure was painted black along the top. The first Rapala lure had been born.

The family grows

Lauri and Elma's fourth son, Esko, was born in the cottage in 1937. The traditional Finnish saying 'to be born with a golden spoon in one's mouth' was certainly not apparent at the time of Esko's birth; times continued to be hard for the Rapala family. However, Esko was the first son to be born into the infant Rapala dynasty. It was a busy time for Elma; although she had four young sons to look after, she still helped Lauri catch and transport live bait for his long-lines. Lauri continued to work on farms and in forestry during the day, and fish in his spare time.

Lauri and Elma obtained work wherever they could, while the growing boys were left to entertain themselves playing in the farmyard or in the nearby forests. In addition to the farm produce they received, Elma had a small kitchen garden near the cottage where she grew both vegetables and currant bushes. Each spring Lauri and Elma would obtain a piglet as part of their pay from a local farmer. They raised the pig through the summer and autumn, then slaughtered it in early November. The meat was salted down to preserve it, and it was eaten at Christmas and throughout the winter months. Each autumn the whole Rapala family would go into the forests in search of blueberries, wild raspberries, lingonberries and cranberries, some of which were preserved for later use. When each boy reached the age of seven he started to attend the local school at Riihilahti, which was some two miles (three kilometres) from the house. They went to school until they reached the age of 14.

As part-payment for her work, Elma would sometimes accept wool and flax. She would clean the wool and spin it. The wool was rarely dyed, therefore knitted clothes tended to be white, grey or black. She would process the flax and weave material that she then used to make clothes such as shirts and trousers. Material for more formal clothes was given to a local professional tailor who would make better quality outfits for the family when they could afford it. Footwear was always a problem. Many children at this time did not have proper shoes. In the summer the boys were

Riihilahti School today.
(John Mitchell)

28

happy to run around in bare feet, but for the winter they had felt boots made by a travelling shoemaker, or cloth boots made by their mother Elma.

A man in demand

News of Lauri's lures had spread amongst the fishermen of Lake Päijänne, and he continually received requests to make samples for other people. Lauri and his friends Toivo Pylväläinen and Akseli Soramäki all became involved in making lures based on Lauri's design with subtle alterations and modifications. As an increasing number of people got to hear about the 'Rapala' lure, and eventually got their hands on one, more and more examples were produced around the shores and on the islands of Lake Päijänne. In fact the area around the southern shores of the lake became the centre for lure production in Finland; to this day Rapala and Finlandia-Uistin (the makers of the famous Nils Master lures) still have their factories in the area where it all started. Coincidentally, Finlandia-Uistin have their offices in the old Riihilahti school that the Rapala children attended.

Lauri's first commercial breakthrough came in 1938 when the local co-operative store in Kalkkinen village, which is still standing today, purchased a small number of lures to sell to its fishing customers. It was a modest start, and unfortunately it was to be short-lived. The shadows of war were looming over Europe.

Lauri dearly wanted to produce a lure with a reflective silver finish. Until now his lures had been gold, but the majority of bait-fish in the lake were silver. Fortunately, inspiration was near at hand. Elma's cousins worked in a printing house in Helsinki. They suggested to Lauri that he might try the silver foil that was used in the printing industry, and they arranged to provide Lauri with some sample material.

The silver foil was very thin and flexible. Lauri found that he could easily cut it to shape and glue it to the sides of his lures. However, he had no way of sealing the lure; the water would quickly dissolve the glue, and the silver foil would fall off. By coincidence, whilst Lauri was fishing on Lake Päijänne he met a professional photographer called Linnala who was himself a keen fisherman. Lauri showed Mr Linnala his lures; firstly his gold ones, then his prototype silver models. Lauri explained his waterproofing problem to Mr Linnala who suggested that he might be able to supply Lauri with used film negative material. He explained to Lauri that he would

The Kalkkinen village store in the 1930s.
(Kalkkinen Area Village Association)

The interior of the Kalkkinen village store.
(Kalkkinen Area Village Association)

have to dissolve the negatives in acetone to make them soft, and then he would be able to mould the softened material around his lure to seal it. True to his word, Mr Linnala supplied some negatives to Lauri. Acetone was obtained, and a series of experiments followed to ascertain the best method of sealing the lures. Eventually it was found that the softened negatives could be cut to shape and applied to the lure body. The negatives were then cut to an exact fit, and acetone applied to seal the joints. Lauri's problem had been solved.

Lauri continued to work and fish throughout 1938 and 1939, but he already had plans to develop his lure business into something bigger to help support his family. In fact, his second son Risto remembers a fishing trip sometime in 1939 where he accompanied his father and his mother's two cousins Uuno and Urpo Laaksonen on Lake Päijänne. They fished with their own lures and spent the night with Toivo Pylväläinen on Koreakoivu Island. Risto recalls that Elma's cousins were to be involved in lure production as they both had technical and production skills that Lauri lacked. However, the events of 1939 would swiftly put an end to those plans, and have dire consequences for Lauri and his family.

The outbreak of war

In 1939 Germany invaded Austria, Czechoslovakia and Poland, and the Second World War begain. The Russians felt vulnerable. One of their longest land borders was with Finland, and the Gulf of Finland gave naval access to important cities such as Leningrad (St Petersburg), Novgorod and ultimately Moscow. During the preceding year the Soviet Union had continually tried to negotiate various treaties with Finland that would protect the Finno-Soviet border against attack from the Finnish mainland. Finland had consistently declared its neutrality and confirmed that it would defend its land from all attackers regardless of their nationality.

In early October 1939, sensitive to the tense European political situation, Finland had mobilised over 21,000 soldiers to its eastern frontier with what was formerly Russia, and to its southern coast. Soon Finland mobilised virtually all its armed forces, and Lauri Rapala received his call-up papers informing him to report for army duty with Infantry Regiment 33 on 13 October. In fact all the eligible men from the Kalkkinen and Asikkala areas were called up to join the same regiment. In total some 60 men were called up at this time. By the end of October almost 300,000 men had been mobilised to emergency deployment positions.

Despite Finland's declared neutrality, on 30 November 1939 the Soviet Union invaded Finland after falsely claiming that Finnish troops had bombarded the village of Mainila killing four Soviet soldiers. The 'Winter War' had begun.

The Soviet Union invaded Finland on two primary fronts, the most important being through Karelia in south-eastern Finland, with the second north of Lake Ladoga. Lauri's Infantry Regiment 33 was stationed in the area north of Lake Ladoga where they played a key part in the heavy fighting. In Karelia the Finnish Army held firm despite concerted attacks on both the east and west sides of the isthmus. The Soviets lost a surprising number of tanks, and the Finns even launched a counter-attack, but were driven back. At the end of December 1939 the fighting in Karelia had reached a stalemate.

In the north the Finnish Army enjoyed greater success. The Finns were good skiers and were able to move quickly and silently through the deep snow of the northern forests. Their tactics can almost be described as guerrilla ones, isolating and dealing with smaller Soviet units whilst keeping the major units penned in and unable to help. During the Winter War thousands of professional Soviet soldiers were either killed or rendered totally ineffective by a fraction of their number of Finns.

Lauri and all the men from Kalkkinen and Asikkala were transferred to Infantry Regiment 6 on 1 January 1940 and saw active service in and around Salmenkaitajoki in Karelia, Finland's south-eastern border with The Soviet Union.

Air operations during the Winter War gained much publicity. The Soviet Union adopted a policy of widespread indiscriminate bombing of civilian targets in an effort to panic the Finnish population. Although a high number of civilians were killed or injured, panic was not widespread. Helsinki was bombed on 30 November, as was Lauri's home town of Lahti. During the Winter War almost 4,000 bombs were dropped on Lahti. The town was an important strategic target due to its major railway connections to the eastern front, the establishment of the Finnish National Radio Station, its large number of machinery and heavy industrial factories, and the Lahti Army Garrison, which had large barracks in the town. The heaviest of the bombing took place on 27

December 1939, during which over 500 homes were destroyed. Families living in major towns and cities that suffered air raids took the decision to send the mothers and children to safety in the countryside. Some families even sent their children to Sweden where Swedish families undertook to look after them.

During early 1940 Finnish Prime Minister Risto Ryti authorised approaches to be made to the Soviet Union via Sweden, the United Kingdom and France to discuss a possible peace treaty. Moscow's terms were severe, but the Finnish Army was in a desperate situation especially in Karelia, and there was no alternative but to accept the Soviet conditions. Hostilities ceased on 13 March. Finland lost 35,000km² (22,000 square miles) of national territory including all of Karelia for which they had fought so hard. In fact the Soviet Union gained all the land it had previously tried to negotiate treaties for prior to its invasion of Finland, plus other significant areas. The Winter War was over.

Had Finland continued to fight there is no doubt that it would have been overwhelmed and occupied, remaining under Communist domination. It did however preserve its independence, and proved to the world that it would not bow to threats or flinch from war.

Lauri's army record shows that on 13 February 1940 he broke his left ankle whilst running to an air-raid shelter. He was treated in a military hospital, and remained there until the end of May 1940. His record goes on to show that he was discharged from the army on 31 May 1940.

For the Rapala family, the good news of 1940 was the birth of Lauri and Elma's fifth son, Kauko, on 12 May. However, on 31 July 1940 Lauri's mother Maria died. Maria had suffered from rheumatism for many years, and had spent her last years in an old people's home close to the church at Asikkala. She was buried in the churchyard there, and only Lauri attended the funeral. Parish records do not register the actual site of Maria's grave, however, they do contain one surprise. At some time between the date of Lauri's registration in 1914 when he was wrongly given the family name Rapala, and the date of Maria's death, she had adopted the Rapala name. The details of her death are therefore recorded under the name of Maria Rapala.

Peace, but not for long

At the end of the Winter War more than 10 per cent of Finnish territory had been ceded to the Soviet Union. Finland had lost three large towns, considerable industrial capability, a third of its electricity generating capacity, and ten per cent of its agricultural land. The country had to start the long job of rebuilding itself yet again. An additional problem was the housing in Finland of over 400,000 evacuees from Karelia. This equated to over ten per cent of the Finnish population. A law was passed to aid the efficient relocation of the evacuees mainly in southern Finland where land was requisitioned to establish 40,000 new farms. Families previously farming in Karelia were given new farms whilst people who had lived in towns or cities were found accommodation in towns in southern Finland.

In April of 1940 Germany invaded Denmark and Norway. The Soviets countered these invasions by incorporating Latvia, Estonia and Lithuania into the Soviet Union. Between September 1940 and April 1941 Germany planned its attacks on The Soviet Union. The Finns were aware that relations between Germany and the Soviets were reaching an all-time low, and they desperately tried to maintain their independence and neutrality. The Germans expected Finland to offer military assistance and to make Finnish airfields available to the German Luftwaffe.

The Finns desperately needed to retain the friendship of the Western Allies and the USA, and they could only do this if they were able to convince the Allies that Finland was not collaborating with Germany. Finland therefore decided that it should invade the Soviet Union separately from Germany and immediately declare that the sole aim was to recover the lands lost to the Soviets in 1939.

In June 1941 Finland mobilised one full army division to its eastern border with the Soviet Union. Lauri was called up again on 18 June to join Infantry Regiment 22, which was part of the Finnish Army's 5th Division. The 5th Division was posted to Karelia in an area between Lake Ladoga and Lake Ääninen. This was described as a defensive measure due to the worsening relations between the Soviet Union and Germany. A further mobilisation shortly after brought three more army divisions to readiness in the north of the country. The third and by far the largest mobilisation would take place when Germany invaded the Soviet Union in the Arctic and through the Baltic States.

In July 1941 Germany attacked the Soviet Union from Poland, and the Finnish army invaded Soviet territory. The Finns of course did not see it that way. They were liberating land that was originally Finnish, and returning it to Finnish rule. Their idea was to stop at the 1939 border, which would return substantial parts of Karelia to Finland.

The 5th Division advanced south deeper into the Olonets Isthmus, and there was heavy fighting in the area of Säntämä. The Soviets suffered heavy casualties, and the 5th Division also suffered losses, including men that Lauri knew well. The Division then moved further south to the town of Aunus and continued to the banks of the River Syväri. They were stationed in and around this area for a period of two years. Records show that Lauri was listed as a 'horseman' at this time. His experience of using horses on the farms obviously made him the ideal person for this work.

The Finnish Army spent December 1941 consolidating its positions along the length of its border with the Soviet Union. The 1939 border had in fact been crossed in many areas. The end of the invasion of 'old Russia' and the establishment of a static line of trenches brought relief to Finland. The economy was extremely fragile and was desperately in need of manpower to keep it functioning even at a minimal level. During the Russian offensives Finland had half a million men and women in the armed forces or working in support of the war effort. Early in 1942 twenty per cent of these were demobilised to return to agriculture and industry.

During the war Elma looked after the five sons and her aging mother, Hilma Leppänen, who had moved from the Leppänen home to be with Elma. In their evening prayers the family begged for Lauri to return back home safe and sound.

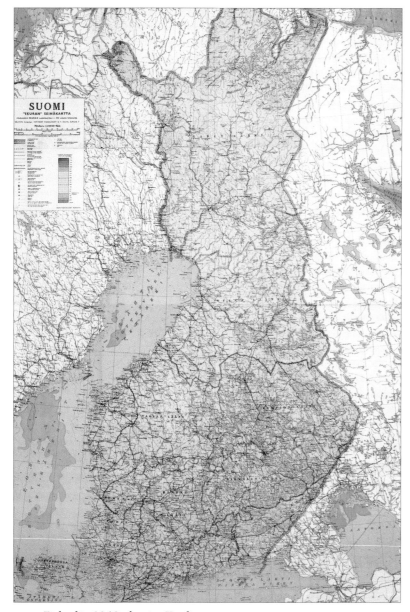

*Finland in 1940, showing Karelian
territory lost to the Soviet Union.*
(Eero and Erkki Fredrikson)

During 1942 Mannerheim drew up plans for rear defensive positions to be prepared, but little work was done until 1943. There was virtually no contact with the Soviet Army and the Finnish troops were becoming lethargic. There were rumours of peace treaties and an armistice.

In January 1944 the Soviet Army relieved Leningrad. This signalled the start of a number of Soviet offensives. The first one began with an attack south of Leningrad that drove the German Army back to Narva on the Estonian frontier. The second offensive saw the Soviet Air Force bomb Helsinki every ten days from the 6th to the 26th of February.

The Soviet Army assembled a force of 450,000 men with tanks, artillery pieces and aircraft for a final offensive to drive Finland out of the war. Finland made an approach for peace via Sweden, but the Soviet terms were totally unacceptable to the Finnish government.

The Soviet attack began on 9 June 1944. Their army made steady progress for six days, forcing the Finnish Army to withdraw to new lines of defence. On 19 June Mannerheim appealed to the German High Command for help. Germany replied with a squadron of Stuka dive-bombers, a division of soldiers, and an assault gun regiment. They also supplied several thousand bazookas. The recall of Finnish reserve soldiers gave hope that the Soviet Army might be held until peace terms could be agreed.

It was about this time that Mannerheim and President Ryti were convinced that if a Soviet occupation of the whole of Finland was to be avoided a peace plan had to be drawn up in very short time. However, before they could sue for peace Finland had to be in a stable military position from which they could open negotiations with the Soviet Union. Hitler, however, demanded that the Finns did not negotiate a separate peace treaty. President Ryti wrote to Hitler and informed him that Finland would not begin independent negotiations with the Soviet Union. In return Germany supplied Finland with sufficient air support and anti-tank weapons to stabilise Finland's eastern fronts.

The letter to Hitler was in fact a lie. Finland again enquired through their Stockholm embassy about a peace treaty with the Soviet Union. When the response was received Ryti resigned as President and was replaced by Mannerheim. Mannerheim immediately repudiated Ryti's letter to Hitler and opened peace negotiations with Stalin. On 2 September Finland broke off all diplomatic relations with Germany.

A cease-fire between Finland and the Soviet Union came into effect on 4 September 1944, but the price was very high. Stalin demanded that Finland intern 220,000 German troops in Lapland, or drive them out of the country. So Finland had its peace, but there was one more campaign to be fought.

Detailed negotiations were opened with the Soviet Union on 14 September. They lasted four days, and at the end of the meetings the Soviets made their final demands:

- A return to the Treaty of Moscow frontiers of 1940.
- The disarming and internment of all German troops in Finland.
- The return of Finland's armed forces to a peacetime basis within three months.
- Payment of $300 million in goods specified by the Soviet Union as reparations over the next six years.
- The lease of the Porkkala Peninsula as a Soviet naval base in perpetuity.
- Use of Finnish airfields and territorial waters for operations against Germany for as long as the war lasted.
- The abolition of all Finnish organisations of a Fascist nature.
- The trial and punishment of war criminals.

If the terms were not accepted, the Finnish delegation was left in no doubt that the whole of Finland would be occupied by the Soviet Army. Unsurprisingly the Soviet terms were accepted immediately, for Finland was at least to remain an independent state.

Wartime lures of 1940 and 1944.
(Normark Corporation archive)

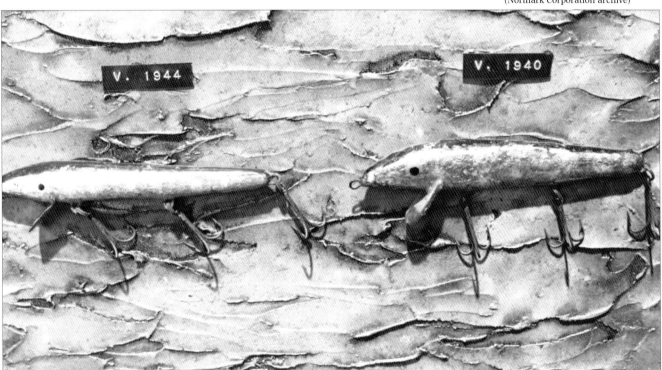

One must appreciate that northern Finland was completely occupied and controlled by German forces at this time, and Finland was at risk of being invaded by the Soviet Army if it did not meet its obligations to either evict or intern all German troops as agreed in the meetings of 14–18 September.

The Finnish Army was committed to demobilisation under the terms of the cease-fire agreement with the Soviet Union at the same time as it was fighting the retreating German Army in the north. Lauri Rapala served for a short time in Lapland fighting the Germans before he was discharged from the army on 7 October 1944, after having served for more than three years. During his service Lauri had served in a number of companies. He had served as a rifleman, a guard, a machine gunner, and a field medical orderly. He left with an excellent disciplinary record and in common with those who fought in the war he was awarded the 1941–45 Service Medal.

Elma's cousins, Uuno and Urpo Laaksonen were not to return from the war. Unfortunately they both died either in battle or due to severe injuries, sustained whilst fighting for Finland's independence. Their plans to set up a lure-manufacturing business with Lauri died with them.

Finally, on 29 November the Germans broke off contact in the Kaaresuvanto area. The active operations between German and Finnish troops had come to an end. However, it was not until April 1945 that the last German troops left Finnish territory, crossing the border into Norway at Kilpisjärvi.

Lauri's war did not consist of continuous fighting. There were days, sometimes weeks, when his army unit did not move, and was not engaged with the enemy. Being a married man, Lauri was not always in the front line. The Finnish Army had a policy of protecting its married men as much as circumstances allowed. However, there are accounts in a local history book of Lauri taking a very active role against a Soviet patrol that his own patrol encountered one winter day. The story goes that the Soviet patrol opened fire first, and Lauri waited for his commanding officer to order him to open fire. The order never came, and Lauri left it as late as possible before opening up with his sub-machine gun and running for cover. Lauri waited in the snow, but there was only silence. When he finally ventured out he found that all the members of his patrol were dead. So were the Soviet soldiers.

Lauri did not like to talk about the war, but he used to tell stories about the opportunities he had to go fishing during his army service. Karelia has many lakes and rivers and Lauri saw them as a challenge. He fished whenever possible and brought pike, perch and the occasionally trout back to the mess tent. No doubt Lauri's fresh fish added some welcome variety to army rations.

Lauri took some of his lures to war with him, but he also carved and whittled new ones when there was little or no action on the front. One person took a great interest in Lauri's new lures. He was Captain Pekka Myyryläinen, a senior officer in Lauri's regiment. Lauri and Pekka used to fish together whenever possible, and formed a firm friendship. Lauri told the story of the night he and Captain Myyryläinen fished a lake together, with his lure accounting for 70 pike that were taken back to the army camp. Lauri and Pekka maintained their friendship after the war, and often fished together.

Lauri's army record, part one. (Finnish military archive)

Lauri's army record, part two. (Finnish military archive)

Countdown

The history of the Countdown

1965 First introduced in 7cm, 9cm and 11cm models in Gold (G), Silver (S) and Blue (B).

1966 13cm model introduced.

1967 5cm model introduced.

1977 Perch (P) colour introduced.

1979 Rainbow Trout (RT) colour introduced.

1988 Minnow (MN) colour introduced.

1989 3cm model introduced.

1991 Trout (TR) colour introduced.

1992 Firetiger (FT) colour introduced

1997 Clown (CLN) introduced

1998 Red Clown (RCL), Vampire (V) introduced.

2000 Rapflash holographic colours introduced: Blue Shiner (HBSH), Emerald Shiner (HESH), and Shiner (HSH).

2001 Silver Minnow (SMN) and Fathead Minnow (FH) introduced.

2002 Fire Minnow (FMN) and Muddler (MD) introduced.

2003 Countdown 01 introduced. New colours introduced:
Golden Muddler (GMD)
Bleeding Minnow (BLM)
Redfin Spotted Minnow (RFSM)
Silver Spotted Minnow (SSM)
Blue Spotted Minnow (BSM).

Fishing the Countdown

To use the Countdown method, follow these simple steps:

• Immediately after casting take up any slack line, and begin counting just as the Countdown hits the water.

• A good, uniform way to count is 'one thousand one, one thousand two, one thousand three' etc.

• Keep counting until the lure settles on the bottom or has found a resting place in the weed. The line will go slack at this point.

• Remember the count at this moment.

• By reducing the count by one or two numbers on subsequent retrieves and picking up the lure with your reel, the Countdown will stay just above the weeds or off the bottom.

• Keep reducing the count to comb each layer of water, until you locate the fish.

Tips from the pros

• Take advantage of the wind when you're fishing. When waves are pounding in on a spot, it increases the chance that feeding fish will be using it. Waves break up and reduce light penetration, making predator fish more likely to venture shallow. Bait-fish and other prey items often get dislodged from hiding places, and tossed around. The big fish take advantage of it. Get your lure in there, before the fish all get filled.

• Do you use bottom bouncers or other heavy weights to get shallow running Rapalas down to deeper fish? Pay attention to the distance between your lure and the weight. Start off with your lure three feet behind the weight, but if you think that the weight is spooking the fish, don't hesitate to extend this distance to six feet or more.

• Did you know that knot placement can have a huge impact on the action of a Rapala minnow imitation that you tie directly to the eye of the lure? Actually a loop knot like the Rapala knot can be an excellent choice, because it allows the lure freedom of movement – which means maximum action. But you can also affect the action by tying a 'jam' knot, such as an Improved Clinch, and adjusting the knot's position on the lure eyelet. Push the knot downward, into the lower half of the lure eyelet, and the side-to-side wobble of the lure will be more pronounced. This can be an advantage when you're using the lure in the traditional manner, swimming it below the surface. Push the knot upward, into the upper half of the lure eyelet, and the lure will have very little swimming action. You can use the lure as a successful jerk bait with the knot in this position.

Countdown

Code: CD   Freshwater – Sinking

Main features:

- A sinking lure based on the Original
- Weighted balsawood body
- Improved casting in windy weather
- Specially designed for longer casting
- Useful for controlled-depth fishing
- Typical wounded minnow action

Fishing tips:

- Use the Countdown fishing method
- Count how long it takes for the lure to reach the bottom
- Adjust the count each cast to control the depth at which the lure is fishing

Target predators:

Asp, perch, chub, trout, black bass, salmon, zander (walleye), pike, sea trout

Technical features:

Code	Body length	Weight	Treble hooks	Swimming depth
CD-01	2.5cm / 1in.	2.7g / $^{1}/_{16}$ oz.	One No. 12	0.3–0.9m / 1–3ft.
CD-03	3cm / 1$^{1}/_{4}$in.	4g / $^{1}/_{8}$ oz.	Two No. 12	0.6–0.9m / 2–3ft.
CD-05	5cm / 2in.	5g / $^{3}/_{16}$ oz.	Two No. 10	0.9–1.8m / 3–6ft.
CD-07	7cm / 2$^{3}/_{4}$in.	8g / $^{1}/_{4}$ oz.	Two No. 7	1.5–2.4m / 5–8ft.
CD-09	9cm / 3$^{1}/_{2}$in.	12g / $^{7}/_{16}$ oz.	Two No. 5	2.1–3.0m / 7–10ft.
CD-11	11cm / 4$^{3}/_{8}$in.	16g / $^{9}/_{16}$ oz.	Two No. 3	2.7–3.9m / 9–13ft.

Jigging Rap

The history of the Jigging Rap

1965 The first Balanced Jigging lures are introduced in 3cm, 5cm, 7cm and 9cm sizes.

1973 The Vertical Jigging lure is launched in 45mm, and 65mm sizes.

1978 A 50mm Vertical Jigging lure is launched.

Fishing the Jigging Rap

Pro anglers in their constant quest to out-fish the competition sometimes go 'outside the box' to make it to the winner's circle. In the heat of summer when big fish are holding on sunken islands and other bottom structures, pro anglers turn to a traditional winter lure, the Rapala Balanced Jigging lure. Planting right on top of marked fish, they can repeatedly swim this tantalising lure in circles right in the middle of deep or suspended game fish.

The Jigging Rap of the icy north countries is now being used on soft water too. From the 20 lb. (9kg) bass they are catching in the deep reservoirs of California to the 14 lb. (6.3kg) suspended zander (walleye) in the Great Lakes, anglers know this is not just another ice-fishing jig.

Mind you, the Jigging Rap makes a superb ice-fishing lure too.

Tips from the pros

• The Jigging Rap isn't a straight-up-and-down jigging lure, but you've got to get the timing right for it to work well. The trick is to lower the rod tip quickly so that there is slack line between the Jigging Rap and the rod tip. When there is slack line, the lure picks up speed and the flow of water past the special tail makes the lure move forward. Because the lure is fished vertically, this forward movement is translated into a circular swimming pattern, which can be irresistible to predators.

• A secret of west-coast bass chasers – using the 'winter' jigging Rapala in open water – is producing huge fish for anglers everywhere. The 'Jigging Rap' as it's known in some circles, has a unique action, a sliding, circling movement that flashes and really pulls the trigger on predator fish. It's not just for ice-fishing any more.

Jigging Rap

Code: W   Freshwater – Saltwater – Jigging

Main features:

- Metal jigging lure
- Fixed nose and tail hooks with belly treble
- Suitable for summer and winter use
- Specially shaped tail to make it swim
- Large range of colours and sizes
- Balanced design allows for deep jigging

Fishing tips:

- Designed primarily for fishing through the ice for perch and pike
- Is now used in hot summer weather for vertical jigging from a boat
- Find an underwater structure and concentrate your jigging around it

Target predators:

Perch, pike, zander (walleye), black bass, lake trout

Technical features:

Code	Body length	Weight	Treble hooks	Swimming depth
W-2	2cm / 3/4in.	3.5g / 1/8 oz.	2 single / 1 treble	Variable
W-3	3cm / 11/4in.	5.5g / 3/16 oz.	2 single / 1 treble	Variable
W-5	5cm / 2in.	9g / 5/16 oz.	2 single / 1 treble	Variable
W-7	7cm / 23/4in.	14g / 1/2 oz.	2 single / 1 treble	Variable
W-9	9cm / 31/2in.	21g / 3/4 oz.	2 single / 1 treble	Variable
W-11	11cm / 43/8in.	32g / 11/8 oz.	2 single / 1 treble	Variable

Countdown Magnum

The history of the Countdown Magnum

1969   Countdown Magnum introduced with the 18cm model.

1971   13cm model introduced.

1976   Mackerel colours introduced to the Magnum range.

1981   11cm, 14cm and 26cm models introduced.

1981   Red Head (RH) and Green Mackerel (GM) colours introduced.

1982   18cm model improved.

1983   9cm model introduced.

1986   7cm model introduced.

1990   Special Magnum Constant Guigo (CG) colour introduced.

1991   10cm model introduced.

1992   Firetiger (FT) colour introduced to the Magnum range.

1994   8cm and 22cm models introduced.

1996   Dorado (D) colour introduced.

1997   Purple Mackerel (PM), Black Red Head (BRH), Silver Shadow (SSH) introduced.

1998   Magnum Stainless Steel colours introduced.

1999   Sardine (SRD) colour introduced.

2002   New colours introduced: Pink Mackerel (PIM), Shiner (SH), Blue Shad (BSH), Redfin Shiner (RFSH) Blue Sardine (BSRD) and Red Dorado (RD).

2003   New colours introduced: Bonito (BTO), Donzella (DZ) and Pike (PK).

Fishing the Countdown Magnum

When casting, use the 'Countdown' method of fishing to determine the depth, then fish the Magnum just above the bottom or just over the weed beds. If the lure touches the bottom or the weeds, you are doing it right.

The Countdown Magnum is a great trolling lure in fresh and saltwater. Just make sure that it is properly tuned before you start trolling. If you are using an echo sounder make note of the underwater obstructions you find, then go back around and search them thoroughly.

The Countdown Magnum is a big lure designed for big fish. Keep those hooks sharp because big fish don't come by every day.

Tips from the pros

• A secret of top anglers is to use larger baits when fish are on the bite. On those days when fish are 'hitting', you can actively fish for bigger fish by tempting them with bigger lures. In a way, what you are doing is deterring more of the smaller fish.

• Here's a trick used by musky hunters, shared by the experts at Rapala. If a big fish follows your lure but won't hit, try moving away and coming back at another angle. It also helps if you position the sun at your back, so the fish has to look into it while approaching your boat. That lighting condition makes it harder for the fish to see your movement.

• When you're trolling and you get a strike, but the fish doesn't get hooked, keep that lure in the water. If the rod is in a rod holder, take it out and begin to manually pump it, then let it stall out. Frequently 20 or 30 yards down the line, they'll come back and crush it.

• If you use lures intended for saltwater in freshwater, there's no need to replace the saltwater-resistant hooks. About the only thing anglers ever need to worry about is checking the sharpness of the point and barb of each saltwater resistant hook, because the hooks are sharpened and then treated. If the coating builds up a bit, it is sometimes necessary to sharpen the points. But there is virtually no difference in their ability to hook fish as compared to a traditional freshwater hook.

• If you're new to saltwater fishing and think that live bait is the only way to take good numbers of fish, try speed-trolling with Rapala Magnums. Top saltwater anglers routinely run these baits at eight knots and faster for everything from calico bass to yellowtail, bonito, barracuda, wahoo and even small sharks. The high speed, it is believed, is the ticket to the action.

• The diameter of your line can make a tremendous difference to the trolling depth of your lure. The greater the diameter of the line, the more resistance it creates, which pulls the lure towards the surface. If additional depth is a critical factor then try one of the new 'super lines' or select a monofilament with a reduced diameter.

Countdown Magnum

Code: CD-MAG   Saltwater – Freshwater – Sinking

Main features:

- Hardwood body for maximum strength
- Can be trolled up to seven knots
- Tight, wounded minnow action
- Fitted with VMC Perma Steel hooks
- Special steel diving lip for added strength
- Very long casting lure

Fishing tips:

- Try high speed trolling for tuna and wahoo
- Use matching leaders, and snap-locks for safety
- Concentrate around both floating and submerged features for the best action

Target predators:

Zander (walleye), pike, bonito, tuna, wahoo, tarpon, musky, bluefish, snook

Technical features:

Code	Body length	Weight	Treble hooks	Swimming depth
CD-07-MAG	7cm / 2³/₄in.	12g / ⁷/₁₆ oz.	Two No. 3	2.7–3.3m / 9–11ft.
CD-09-MAG	9cm / 3¹/₂in.	17g / ⁵/₈ oz.	Two No. 2	3.6–4.2m / 12–14ft.
CD-11-MAG	11cm / 4³/₈in.	24g / ⁷/₈ oz.	Two No. 1	3.9–4.5m / 13–15ft.
CD-14-MAG	14cm / 5¹/₂in.	36g / 1¹/₄ oz.	Two No. 2/0	4.5–5.4m / 15–18ft.
CD-18-MAG	18cm / 7in.	70g / 2³/₈ oz.	Two No. 4/0	5.4–6.3m / 18–21ft.
CD-22-MAG	22cm / 9in.	100g / 3¹/₂ oz.	Two No. 7/0	5.4–7.5m / 18–25ft.
CD-26-MAG	26cm / 10¹/₂in.	130g / 4¹/₂ oz.	Two No. 10/0	5.4–7.5m / 18–25ft.

Floating Magnum

The history of the Floating Magnum

1969 Floating Magnum range launched with the 18cm model.

1971 13cm model introduced.

1976 Silver Blue Mackerel (SM) colour introduced.

1981 11cm and 14cm models introduced.

1981 Green Mackerel (GM) and Red Head (RH) colours introduced.

1987 18cm model improved.

1990 Special Magnum CG colour introduced.

1992 Firetiger (FT) colour introduced.

1996 Dorado (D) colour introduced.

1997 New colours introduced:
Purple Mackerel (PM)
Black Red Head (BRH)
Silver Shadow (SSH).

1998 7cm and 9cm models introduced

1999 Sardine (SRD) colour introduced.

2002 New colours introduced:
Shiner (SH)
Blue Shiner (BSH)
Redfin Shiner (RFSH)
Perch (P)
Gold Fish (GF)
Hot Tiger (HT) and
Yellow Tiger (YT).

2003 Pike (PK) colour introduced.

Fishing the Floating Magnum

Try a pause-and-retrieve method when casting the Floating Magnum to let the lure float upwards beside a likely fish holding area.

Test your lure before trolling to make sure that it maintains its action at the required trolling speed. When you are trolling, don't steer in a straight line. Troll in curves so that your lure will either speed up or slow down as you steer left or right.

If you are fishing for big game fish make sure that those hooks are really sharp. They only have one chance to secure a good hook hold.

Tips from the pros

• Try trolling floating Rapalas along the deep edges of drop-offs, by weighing them down with bottom bouncers. Modern bottom bouncers are amazing in their ability to avoid getting snagged. Even when they do, usually they come off easily if you motor back around the lure and pull from the opposite side. Meanwhile, you can troll with a relatively short line, giving you good control, and run the Rapala right where you want it. You'll feel the strikes, and the bottom bouncer won't interfere much with the fight.

• If you break the lip off a floating minnow lure like a Floating Magnum don't throw it away! It'll make a great surface bait for bass or pike. Just smooth off the lip where it has broken and make sure that the water can't get in to the lure. Then cast it out and twitch it erratically across the top through likely areas. There you are, a new top summer bait for bass and pike.

• If you're stalking big fish in clear, shallow water situations, try making them look into the sun. It can help you avoid spooking big fish that are holding in the clear shallows if you position yourself so that the sun is at your back. This doesn't help when the sun is high in the sky, but as it slips lower on the horizon, it can help tip the odds in your favour.

• Make your lure behave as if it's wounded. No question about it; predator fish can detect the erratic low-frequency waves created by a 'bait-fish in trouble' through their lateral line sense. A bait-fish swimming normally presents an entirely different impression on the predator's lateral line. Make them think your bait is easy pickings!

• Just because a lure label says it's intended for freshwater, it still might be deadly in saltwater, and vice versa. For years, some anglers have been using 'saltwater' Magnum Rapalas for walleyes, bass, pike, muskies and other freshwater species with great results. And with the addition of saltwater-resistant hooks, several Rapala models originally intended for freshwater have become 'secret staples' of inshore and offshore anglers.

Floating Magnum

Code: **FMAG** Freshwater – Saltwater – Floating

Main features:

- The largest Rapala lures for the biggest fish
- Made of hardwood for strength
- Fitted with VMC Perma Steel hooks
- Use in fresh and saltwater
- Very long casting
- Can be successfully cast or trolled

Fishing tips:

- Use heavy duty leaders, snap-locks or oval rings
- Select the correct size according to your target species
- Fish fast or slow, and use the rod tip to impart more action

Target predators:

Zander (walleye), pike, bonito, tuna, wahoo, musky, bluefish, snook, tarpon

Technical features:

Code	Body length	Weight	Treble hooks	Swimming depth
F-07-MAG	7cm / 2³/4in.	7g / ¹/4 oz.	Two No. 3/1	0.9–1.8m / 3–6ft.
F-09-MAG	9cm / 3¹/2in.	13g / ⁷/16 oz.	Two No. 2	1.2–2.1m / 4–7ft.
F-11-MAG	11cm / 4³/8in.	15g / ⁹/16 oz.	Two No. 1	2.7–3.3m / 9–11ft.
F-14-MAG	14cm / 5¹/2in.	22g / ³/4 oz.	Two No. 1/0	2.7–3.3m / 9–11ft.
F-18-MAG	18cm / 7in.	40g / 1 ¹/2 oz.	Two No. 4/0	2.7–3.3m / 9–11ft.

Jointed

Fishing the Jointed

This articulated lure commits more of that wiggling action that fish can't seem to resist. The Jointed Rapala is ideally suited to an extremely slow retrieve without sacrificing any of that famous action.

Use it when fishing windswept shorelines. Keep the lure just below the surface. The pronounced action will attract attention and trigger fish that are actively feeding on both surface and sub-surface food items.

In the winter when the water is cold, during flood conditions when the water is dirty, and at times when the weather pattern is disturbed, the extra movement and vibration of the Jointed Rapala can make the difference between a good day and a failure.

Tips from the pros

• We now realise that numerous species of fish roam open basin areas from late spring through to the autumn on many systems. Big, predator fish are often suspended at some depth in the water column, following pelagic (open water) bait-fish and other food sources. These fish can be very catchable, and chasing them can be the best game plan for an angler looking for a trophy. The most successful basin anglers troll, usually with crank baits. What we're learning is that a wide side-to-side action, a lure with an 'aggressive' wobble, is often the best producer in basin situations. One lure, the Jointed Rapala (sometimes called the 'broken-back' Rapala) has become a secret weapon for basin trollers, because of its appeal to open-water fish.

• When fishing, make a conscious effort to change your presentation until you find what the fish want. One important way to change things is to try crank baits that have distinctly different wobbles – that is, begin with a bait that has a tight wobbling action, and if it doesn't catch fish that day, switch to a lure with a wider wobble.

• Shallow running, floating crank baits and minnow lures can be deadly on deep-water fish. Today's new generation of adjustable bottom bouncers let you change the amount of weight you have on the wire arm of the 'bouncer' without cutting and re-tying.

• When fishing from shore, be very aware of how you approach fishing areas. Walk softly and carefully, especially on spongy ground. And avoid silhouetting your body or fishing rod against the sky. If necessary, kneel or crouch and make sidearm casts.

• When the water is very cold or a weather change has put the fish off the feed, try a lure with a more exaggerated action like the Jointed Rapala. It's not only the action that might make a difference. Jointed lures emit a clicking noise as they move from side to side, and the wider action increases fish-attracting vibrations. Remember to fish the lure slowly, with occasional rod tip jerks to impart just a little flash. It might just be enough to get one of those reluctant predators to strike.

Jointed

Code: J   Freshwater – Floating (J-13 Saltwater)

Main features:

- Two-piece balsawood body
- A good lure when the fish are not active
- Wide swimming action and more vibration
- Maintains its action when fished slowly

Fishing tips:

- Move the rod tip to impart more action when using a slow retrieve
- Match the size of the lure to the target fish
- Use this lure in cold water to stimulate the fish into action

Target predators:

Asp, perch, chub, trout, black bass, salmon, zander (walleye), pike, sea bass

Technical features:

Code	Body length	Weight	Treble hooks	Swimming depth
J-05	5cm / 2in.	4g / $^1/_8$ oz.	Two No. 10	0.9–1.5m / 3–5ft.
J-07	7cm / 2$^3/_4$in.	4g / $^1/_8$ oz.	Two No. 6	1.2–1.8m / 4–6ft.
J-09	9cm / 3$^1/_2$in.	7g / $^1/_4$ oz.	Two No. 5	1.5–2.1m / 5–7ft.
J-11	11cm / 4$^3/_8$in.	9g / $^5/_{16}$ oz.	Two No. 3	1.2–2.4m / 4–8ft.
J-13* (SW)	13cm / 5$^1/_4$in.	18g / $^5/_8$ oz.	Two No. 2	1.2–4.2m / 4–14ft.

* J-13 is equipped with VMC Perma Steel hooks

CELEBRITY BITES

Jan Eggers on catching pike with Rapala lures

'Quality lures that both pike and I like'

I don't know the exact number of years that I have been using Rapala lures. I made my first contact with Rapala in 1975, and I was certainly using Rapala lures before then. At that time I often used the Rapala Original Floating in 11cm and 13cm sizes in the shallow Dutch polder canals. Later I discovered that the Jointed Floating 11cm was the perfect lure for the fat pike that inhabit these canals. I must have caught thousands of members of the Esox family with this lure, and it is still my favourite for lure fishing from the bank in shallow waters.

As an international sport-fishing journalist I have had the opportunity to fish for pike all over the world, and I have caught them in 19 different countries. I am lucky enough to have taken more than 1,000 pike over the Dutch 'dream length' of one metre. Fishing the international waters that are often much deeper than my Dutch polder canals, I discovered that there is another Rapala lure that pike like a lot. The number one lure for trolling is without doubt the Rapala Super Shad Rap. No matter if I am fishing Lough Corrib in Ireland, the Baltic Sea between Sweden and Finland, or the Great Slave Lake in the very north of Canada, the Super Shad Rap will always catch my dream fish: big pike!

So, wherever in the world I go pike fishing, the Rapala Original, Jointed and Super Shad Rap will ALWAYS be in my tackle box. It is a guarantee that I will catch big pike. The last 30 years prove it!

CHAPTER 3

A business is born

1946–58

Aftter the war Lauri returned home to his wife and five sons and the family home at Lyyranmäki. Life quickly resumed the familiar routine established before the war. Lauri went back to working on the farms and in the forests, supplementing his income and the family diet by fishing, while the children attended the local Riihilahti school

The Rapala family's living conditions were not good, with five children and two adults living in one room. The family made do with the bare essentials. They had a cast-iron stove and a brick-built baking oven for heating and cooking. There was insufficient space for each individual to have a bed, so the children slept together head to toe. Food at least was plentiful, from the farm and from Lauri's fishing. The warm Finnish summers were no problem, but the winters were a different matter. The one wood-burning stove struggled to maintain a decent temperature in the cottage when the outside temperature could drop to minus 25 degrees Centigrade (minus 13 degrees Fahrenheit). Sometimes it was cold enough inside the cottage for the water to freeze in the bucket, and for the potatoes to be frostbitten under the bed.

Risto Rapala tells of a rather embarrassing occasion when he was a young boy. It was around Christmas time, and the weather was cold. Risto was cold as well, and the only warm place in the cottage was close to the stove. Risto climbed onto a bench that was next to it. He had no trousers on so he tried to position his behind over the stove to get warm. Unfortunately he slipped, and actually sat on the stove, which was at cooking temperature. Risto did not sit there for long; his natural reflexes took over and he jumped up and away from the stove. However, he was too late. The iron cooking ring on the stove had scarred his behind. Risto admits that the family could see the rings of the stove and even the stove maker's name branded in the skin of his behind for some time. He will not divulge if the scars are still there today.

The one major thing that the family lacked was a sauna. The sauna has always been a way of life in Finland, and virtually every house had one. However, the Rapala family did not, and they could not afford to build one. Occasionally they were able to use the sauna of a house within easy walking distance as the family in the house felt sorry for them, but this was not always the case. More often than not the Rapalas had to fill a water tank, which they pushed on a sledge over the hill to Elma's parents' house in Riihilahti village, a distance of perhaps a mile. They had their sauna at the house, and then pushed the sledge

- **Lure making becomes a business**

- **Financial security for the Rapala family**

- **The sons join the business**

- **Expansion and mechanisation**

- **The effects of the Helsinki Olympics**

- **The influence of Fritz Schröder**

containing the empty tank back to their cottage at Lyyranmäki. It was not a journey to be undertaken lightly.

Lauri and Elma's family was facing severe hardship. Finland's economic situation after the war was very bad, and the outlook for unskilled workers was bleak. The Finnish government offered all men who had fought in the war a small area of land on which to build a house. Lauri was offered a plot of land in Asikkala, but he refused it, as he did not want to move his family. Considering Lauri's financial circumstances it was highly unlikely that he would ever have raised the necessary money to build the house, and the likelihood of obtaining a loan was almost nil.

The lure of success

However, there was one thing in Lauri and Elma's minds that gave them hope for the future. Lauri had to revive his small lure-making business that had blossomed just before the war. He was now sure that he had found the secret to successful lure design. Because of the war, materials to make lures were hard to come by. The pine bark was no problem – it was a useless by-product of the forestry industry – but acetate, celluloid and metal foils were strictly rationed. However, Lauri was a resourceful man, and he managed to obtain the materials he required or he substituted other materials, like used film negatives, in their place.

Lauri was not the only resourceful member of the family. Risto recalls a time when he had to queue in order to obtain some celluloid sheets. The material was strictly rationed, but he was aware that without it his father could not finish a batch of lures. When Risto reached the head of the queue he was given some sheets, but he did not consider it enough, so he took off his hat and coat and joined the queue again in the hope that he would not be recognised. Unfortunately the same man was issuing the material when Risto again arrived at the head of the queue. Risto was recognised and was lucky to get away without his first batch of celluloid being confiscated.

The Rapala family's first sauna.
(Rapala family archive)

The first major creative innovation to the lures after the war was the use of gold and silver foil in the production process. The choice of colours at once made Lauri's lures more widely acceptable to both game and coarse fishermen, and his business began to gain momentum. The foil was often embossed with a pattern by simply pressing a sharp point (such as a pen nib) into it before it was applied to the body. However the business was still not able to feed his family, and so Lauri had to continue fishing and working on the farms. At least his fishing gave him the opportunity to test his new lures. Lauri gradually refined the design over time, making it slimmer and lighter.

The demand for Lauri's lures slowly increased. Elma used to help Lauri when she could, but with five hungry boys to look after she did not have much time. It was now time for Lauri and Elma to make a decision. Should they commit themselves to their new lure business, or should they continue to earn their living as they had done since their marriage?

The decision was probably made when Elma found out that she was expecting another baby. Kauko, the youngest son, was now eight and attending school, so Elma had been able to help Lauri. Now she was pregnant again and would have little time or energy to do the physical work that she had done before. In 1948 Lauri and Elma's first daughter, Marja, was born. Elma did not have an easy pregnancy, and for the first time she was in hospital for the birth. All the other children had been born at home with a local midwife in attendance. No doubt Elma was relieved that at last she had a daughter, and looked forward to the time when Marja could take care of some of the household chores.

In 1948 Lauri and Elma were awarded a loan from the state in recognition of Lauri's military service during the war. Two local farmers guaranteed the loan. With this money, cashed from the Kalkkinen Cooperative Bank, they managed to purchase the Lyyranmäki cottage and a piece of land from Miina Lyyra. Their first priority was to build a proper sauna! They also built a small room adjoining the sauna into which Reino and Risto moved. The Rapala family home now contained the two parents, Elma's widowed mother (who had moved to Lyyranmäki to live with the Rapala family), and six children, so the extra space made a very significant difference to their quality of life. For the first time the future looked promising for the Rapala family. The Leppänen cottage where Elma's parents used to live was quickly converted into a lure workshop.

Production takes off

Lauri and Elma were now fully committed to the lure-making business. In 1949 Lauri won a prize for his lures at a local agricultural fair. By the end of 1949 Risto and Ensio were helping their father to manufacture lures whenever they could. Esko started full-time work in the business immediately after leaving Riihilahti school. The family soon adopted a simple system of batch production, each of them responsible for a different part of the manufacturing process. The eldest son Reino had shown little interest in the fledgling business and had moved away the previous year in order to study engineering. In 1950 Lauri improved on his previous year's performance by winning first prize for his lures at the local agricultural show. All the lures were now

The Rapala family working in the fields.
(Rapala family archive)

Rapala lures from 1946 and 1949.
(Normark Corporation archive)

Risto Rapala in his army uniform.
(Rapala family archive)

properly boxed, and it was Elma's job to fold the boxes from flat, printed cardboard sheets. Lauri and Elma had taken advice from Mr Kanerva, the manager of a local printing works whom they approached to print their boxes. He left them in no doubt that they should call their lures Rapala.

Ensio began studying at the carpentry school in Lahti to learn as much as he could about working with wood. This was to prove a great asset to the company in the years to come. He also attended a course of evening classes to learn the basics of bookkeeping. Risto completed his national service between 1952 and 1953 at the Kouvola Garrison, just like his father, and started working full-time for the company as soon as he returned home.

Mechanisation first entered the production process at about this time. Wool and other materials were now more readily available in the shops, and people had more money with which to purchase them. Spinning wheels were standing idle and so a redundant spinning wheel was obtained and stripped down. A thin strip of sandpaper was glued to the rim of the wheel. The operator worked the spinning wheel with his foot and sanded the lure body smooth against the revolving sandpaper.

Due to the fact that all the lures were made by hand, Lauri insisted on testing every lure to make sure that the action was just as he wanted it. There were inconsistencies in the density of the pine bark, and of course each lure had a slightly different shape. Lauri discovered that he could fine-tune his lures by adjusting the angle of the wire nose loop, and by shaving the diving lip. Lauri used to test them in the clear, fast-moving waters of the Kalkkinen Rapids, not far from his home in the summer, and during the winter he used a sheltered boat house on the water owned by one of the many companies who floated cut timber down the rivers and through the lakes.

The Kalkkinen Rapids were (and still are) a favoured fishing location. The fishing rights were owned by the members of the Kalkkinen Hunting and Fishing Club, which was formed in 1886 and is the oldest fishing club in Scandinavia. The members traditionally fished with flies, a method introduced to Finland in the early 1800s by English sport fishermen. Lauri was testing his lures one day when a gentleman approached him. He introduced himself as Fritz Schröder. Mr Schröder asked to look at Lauri's lures, and was impressed enough to purchase two of the ones that Lauri was testing. Little did Lauri know that he was talking to the owner of the best fishing-tackle shop in Helsinki[7].

---

[7] The Schröder shop continues to sell fishing tackle in Helsinki to this day, although the Schröder family no longer owns it.

In 1951 Lauri decided that he had to expand the business. His 11cm (4.5in.) lure was selling well, but it was obvious that he could increase his business by offering a greater selection. Introducing a greater range was the first step, so Lauri designed a smaller 9cm (3.6in.) lure. He was just as meticulous with this lure as he was with his original 11cm (4.5in.) version. It still had to swim with a slightly off-centre wobble to attract the attention of the predatory fish. The 9cm (3.6in.) lure was introduced later that year in the standard silver and gold foil colours.

In 1952 the Rapala family was made complete by the birth of their second daughter and seventh child, Irja. However, another important event was to take place that year, which would have a momentous effect on both the family and the business. In the summer of 1952 the Olympic Games were held in Helsinki. Athletes, coaches, trainers and sports delegations from around the world converged on the city for a two-week festival of sport. Risto was completing his national service in the Army at this time, and his regiment was moved to Helsinki to undertake security duties at the games. A few of the privates, Risto amongst them, were selected to release the white doves in the stadium at the opening ceremony.

It was little wonder that some of the many thousands of visitors were keen fishermen, and that they visited Fritz Schröder's shop in Helsinki. It was in Mr Schröder's shop that Rapala lures were first exposed to the world sport-fishing market. It is not possible to know where Lauri's lures were taken when the Olympics ended, but some certainly found their way to the lure-fishing capital of the world, the USA.

The Olympics were not the only means by which the fame of Lauri's lures spread across the Atlantic ocean. Viktor Tommola, the brother of Santeri Tommola, the farmer whom Lauri's mother occasionally worked for when he was a child, had emigrated to the USA in 1910. Viktor returned to Finland in the early 1950s and visited his brother at his farm in Kalkkinen. Santeri told his brother of Lauri's success, and Viktor purchased some lures from Lauri to take to his fishing friends when he returned to America.

Rapala lures were now becoming famous in southern and central Finland. Fishermen converged on Lauri's home to buy them. His

*The first stages of mechanisation –
a spinning wheel.*
(Rapala company archive)

*Ensio and Risto Rapala making
lures at Kulmala.*
(Rapala company archive)

Prize-winning Rapala lures of the 1950s.
(Rapala company archive)

major customers were the members of the Kalkkinen Hunting and Fishing Club. Lauri continued to test the lures in the rapids, and he used to tell the club members, 'If you don't catch a fish with this lure, bring it back, and I will change it for another one.' No lures were ever returned to Lauri.

The business was now viable for supporting the Rapala family, so Lauri and Elma took the decision to stop commercial fishing, and farm working. Lauri eventually gave up the stall at Lahti market that had done so much to provide his family with food and clothing over the years. During the early 1950s Lauri began to employ some of his neighbours to carve the lures. Kalkkinen village soon became the wobbler Mecca of the world with five individual lure workshops in the area, and when the American boom started a few years later, there were even more[8].

Lure and order

The house the Rapala family built in 1953, since extended.
(Rapala family archive)

In 1953, Fritz Schröder placed an order for 300 lures with Lauri. It was by far the largest order that the Rapala family had ever received. The receipt of the order gave Lauri and Elma the confidence to make their biggest financial decision to date; with the remainder of their state loan, they built a new house and a decent-sized workshop on the site of their cottage. The original site was too small for the new buildings, so Esko used his savings to purchase an adjoining plot of land from a neighbour. The original Lyyranmäki cottage was demolished, although the stone steps can still be seen to this day.

[8] Finlandia-Uistin, the manufacturer of Nils Master lures, was also established here in 1963, and along with Rapala is one of the few survivors of this era.

The family called their new house 'Noukkahonka', after the name of the site on which it was built. The house consisted of a large kitchen, two ground-floor rooms, a hall and a cellar. The upstairs remained unfinished, until a few years later when Risto, having recently married his wife Lea, financed the building of a further two rooms upstairs. Risto and Lea lived in the upstairs rooms until the 1960s. In 1956 Risto also bought a house called 'Kulmala', near the Rapala family's new home. This house was immediately converted to a workshop in order to satisfy the demands of increased production.

Once the house and workshop were complete the production of lures increased, and Lauri gradually increased his workforce to 25. The majority of these people worked from home. They collected the pine bark from the forest, and returned the carved lures to Lauri. They were paid according to the number of lures they produced. The rest of the production process was carried out in the new workshop.

It was in 1953 that the third Rapala lure was launched. Having introduced the smaller 9cm (3.6in.) model in 1951, Lauri decided that he had the production capacity to produce a larger lure. The new 13cm (5.3in.) floating lure was

Esko Rapala tests lures at the Kulmala workshop.
(Rapala company archive)

produced in the customary silver and gold colours. It had the same off-centre wobble as the other lures, perhaps a little slower due to its larger size. It was an immediate success with the local fishermen who targeted northern pike and zander[9], and it quickly gained a reputation as an excellent salmon lure. At last Lauri was able to install a testing tank in his new workshop. Now he could test and fine-tune each lure without having to travel to the Kalkkinen Rapids or the boat house.

In 1954 Lauri won yet another first prize for the craftsmanship of his lures at a local agricultural fair. This was the last prize that the Rapala lures would win at such events, as the business had now become too large to qualify for local trade status.

From the very start of the business in 1936 the Rapala family kept records of the lures that they had made. These archives reveal that in the years from 1936 to 1955 Lauri, Elma and their sons made 51,404 lures, an incredible achievement bearing in mind that every lure was made by hand. It should be remembered too that production during the war years was virtually nil.

Fame and success beyond Finland

The way was now open for Rapala lures to start making their mark on the international scene. In 1955 Fritz Schröder acted as the Rapala family advisor when he introduced them to possible distributors in Sweden and Norway. Contracts were signed later in the year, and for the first time the Rapala family became official exporters. The first official export licence was granted on 5 October 1955 for 1,120 lures, and on 28 November 1956 a subsequent licence was granted for the export of 10,000 lures to Sweden. The Schröder company handled the export administration for the family. During the first year of the agreement Lauri sold 5,960 lures to his new distributors in Sweden and Norway.

Irja and Marja Rapala in Häme national costumes.
(Rapala family archive)

In July 1957 Pelle Lagerström contacted Ensio Rapala on behalf of the Schröder company, and suggested that he visit Rapala for a meeting. Mr Lagerström estimated that his company could sell between 40,000 and 50,000 Rapala lures in Sweden before the end of 1957. The problem was that the Rapala company could only produce around 3,000 lures each month. The letter also suggested that Rapala should have no problem recruiting additional staff because unemployment always increased in Finland during the winter months. Mention was also made of importing celluloid from France and regular supplies of balsawood.

It was in 1957 that the first steps were taken to establish the business on a formal

---

[9] A large pikeperch, known as walleye in North America.

basis in Finland. Lauri and Elma formed Rapala-Uistin, 'Lauri Rapala and Sons'[10]. The owners of the new company were Lauri himself, and his second and third sons Risto and Ensio. Official notes were added to the company's articles to the effect that both Esko and Kauko would receive their share of the company when they came of age. This they duly did.

In 1959 Lauri made his first trip abroad. He and Ensio visited Victory Produkter AB, their distributor in Sweden, only to find some extremely disturbing news. They established that Victory Produkter had registered the 'Rapala' name in Sweden, and had started to produce what they described as a 'Super-Rapala' lure made of plastic for the Swedish market. Lauri and Ensio realised the seriousness of the situation and threatened the company with legal action for registering the name without their consent. Eventually Lauri and Ensio managed to reach an agreement with Victory Produkter's manager Bengt Johansson and a contract was signed on 10 October 1959 securing Victory Produkter the Swedish distribution of Rapala lures until the end of 1960. The agreement also required Victory Produkter AB to gift them a lathe worth 6,200 Swedish Krona as compensation for the use of the Rapala trademark in Sweden. However, the Rapala name remained registered with them.

During the trip Ensio managed to purchase a Sandvik saw blade and a planing tool in order to build a band saw and a circular saw to speed up the production of the wooden lure blanks. The saws would also enable them to handle balsawood more efficiently. It was obvious to the family that balsawood would prove to be the most-suitable long-term raw material for the Rapala lures. Supplies of balsawood were becoming more reliable, but the family would not commit entirely to balsa just yet.

Upon returning to Finland, Ensio built the band saw and the circular saw. The lathe eventually arrived in December 1959, and was set up in the workers' room at the Mattila farm in Riihilahti, where Lauri and Elma had been married in 1928. The family needed someone with good woodworking skills to operate the lathe, so they employed Hugo Siljander, who had gathered the necessary experience during his time at the local saw mills. Eventually the lathe was moved from the Mattila farm to a newly constructed hut adjoining the sauna at Lyyranmäki.

Records kept by Ensio Rapala show that people working from home carved the lure bodies according to Lauri's pattern. In 1957, 24 people were listed in the company records; in 1958 this figure was reduced to 21, and in 1959 it was reduced further to 17. This reflects the gradual automation of the manufacturing process during these years. Ensio had to maintain accurate records of the home workers' wages for submission to the municipal offices each year so that their income tax could be properly calculated. Records also show that Lauri Rapala's business was properly registered for VAT (purchase tax) as early as 1954. The business was growing rapidly.

---

[10] The word 'Uistin' is Finnish for lures.

Fat Rap

The history of the Fat Rap

1977 The Fat Rap is introduced in sizes 5cm and 7cm in a deep-running version.

1978 A Fat Rap shallow-running version is introduced in 5cm and 7cm models.

1991 A Rattlin' Fat Rap is introduced in 4cm and 5cm models.

1992 A Rattlin' Fat Rap 7cm model was introduced.

1993 A Down Deep Rattlin' Fat Rap 7cm is introduced.

1994 A Down Deep Rattlin' Fat Rap 5cm is introduced.

2000 Crayfish imitation colours introduced in Fat Rap:
Brown Crawdad (BCW)
Crawdad (CW)
Fire Crawdad (FCW)
Red Crawdad (RCW).

Fishing the Fat Rap

The Fat Rap has a well-earned reputation for taking finicky fish. When crank bait anglers encounter open water and weary fish they reach for their lightweight outfit, and tie on a Fat Rap. The tight swimming action of this balsa lure is perfect for these conditions.

The Fat Rap works great using the 'bump the stump' method, based on the fact that big bass and often smallmouth will be concealed near the shelter of an ambush point. Hunt out these ambush points (lily pads, log pilings, submerged vegetation, docks, boat houses and of course stumps), and cast to them literally bumping against them on retrieve.

The lure's strong plastic lip should fend off most hang-ups, but if you pick up a weed, give your rod tip a strong backward sweep.

Another technique that really benefits from the Fat Rap's swimming action is cranking. When over points, rock piles or sloping weed beds, cast to the shallow area of the structure and retrieve down the slope bumping the bottom.

Tips from the pros

• When fishing is tough – you've tried every spot you can think of and every presentation you know – try this tip from Rapala pro Larry Dahlberg: take a Fat Rap or Down Deep Rattlin' Fat Rap, which dives at a steep angle, and troll it at high speed – up to 5mph (8kmh) and even faster – along spots that you know should hold fish. Hit the very tips of the points, the little boulder piles, the spot-on-the-spot type of thing. That lure will dive deep while it's still close to the boat, and very much under control, so you can make it go anywhere you want it to go. Make repeated, fast trolling passes over the same spot at a lot of different angles. You can move the boat very fast and catch fish, even in cold water, and even in spring and autumn.

• Strive to develop your sense of feel when retrieving crank baits, suggests bass-pro David Fritts. By paying more attention to the subtle feel of any given crank bait coming through the water (the Down Deep Rattlin' Fat Rap and Fat Rap are favourites) you will just 'know' when something interrupts the normal action. It can mean the lure is out of tune, that it has caught a bit of weed, or that a fish has 'turned on it' and is following the lure. In all cases, valuable information that can help you catch more fish.

• Here's a secret for catching more fish out from under boat docks. Deliberately mis-tune a Fat Rap or Rattlin' Fat Rap, so that it runs either right or left as you retrieve it. Then, position your boat, or yourself if you are shore-bound, so that you can cast to the edge of a dock; as you reel the lure in, it will actually swim under the dock a few feet. Get that bait into the shade and you'll get more bites!

Fat Rap

Code: FR   Freshwater – Floating – Deep Diving

Main features:

- Floating, balsa bodied lure
- Suitable for cranking in deep water
- Fast, dynamic action
- Imitates round-shaped bait-fish
- Long casting and deep diving
- Casts well, even into the wind

Fishing tips:

- A good lure for casting from steeply shelving shorelines
- Stop the retrieve to let the lure slowly float upwards, then start again with a jerk
- Bump the lure along the bottom to imitate a feeding bait-fish

Target predators:

Asp, perch, chub, black bass, zander (walleye), pike, Pacific salmon

Technical features:

Code	Body length	Weight	Treble hooks	Swimming depth
FR-05	5cm / 2in.	8g / $5/16$ oz.	Two No. 4	2.1–4.2m / 7–14ft.
FR-07	7cm / $2^3/4$in.	14g / $1/2$ oz.	Two No. 3	2.7–6m / 9–20ft.

Mini Fat Rap

The history of the Mini Fat Rap

1977 The Fat Rap Deep Runner is introduced in 5cm and 7cm sizes.

1978 The Fat Rap Shallow Runner is introduced in 5cm and 7cm sizes.

1979 The Mini Fat Rap 3cm is introduced.

2000 Crayfish imitation colours are introduced:
Brown Crawdad (BCW)
Crawdad (CW)
Fire Crawdad (FCW)
Red Crawdad (RCW).

Fishing the Mini Fat Rap

It is most important to use ultra-light tackle with this lure. A light rod and supple, low-diameter line will ensure that this lure will cast and perform to ts best.

Use the Countdown method to control the depth of this lure, but also hold the rod tip up to use this lure as a sub-surface lure.

Try this lure when you see fish feeding on or near the surface. If you are fishing a river or stream, try casting upstream and fast winding downstream towards the fish.

Tips from the pros

• Small lightweight lures demand matching tackle. One of the delights of lure fishing is to cast with a completely balanced outfit. A light lure like the Mini Fat Rap can only be cast effectively with a matching rod, reel and line. A lightweight rod with a soft tip, and soft, low-diameter line will always get the best performance from an ultra-light lure. Decide which lures you will use during a day's fishing and make sure that you have the matching rods, reels and lines for them.

• Looking for a modern, yet simple solution to getting crank baits down to depths beyond which they naturally dive? Go to your local tackle shop and ask for the new snap-weight systems, or the new adjustable bottom bouncers, both of which let you put on more or less weight without having to re-tie your rig.

• A predator fish's instincts to strike are brought to the surface when a small fish reacts in a panicky way. Especially when predator fish are in what anglers term a 'neutral' mood (in other words, they can 'take it or leave it' at the moment). A fleeing response can actually trigger the big fish into eating little fish. Fish your crank baits with this in mind: put at least one 'fleeing' move into each cast, as you retrieve your bait, and you should notice an increase in the number of following fish that hit.

• There may be something in the notion that long, slender, minnow-shaped lures attract species like zander (walleyes) and northern pike; and shorter, fatter crank baits attract bass – but that notion may be overemphasised. All species of fish get caught on all types of lures. The most important thing is where a fish is, and whether your lure is similar to forage that fish is feeding on. Zander (walleye) eat short, fat prey, and bass eat long, skinny prey, and saltwater fish eat anything that swims. Which fish strike at which lure will always be a mystery, and the only way to solve the puzzle is to keep fishing.

• In this age of superlines, some anglers aren't aware of the major differences between the no-stretch line and monofilament when putting together the details of a successful pattern. If two people are using the same lure, but one is using monofilament and the other a no-stretch superline, the lure on the superline is probably not only diving deeper, but is behaving differently in the water too. Don't expect identical results with the two very different rigs!

Mini Fat Rap

Code: MFR   Freshwater – Sinking

Main features:

- Popular, long casting, ultra-light lure
- Fast, tight action irritates fish
- Shallow-running lure
- Goes where bigger lures can't go
- Two treble hooks hold fish effectively
- An effective sub-surface lure

Fishing tips:

- Use the Countdown method to control the swimming depth of this lure
- Try it in rivers and streams
- Remember to use ultra-light tackle to balance this lure

Target predators:

Asp, perch, chub, trout, black bass, panfish

Technical features:

Code	Body length	Weight	Treble hooks	Swimming depth
MFR-03	3cm / 1¹/4in.	4g / ¹/8 oz.	Two No. 12	0.9–1.8m / 3–6ft.

Shad Rap Deep Runner

The history of the Shad Rap Deep Runner

1982 Shad Rap Deep Runner 7cm introduced.

1983 Shad Rap Deep Runner 5cm introduced.

1985 Shad Rap Deep Runner 9cm introduced.

1990 Shad Rap Deep Runner 8cm introduced.

1992 Foil colour (B) introduced to the Shad Rap range.

1996 Roach colours introduced:
Blue Roach (BRO)
Gold Roach (GRO)
Orange Roach (ORO)
Roach (RO).

2000 Rapflash holographic colours introduced:
Blue Shad (HBSD)
Emerald Shiner (HESH)
Shad (HSD).
Baby Bass (BB) colour introduced.

2001 Bluegill (BG) and Silver Baby Bass (SBB) colours introduced. Blue Foil colour (BF) reintroduced to the Shad Rap range.

2003 New colours introduced:
Walleye (W)
Silver Shiner (SSH)
Blue Shiner (BSH)
Fire Perch (FP)
Redfin Shiner (RFSH).

2004 New colours introduced:
Hot Steel (HS)
Purpledescent (PD).

Fishing the Shad Rap Deep Runner

The Shad Rap naturally works its way down to its optimum depth. It does not require a fast crank or high troll speed.

You can jig or snap-retrieve your rod tip on the slack line causing the lure to respond with an erratic darting action that simulates a startled or injured bait-fish.

The Shad Rap will maintain its action at very slow speeds so that the fisherman can search all likely fish holding areas thoroughly.

Tips from the pros

• When trolling open basins, make sure you present your spread of lures by motoring in S-curves. Not only does this help you to cover more water, but it creates triggering action by slowing down the inside lines and speeding up the outside lines. Many times, it's the change in speed that brings a strike from a following fish. Also, while you're turning, you're moving the lure away from the possible spooking influence of the boat, allowing even those anglers without planer boards to 'get some spreads to their spreads'.

• When fishing is really tough, here's a little trick gleaned from tournament bass fishermen that can turn the trick on other species too: tie a Shad Rap onto a light line (about 6 lb./3kg) monofilament works well), fishing the lure on a spinning rod. The equipment will allow you to make relatively long casts with the lightweight lure. Now, crank the lure down to the depth you want to reach and begin retrieving. (Choose a Shad Rap based on how deep you are fishing.) At certain points during the retrieve, 'jig' or 'snap' the rod tip, creating slack line and causing the lure to respond with an erratic, darting action similar to a fleeing bait-fish. While you are recovering slack line, your lure is sitting motionless in the water. Predator fish recognise the panic in the darting action, and they recognise the pause as their chance to pounce. This presentation can trigger strikes when many other approaches fail.

• A quick review of how to tune a crank bait that's out of kilter. First bring the Rapala up to eye level and sight along its bottom axis, from the eye of the lure toward the tail. If any of the treble hooks are hanging off centre, use needle-nose pliers to gently bend the hook hanger back into alignment. Always carefully check the 'hanger ring' on the tail of the lure, that holds the rear treble, and carefully bring it back to shape if necessary. If the lure runs off to the side while being trolled or retrieved, bend the eye in the opposite direction the lure is running. Do this only in very tiny stages, checking the lure in the water after each try, until it runs true again.

• Shallow-running lures can be the best choices for deep trolling. That might seem odd, but lures that don't dive deep on their own are often the best option for trolling behind weighted systems such as bottom bouncers, three-way swivels rigs, 'snap-weights' and downriggers.

Shad Rap Deep Runner

Code: SR   Freshwater – Floating – Deep Diving

Main features:

- Specially designed lip for deep diving
- Natural shad-shaped body profile
- Can be cast and trolled
- Maintains its dynamic action at all speeds
- Balsawood body reacts to rod tip movement
- A superb crank bait

Fishing tips:

- Specially designed to imitate bottom-feeding fish in deep water
- Bump this lure along the bottom to kick up little puffs of muddy water
- Search deep holes in rivers by reeling fast to make the lure dive steeply

Target predators:

Asp, perch, chub, trout, black bass, salmon, zander (walleye), pike

Technical features:

Code	Body length	Weight	Treble hooks	Swimming depth
SR-05	5cm / 2in.	6g / 3/16 oz.	Two No. 6	1.2–2.7m / 4–9ft.
SR-07	7cm / 2 3/4in.	8g / 5/16 oz.	Two No. 5	1.5–3.3m / 5–11ft.
SR-08	8cm / 3in.	11g / 3/8 oz.	Two No. 3	2.4–4.5m / 8–15ft.
SR-09	9cm / 3 1/2in.	15g / 9/16 oz.	Two No. 1	2.4–4.5m / 8–15ft.

Shallow Shad Rap

The history of the Shallow Shad Rap

1983 5cm and 7cm models introduced.

1985 Shallow Shad Rap 9cm model introduced.

1990 Shallow Shad Rap 8cm introduced.

1992 Shad Rap Blue Foil finish (B) introduced.

1996 Roach colours introduced:
Blue Roach (BRO)
Gold Roach (GRO)
Orange Roach (ORO)
Roach (RO).

1998 New shiner colours introduced:
Red Shiner (RSH)
Shiner (SH)
Blue Shiner (BSH).

2000 Rapflash holographic colours introduced:
Blue Shiner (HBSH)
Emerald Shad (HESH)
Shiner (HSH).
Baby Bass (BB) colour also introduced.

2001 Bluegill (BG) and Silver Baby Bass (SBB) colours introduced.
Blue Foil (B) colour re-introduced.

2002 Walleye (W) colour introduced.

2003 New colours introduced:
Silver Shiner (SSH)
Blue Shiner (BSH)
Fire Perch (FP)
Redfin Shiner (RFSH).

2004 New colours introduced:
Hot Steel (HS)
Purpledescent (PD).

Fishing the Shallow Shad Rap

The Rapala family claims that the Shad Rap has the best action of any lure they have made to date. Ideal for fish in skinny water, it can be twitched on the surface as a top-water lure, cast and retrieved, or slow trolled. When you are fishing, you can't wait for the fish to find you; you have to find the fish.

Start with the Shallow Shad Rap, which runs 0–4ft. (0.3–1.3m), then move to the original Shad Rap (size 5 runs 6–8ft./1.8–2.4m). The larger the Shad Rap, the deeper it will run (size 9 goes all the way down to 14ft./4.3m).

After a cold front and on days when the fish are not aggressive, try to entice them with a suspending Shad Rap such as the Jointed Shad Rap or the Glass Shad Rap.

The Shallow Shad Rap is a great lure for fishing over weed beds and submerged islands. In rivers it can be fished through the shallow runs that deeper diving lures cannot fish.

Tips from the pros

• There are lots of situations where a shallow-running, minnow-imitating lure can bring up active fish. Even over relatively deep water, you should always consider the possibility that active fish are cruising 'high' in the water column or would be willing to shoot up out of holding areas to take a minnow that's struggling at the surface. The Shallow Shad Rap is an often overlooked casting weapon, because it can be used to churn up the surface, can be twitched on the top, or can be worked slowly so it bulges the water.

• Make sure you keep your lure moving if you see a fish following it! A general guide is to speed up the retrieve slightly as the fish gets closer. That usually triggers a strike. When you see a following fish, that's when you 'work' the lure a lot, put in some twitches and changes of direction. When it darts, a lot of times, they grab it.

• When the wind is pounding into a shoreline that has a 'wall' to it (in other words, it's not a gradual taper onto dry land), predator fish often move in to feed on hapless bait-fish and insects that get bounced back against the wall. The big fish will face the shoreline, much like basketball players looking for a rebound. To catch them, you need to land your casts tight to the shore. Try casting a small Shad Rap so it actually hits land, and pull it away from shore. The strike will usually come in the first few cranks of the reel.

• Don't be in such a hurry to start fishing that you place the importance of presentation in front of finding fish in the first place. It's common for top professional tournament anglers to spend an entire day 'running the water' looking it over with their depth finders before they actually start presenting lures to fish. You can put a Shad Rap or something over the side of the boat to troll while you look things over if you want to. But realise that you need to look for fish before you start fishing.

Shallow Shad Rap

Code: SSR   Freshwater – Floating – Shallow Runner

Main features:

- The world's number one crank bait
- Balsawood body
- Excellent for either casting or trolling
- Lifelike shad shape design
- Lifelike swimming action at all speeds
- Special angled lip to control depth

Fishing tips:

- Very effective in the shallowest water
- Specially suited to rivers and streams
- Fish this lure slowly around sub-surface features

Target predators:

Asp, perch, chub, trout, black bass, salmon, zander (walleye), pike

Technical features:

Code	Body length	Weight	Treble hooks	Swimming depth
SSR-05	5cm / 2in.	5g / 3/16 oz.	Two No. 6	0.9–1.8m / 3–6ft.
SSR-07	7cm / 2 3/4in.	7g / 1/4 oz.	Two No. 5	1.2–1.8m / 4–6ft.
SSR-08	8cm / 3in.	9g / 5/16 oz.	Two No. 3	1.8–2.4m / 6–8ft.
SSR-09	9cm / 3 1/2in.	12g / 3/8 oz.	Two No. 1	1.8–2.4m / 6–8ft.

Sliver

The History of the Sliver

1985 The Sliver is introduced in a 20cm size in just four colours.

1987 The Sliver 13cm model was introduced.

Fishing the Sliver

A trolling lure by design, the Sliver can be used in many ways from flat-lining to downrigger fishing. It is just as good around the coast as it is in the blue water of the deep oceans.

The Sliver does not troll deep and therefore attracts the many game fish that feed on or near the surface. However, the use of a downrigger, or the Countdown method when casting, can get this lure to a good depth where it will pick up the fish schooling near the bottom or in mid water.

The ability of the Sliver to maintain its action at high speed makes it an ideal lure for fishing fast tide rips where game fish often congregate to find their food.

Tips from the pros

• 'Super tune' your trolling lures. The pros like to run their Rapalas at boatside on a fairly short lead, trolling them slowly, making sure that they run true. Then they speed up until they can force the lure to run off to one side. They then tweak the tuning, until it holds true at higher and higher speeds. It's a job that the pros make time for when practising. They believe a 'super tuned' bait will dive deeper, run better and catch more fish. 'Super tuning' might be one of the big secrets of the future. You know how some lures seem to catch more fish than others? Those good fish-catching lures all seem to run well. But if you tune the others, you'll catch more fish with them too.

• A safety tip for anglers who fish saltwater beaches, and wade out in order to reach farther with their casts. Wear protective wading shoes, and shuffle your feet, so you don't step on one of several varieties of rays and fish that can pack a mighty poisonous sting.

• When you make 'S-turns' while trolling, the outside lure speeds up and the inside lure slows down. If most strikes come on the outside line while you're turning, traditional wisdom says the fish 'want the lure speeded up'. But the experts say things aren't always this simple. First, speed the boat up, and troll without turning. If you work the same type of spots, or the same area, and come up empty, it could be that the fish want the baits zigging and zagging, and you have to make more turns to get more strikes.

• If you're trolling multiple lines, don't forget to match up lures that all work at the same speed. A mistake many anglers make is to set out several lines with lures that work well at high speed, and others that have their best action at a much slower speed. That's a mismatched set-up, and one that won't produce good results.

• Fish come in close to a rocky shoreline to feed, and the good angler can take advantage of this. Whether fishing from the shore or from a boat, systematically search the gullies along the shoreline to find the feeding fish. The best time is just after a good on-shore 'blow' when the wave action has churned up the sea bed and forced small fish out of the rock crevices.

Sliver

Code: SL   Saltwater – Sinking

Main features:

- A hardwood, jointed, saltwater lure
- Fitted with VMC Perma Steel hooks
- Fast yet sensitive swimming action
- A superb trolling lure
- Specially designed for big-game fishing
- Runs straight and true at high speed

Fishing tips:

- Don't be afraid to retrieve or troll this lure fast
- Good for casting around rocky coastlines
- Use a suitable knot and leader with this lure

Target predators:

Bonito, tuna, zander (walleye), pike, sea bass, snook, redfish, kingfish

Technical features:

Code	Body length	Weight	Treble hooks	Swimming depth
SL-13	13cm / 5¼in.	17g / 9/16 oz.	Two No. 2	2.7–3.3m / 9–11ft.
SL-20	20cm / 8in.	38g / 1⅜ oz.	Two No. 2/0	3.6–4.2m / 12–14ft.

CELEBRITY BITES

Constant Guigo on Rapala and big-game fishing

When I first used the Rapala CD-18 Magnums in the early 1970s in the Mediterranean Sea, all my fishermen friends laughed at me, saying that only 'white feather jigs' would catch bluefin tuna.

In the early days the Magnums needed some tuning, but we outfished everybody in tournaments. I won my first European Bluewater title in 1972 using only Rapala lures. Since then, everybody has taken to using Rapala lures worldwide, and they are the best bluewater trolling lures ever made. The tuna cannot resist them.

The Rapala brand holds more world-record fish than any other brand. Rapala lures are always easy to fish, and certainly catch more fish than other lures. I have been fishing all around the world for over 40 years now, and Rapala lures are always with me wherever I go.

Constant Guigo

- Winner of the 1st Marlin World Cup in Mauritius
- Three times European Champion
- Winner of over 20 trolling tournaments
- IGFA Representative

CHAPTER 4

The American dream

1959–62

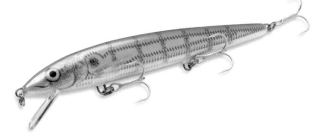

Ron Weber was born in 1928, and graduated from the University of Minnesota Duluth in 1952. He joined Goodyear as a sales engineer, but his love of fishing guided him to Pflueger Fishing Tackle where he was employed as the Midwest regional sales manager. Towards the end of the 1950s Ron left Pflueger in order to start his own fishing tackle sales company, R.W. Weber Sales. Ron was based in Minneapolis where he lived with his wife Mary Ann and their family. His sales territory included Minnesota, Wisconsin and North and South Dakota, one of the premier fishing areas of the USA.

In August 1959 Ron and some friends were heading to north-west Ontario for a week's fishing on Gull Wing Lake. They stopped off to see Ron's friend George Balmer in Duluth. George suggested that they need not travel to Canada for their sport, as fishermen were catching good fish from Pike Lake just outside Duluth, a town situated in the western corner of Lake Superior. Ron asked what the fish were being caught with; George replied, 'Oh, some Finlander plug,' and the matter was dropped.

The fishing trip to Gull Wing Lake was not going well; high winds were making it difficult to catch the walleyes. One member of the group, Al Wallin, took a lure out of his tackle box that Ron Weber had never seen before. Al had received the plug from his uncle, who worked in the American Embassy in Helsinki. He carefully attached the lure to his line and they continued to troll. Suddenly Al's rod arched over as a fish hit the lure. It was boated, and they continued to troll. It was not long before Al's rod assumed a steep curve as another walleye attached itself to his lure, and so it continued.

Ron Weber comments: 'I had been fishing since I was five years old, and I thought that I was a pretty good fisherman. It wasn't every day that I would get out-fished, but when I saw my friend catching fish after fish, I became a believer on the spot. There was something different about this wobbler.' It was a Rapala.

During the first half of the twentieth century many Finns emigrated to the USA to seek their fortune (including, as we have already noted, Viktor Tommola). Consequently there was a significant Finnish population in Minnesota and to the north of the Great Lakes where the timber industry flourished. The size of this community was significant enough for the Finnish government to appoint a Finnish consul to Northern Minnesota. The consul was based in Duluth. His name was Alex Kyyhkynen, and he ran the Dove Clothing Store (*kyyhkynen* is the Finnish word for dove). Together with Koski's

- **Ron Weber discovers Rapala lures in the USA**
- **The start of a long-term relationship**
- **Ron Weber and Ray Ostrom start their first business**
- **'A Lure Fish Can't Pass Up'**
- **Overnight success in the USA**
- **From workshops to factories**

in Minnesota, Karjala and Sons in Illinois, and Hans O. Elmgren of Toronto, Alex imported and sold Rapala lures. It was to Alex Kyyhkynen's shop that Ron Weber headed on his way back to Minneapolis. Ron purchased a few Rapala plugs, and tested them over the next few weeks. They were just as good as the lure that Al Wallin had used to catch all those walleye in Gull Wing Lake.

The more Ron thought about it, the more he believed that he had hit upon a product that could revolutionise fishing in America. He approached his friend and regular customer Raymond Ostrom, another die-hard fisherman; together with his wife Norma, Ray owned a store in Minneapolis called Ostrom's Marine and Sporting Goods. Ray tried the lures that Ron had purchased, and he rapidly came to the same conclusion as Ron. There was something special about the wobblers, and they certainly caught more fish than anything else currently available.

Together they decided that they should try to track down the manufacturer of the Rapala lures in Finland and attempt to purchase some plugs. If they were successful their intention was to start a small distribution company. Ron's wholesale experience and Ray's retail knowledge would form the basis of this new venture. Ron was aware that other people in the fishing tackle trade had seen these new lures, but had turned them down as being difficult to cast, too delicate or too expensive. However, he and Ray could see their full potential as fishing rods and monofilament lines were becoming lighter and more responsive.

Contact is made

Ron and Ray eventually managed to trace the Rapala company through the Finnish Trade Council in Chicago, and on 23 September 1959 Ray Ostrom wrote a letter to Rapala-Uistin in Finland that was to change the history of fishing in the USA, and the lives of the Rapala family and many people around Asikkala, Kalkkinen and Vääksy in Finland. Ron remembers, 'We dictated the letter to Ray's secretary, and she typed it on Ostrom's Marine and Sporting Goods headed paper to make it look more official.'

Rapala lures from 1955 and 1960 (below) compared with the traditional shape that we see today (above).
(Normark Corporation archive)

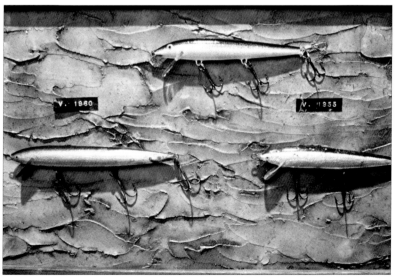

Risto Rapala recalls the letter arriving at their home. 'It took us by surprise,' he said. 'No-one in the family could read it, so my father walked several miles to Särkijärvi village where Mrs Tonttila, a local schoolteacher, translated it for him. We knew that some of our lures were going to America, and we exported a small number ourselves, but we never thought that someone would want to distribute them.' If the truth be told, Ron and Ray's letter arrived just in time. The Rapala family had realised that their business could not support them all. Risto had got a job with a company that was building a local canal, and Ensio was planning to go into further education.

25

OSTROM'S MARINE & SPORTING GOODS
3540 East Lake Street
MINNEAPOLIS 6, MINNESOTA
PA. 2-6601
Boats—Canoes—Motors—Trailers—
Sporting Goods—Camping Equipment
Rentals

Johnson Sea-Horses ● FIRST IN DEPENDABILITY

September 23, 1959

Rapala-Uistin Lauri Pohjala & Pojat
Asikkala, Kalkkinen
Finland

Gentlemen:

Two lures of Finnish manufacture have come to our attention.
We are interested in importing for the purpose of sales and
distribution of these and any other lures which you may manufacture.
We have been informed by the Consulate General of Finland
that you definitely manufacture the plastic minnow labeled on the
diving lip "Original Rapala". The other lure is of the balanced
pimple type that is used for jig fishing. This lure is labeled
Jeppe 3. The trade mark is an Osprey carrying a fish. Do you
manufacture this lure also? If not do you manufacture a similar
balanced pimple type lure?
If a lure of this type is not available from you, would
you put us in contact with the manufacturer. It is imperative
that we have immediate attention on the pimple type lure, as we
hope to introduce it in this area for ice fishing. If possible
we hope to have a quantity of this lure for distribution within
the next six weeks. The "Original Rapala" lure is for distribution
starting after January 1, 1960.
Would you please rush a catalogue of your lures, or if a
catalogue is not available a sample of each. Also, a price
quotation on each item, especially on the "Original Rapala"
and the balanced pimple, indicating any price break on quantities.
If this program is successful in the Central United States,
we intend on a national distribution program. Scandinavian
lures have found good acceptance in the United States, as witnessed
by the success of Abu Fabrik of Sweden and their Abu Reflex lure.
We will work with you on a prepaid basis until credit can
be established.
We have been attempting to contact you since August,
therefore time is at a premium. Please furnish the requested
information by return air mail to enable us to establish an
immediate working arrangement.

Yours truly,

Raymond G. Ostrom

Raymond G. Ostrom

Litho. in U.S.A.

Once the full implications of Ray Ostrom's letter were clear to the Rapala family, Ensio travelled to Helsinki to seek advice from the Finnish Foreign Trade Association. The administration of import and export shipments was far more complicated in the late 1950s than it is today, and Ensio knew that he had to get some assistance if the family business was to succeed overseas. Export shipments in particular required complicated licences from the Finnish government offices in Helsinki.

The original letter to Rapala-Uistin from Ray Ostrom. (Rapala company archive)

MERCHANDISE ORDER

10.01.1960

No. 07402   Req. No. _____   Date Feb 10 19 60

To H Brunou   For _____
Address Commandite Co, Helsinki, Finland Date Required ___
Ship To OSTROM'S MARINE + SPORTING GOODS How Ship ___
Address 3540 EAST LAKE ST. MINNEAPOLIS 6, MINN. U.S.A.   Terms

NUMBER	QUANTITY	DESCRIPTION	PRICE	AMOUNT
1	250 only	7CM length Silver Rapala Floating Spoon Bait		
2	150 "	7CM " Gold	0.44 "	176.0
3	250 "	9CM " Silver	0.44 "	176.0
4	150 "	9CM " Gold	0.44 "	
5	50 "	11CM " Silver	0.42 "	42
6	50 "	11CM " Gold	0.42 "	
7	50 "	13CM " Silver	0.93 "	42
8	50 "	13CM " Gold		
9				446.0
10				
11				
12				
13				
14				
15				
16				
17				
18				
19				
20				
21				
22				

IMPORTANT
OUR ORDER NUMBER MUST APPEAR ON ALL
INVOICES, PACKAGES, ETC.
PLEASE NOTIFY US IMMEDIATELY IF YOU ARE UNABLE
TO SHIP COMPLETE ORDER BY DATE SPECIFIED.

Please Send   Copies Of Your Invoice With Original Bill Of Lading

Raymond S. Ostrom
Purchasing Agent

IH 149 Rediform   **ORIGINAL**

The very first order from Ron Weber and Ray Ostrom for Rapala lures, February 1960.
(Rapala company archive)

Ensio was advised to contact Harald Brunou who ran an agency in Helsinki that specialised in preparing and obtaining correct export documentation for its clients' shipments. Harald assured Ensio that his agency could handle all the administration for Rapala, which would permit the family to concentrate on the production of the lures. The association between Harald Brunou, Rapala and eventually Normark continued until well into the 1970s.

As well as needing a company to handle the complicated paperwork, Rapala and Sons also required a company that could handle the physical shipping of the goods. Dealing with Sweden and Norway presented no problems, as trucking companies ran almost daily services across Scandinavia. However America was a different matter. Harald Brunou advised Ensio to contact Huolintakeskus Oy in Helsinki. Their manager, Kosti Gustafsson, ensured that the family provided the correct shipping documentation, while the company handled the practical shipping side of the operation, and would do so for many years to come.

With the help of Harald Brunou the family replied to Ron and Ray's letter. Ensio accepted the responsibility of managing the business's administration, and his signature can be found on the vast majority of documents in the company archives from this period. The first order for 1,000 Rapala lures was dated 10 February 1960, and included 7cm (2.8in.), 9cm (3.6in.), 11cm (4.5in.) and 13cm (5.3in.) wobblers. It was shipped on 19 March 1960. Each lure was packaged in a printed cardboard box with a transparent plastic lid, a policy that the company continues to honour today.

The second order from Ron and Ray's fledgling company was for 2,040 lures. It was dated 18 April 1960 and was shipped on 29 April. This time the individual lure boxes were packed in outer boxes containing 12 wobblers. This policy was continued until the 1990s when the outer cartons were reduced in size to contain six pieces.

The Rapala family decided that their new American distributors were doing such a fine job that they informed their other American customers to purchase their Rapala lures from Ron and Ray. Since 1959 Rapala has only supplied lures to one company in the USA.

Up and running in America

Ray Ostrom cleared the basement of his store, which was located on 36th Avenue and Lake Street in south Minneapolis. This was to be the head office of the fledgling company that would eventually become the greatest Rapala distribution company in the world. Initially all correspondence was typed on Ostrom's Marine and Sporting Goods headed paper and letters were signed by Ray Ostrom, who handled the administration.

Weber and Ostrom decided to call their company 'The Rapala Company', and, after receiving written permission from Lauri Rapala they registered the name of Rapala as a trademark in the USA. The written agreement was filed on 9 January 1961 and addressed to the US Patent Office. The Rapala family was happy to entrust the registration of their brand name to the people who were working so hard to sell their lures. Both Ron and Ray understood the value and security of developing a strong brand; it would be their lives' work.

Ron especially considered the Rapala family to be a good long-term prospect. He and Ray were offered lures from other family manufacturers in Finland, but none of these families had four sons to continue the business after the parents had bowed out.

While Ray was based at the shop premises, Ron went out on the road and sold the Rapala lures. In fact for the first two years Ron was the company's only salesman. Gradually, through his contacts, Ron was able to set up a sales agency organisation. Ron's contact with agents around the USA helped him to select the very best salesmen, and the company has always boasted the best sales

Ray Ostrom's tackle shop in Minneapolis, Ostrom's Marine and Sporting Goods.
(Rapala company archive)

agency organisation in the American tackle trade. Ron remembers that it was a difficult task to convince the salesmen to take on the responsibility of selling the Rapala lures.

Bill Cullerton Sr., who along with Jack Wicklund was one of the first sales representatives to sell Rapala plugs, remembers the time well: 'The timing was perfect. With the new mono lines and lighter fishing tackle, the industry needed lighter lures. We had many meetings in Ray's tackle store devising ideas on how to tell anglers about this new wobbler.'

One major problem was the cost of the new Rapala lures. 'How were we going to explain the price?' Cullerton continues. 'Established American plugs like the Lazy Ike and Bass Oreno sold for 99 cents. We were planning to sell Rapalas at $1.95. The lures were light, and difficult to cast. They were not suited to the use of a leader because it impaired the action, and occasionally pike and musky[11] bit them off.' Bill's first order that he took for Rapala lures was to Faber Brothers in 1960 for 500 lures.

During the first 12 months of the American distribution agreement with Ron and Ray (1959–60) Lauri's business shipped 3,040 lures to the USA. However, sales for the next year (1960–61) increased to a staggering 31,135. In the same period sales to Scandinavia had increased to between 20,000 and 30,000 pieces. Sales in the Rapala family's own domestic market of Finland amounted to between fifteen and twenty thousand wobblers. A further 1,660 lures were exported to countries outside of Scandinavia and America. Therefore, in the year 1960–61 the business manufactured somewhere between 42,873 and 68,182 lures – a formidable total.

The news media in and around Minneapolis played an important role in promoting Minnesota's outdoor scene during the 1960s, and Ray Ostrom understood the important role that the media could play in the marketing and sales of a new product. He maintained good connections with the local radio and TV stations along with a host of regional and national newspapers and magazines. In fact Ray was a natural public relations man, intent on getting the story of Rapala spread as wide as possible at every opportunity.

Ray's major contribution to the company was his great affinity with the media. Ray regularly appeared on local TV fishing programmes, and suggested possible stories to magazine writers and TV presenters. Ray ran fishing trips from his shop to Crow Lake, near Lake of the Woods on the Canadian border. A bus would leave his shop on a Friday evening; he would arrange guides, accommodation and fishing permits for a very reasonable fee. A busload of very tired and slightly hung-over anglers would return on the Monday morning.

For years, Ray had been a competitive walleye tournament fisherman. He and his fishing friend Jack Maciosek always enjoyed the camaraderie and thrill of the chase. In addition, for three years, Ray ran an invitational musky tournament with the help of his good friend Mike Baronowski, out of Nestor Falls, Ontario, Canada. The invitations to the musky tournament always included a number of Ray's media contacts. Ray was always promoting his business, and now he began the work of promoting Rapala.

---

[11] A short form of 'muskellunge', a large pike of North America and Canada.

Ron Weber with Lauri Rapala and Thorsten Brunou during Ron's first visit to Finland in 1962.
(Rapala company archive)

In October 1961, Marshall Smith, a reporter with *Life* magazine, visited Minneapolis to interview the Minnesota Vikings, a new professional football team that was grabbing the nation's spotlight with its 'Purple People Eater' front four.

Jim Peterson, then editor of the *Minneapolis Tribune*, had known Smith from years back, and invited him to dinner. He also invited Ray Ostrom to join them. With two die-hard fishermen at the table, it was not long before the subject of the conversation got round to fishing. Ray, the ultimate media relations man, had brought a couple of Rapala lures with him, and he told the story of Lauri Rapala and his family. After the dinner Marshall Smith left with the two Rapala lures secure in his pocket. Along with a short report, he sent them to his boss in New York. Marshall Smith's boss did not try the wobblers until the following spring when he spent some time fishing in Maine. The fishing was hard so he regularly changed plugs and eventually put up a Rapala lure. He caught a bass, and then several more on Rapalas, and decided there and then that there might be a decent story to be told.

Ray recalls, 'Marshall Smith seemed interested in our story, but neither Jim or I heard much more from him. It was only later that we discovered *Life* had sent a reporter and a photographer to Finland to interview Lauri Rapala.'

Some six months later, in March 1962, Marshall Smith's secretary Rose called Ray and told him that *Life* was going to run the story of the Rapala family and its lures in the April edition. 'I was just shaking when I got off the phone,' recalls Ray. '*Life* magazine was huge. Everybody read it back then.'

A few weeks later Marshall Smith's secretary called Ray again and explained that the story had been shelved because the space had been allocated to more important articles. It was the time of the 'space race' when the USA and the Soviet Union were making some of their first manned space flights. Rose informed Ray that once a story was shelved it was usually never used. Ray assumed that perhaps it was not interesting enough, or maybe it did not appeal to the editor of the magazine.

Early in 1962 Ron and Ray decided to change the name of their company to Nordic Enterprises Inc., but the Rapala name continued to be registered in the USA.

Meeting the family

It was in July of 1962 that Ron Weber made the first of many visits to Finland. He recalls, 'I had to fly from Minneapolis to New York, then to Copenhagen and on to Stockholm from where I caught a flight to Helsinki. In all it took me about 20 hours.'

Ron had previously arranged for Thorsten, the brother of Harald Brunou, to act as an interpreter, and an attorney called John Adams, who was on a business trip to Europe, would join him later in case there was any need to formulate contracts of any kind.

The Rapala family extended every courtesy to their guest from America, even to the extent of arranging for Ron to have his first sauna. Ron remembers that he had to undress on the lawn in front of the family, including Elma and the sons' wives. After the sauna he was again expected to stand naked on the lawn whilst he was served a beer, and the family stood around him casually chatting. The last thing that Ron wanted was to casually chat. He just wanted to get his clothes on!

During the visit, Risto Rapala and his wife invited Ron and John Adams to dinner at their house. A cold buffet of traditional Finnish foods was served. The fish dishes were particularly to John's taste. He said to Ron, 'I have had too much. I just can't eat another thing.' As he sat back to relax his overfilled stomach Risto and his wife proudly brought the roast beef main course to the table. Ron whispered to John, 'You know that it is extremely impolite to refuse a meal.' After the main course the men retired to the lounge where they were served chocolate cake and coffee. John Adams was not too far away from bursting at the seams.

The Rapala family were proud owners of a small and old Russian car, but were well aware that relations between the USA and the Soviet Union were cool to say the least. They therefore decided not to embarrass their guest by asking him to travel in it. They parked the car out of sight in the woods and hired a Plymouth Valiant and driver from Lahti. The driver had obviously seen the Indy 500 on television and was intent on displaying his driving prowess to Ron. They were taking a bend on a gravel side road when they came face to face with a motorcyclist coming the other way. Ron remembers that the motorcyclist was wearing

The original agreement between Rapala and Nordic Enterprises, 1962.
(Rapala company archive)

76

breeches, a helmet and goggles. In order to avoid a collision the motorcyclist swerved off the road. Ron looked back through the window, and the last sight he had of the motorcyclist was his head bobbing up and down as he tried to steer his machine through a field of wheat.

During Ron's first visit a contract was signed between Lauri Rapala and Sons and Nordic Enterprises Inc. to clarify the terms of the American distribution, and to establish a long-term distribution agreement. The contract contained the following agreements:

- Nordic Enterprises agreed to purchase as many lures as the company could produce up to a maximum of 300,000 pieces against their written orders between 1 July 1962 and 1 August 1963.

    The agreed prices were:

7cm and 9cm lures	$0.38
11cm and 13cm lures	$0.44
18cm lures	$0.70

- Nordic Enterprises promised to pay for the lures on immediate receipt of the shipping notice. In effect, they were paying in advance.

- Lauri Rapala and Sons agreed that until 1 August 1970, provided that Nordic Enterprises Inc. purchased a minimum of 100,000 lures each year, they would not supply any other company in the USA or Canada, nor would they permit any company to manufacture or sell their wobblers in North America.

- Nordic Enterprises Inc. was to advance Lauri Rapala and Sons the sum of $10,000 against the first $100,000 of purchases, to finance the building of a new factory to increase production capacity to a level where it would meet anticipated orders. They would deduct 10 per cent from the payment of each invoice until the $10,000 had been repaid[12].

Life after Marilyn

In early August, Marshall Smith's secretary Rose phoned Ray again and told him that the Rapala story was definitely scheduled for publication in *Life* magazine that month. This was excellent news – but neither Ray nor Ron could foresee the turn of events that would grip the attention of America and the world within a week.

Marilyn Monroe was found dead in her apartment in Brentwood, California on 5 August. The news rocked America, and every newspaper and magazine published a life history or obituary about America's number one beauty.

On 17 August *Life* magazine's front cover bore a picture of Marilyn Monroe and inside featured a pictorial history of her life. Among the accompanying articles in this edition was one entitled 'A Lure Fish Can't Pass Up'. It is understood that this edition of *Life* magazine broke all circulation records and became the biggest-selling issue of all time.

The front cover of the edition of Life *magazine that contained the Rapala article.*
(Rapala company archive)

---

[12] The advance was fully repaid within a year.

Little did the editor of *Life* magazine know that whilst he was commenting upon the passing of one of America's film icons, he was responsible for the birth of a fishing one – the Rapala lure.

The reaction to the article was both immediate and emphatic. American fishermen wanted Rapala lures, and they wanted them now!

Ron Weber remembers the effect of the *Life* article. 'Rapala wobblers were starting to catch on,' he recalls, 'but this was like pouring gasoline on a campfire. We were overwhelmed with requests and orders for Rapala lures. In no time at all we had orders for about three million pieces.'

Ron and Ray could not cope with the phone calls and the mail. For weeks they received three or more bags of mail a day, and many of the envelopes contained cash with a note begging for as many lures as the cash would cover.

'We didn't have enough plugs, and we did not think it right to keep the money until a new shipment of lures arrived.' explained Ron. 'So we returned almost all of it. We nearly went broke from the return postage charges alone.'

There was no way that Ron and Ray could meet the demand for Rapala lures from their stock, and to make matters worse it was impossible for Lauri's small family company to produce lures in anything like the quantity required. The obvious result was a drastic shortage of Rapala products in the USA. The *Life* magazine article had created such an interest in the lures that demand outstripped supply many hundreds of times over.

Stories started to spread about enterprising resort owners and fishing tackle stores limiting the sales of the Rapala lures that they had in stock. There were other stories about dealers charging as much as $25 for a Rapala wobbler. Some fishing resorts rented Rapala plugs to their customers for a $20 deposit and $5 per day.

The Life *magazine article that catapulted Rapala lures to fame in the USA.*
(Rapala company archive)

The response to the *Life* magazine article from across the USA convinced Ron and Ray that they should both make a full-time commitment to their new business. Ray sold Ostrom's Marine and Sporting Goods to Marty Engel, one of his employees, and Ron turned the management of R.W. Weber Sales over to his friend and associate Bill True.

Whilst the *Life* magazine article was creating a virtual stampede in the USA, Lauri and his family were busy in Finland. Until 1963 production was centred at their Kalkkinen and Vääksy workshops. The Vääksy workshop was on the second floor of Ensio's house, and a small fire in the workshop went some considerable way to convincing the family that a purpose built factory was urgently required. It was built in Vääksy very close to the site of the current Rapala headquarters in 1962, using the $10,000 advance provided by Nordic Enterprises Inc.

Ray Ostrom dealing with the demand for Rapala lures.
(Rapala company archive)

In addition to making the full-time commitment to the American market, Ron and Ray also formed a company called Rapala Limited in Canada. Winnipeg was chosen as the location because it was relatively close to Minneapolis. Marge Emby was their first employee, and with help from her husband Ab, she used her garage and basement as a warehouse from which to ship Rapala lures to customers across Canada. With this move, Ron and Ray secured the distribution of Rapala lures throughout North America for their business.

Phase one of the first Rapala factory at Vääksy, built in 1962. (Rapala company archive)

Rattlin' Rapala

The history of the Rattlin' Rapala

1988 First introduced, in 7cm size.

1989 5cm model introduced.

1990 8cm model introduced.

1992 4cm model introduced.

1999 Saltwater colours Croaker (C) and Pinfish (PF) introduced.

2000 Rapflash Holographic colours introduced:
Blue Shad (HBSD)
Emerald Shad (HESD)
Shad (HSD).
Baby Bass (BB) colour introduced.
Crawfish colours introduced:
Red Crawdad (RCW)
Redfire Crawdad (RFCW).

2002 New colours introduced:
Bluegill (BG)
Blue Shad (BSD).

2003 Two new colours introduced:
Chartreuse Shiner (CHS)
Silver (S).

Fishing the Rattlin' Rapala

Cast out a Rattlin' Rapala and watch the swimming action at slow to very fast rates of retrieve. You will be amazed. This loud-rattling, shallow-running crank bait is equipped with two full-size treble hooks for sure hook-ups. The Rattlin' Rapala can be vertically jigged without hook fouling and has a great forward swimming action. It's a special favourite of bass and northern pike anglers.

When bait-fish are schooling, cast a Rattlin' Rapala into the school, let it drop then rip, drop then rip.

The Rattlin' Rapala has two sound chambers each emitting a different frequency rattle. The combination of these sounds makes the Rattlin' Rapala very effective in dark or coloured water where fish tend to rely on their sound receptors more than their eyesight to locate food.

You can jig the Rattlin' Rapala in holes in weed beds or other underwater obstructions to attract the predators that might be there.

Tips from the pros

- If you're having a problem with floating weeds and other debris travelling down your line and snagging on your crank baits, try this trick: put a small split shot on, a few feet up the line. The sinker can be used to help the lure attain a greater depth – and if you're happy with the depth the lure achieves on its own, a tiny sinker won't add much. The sinker will collect much of the wayward material that would otherwise impair the action of your lures, and you'll catch more fish. (Note: a ball bearing swivel, tied into the line a few feet above the lure, performs much the same job, without adding any weight.)

- In dark or dirty water, the fish might need a little help to find their food. This is where rattling lures like the Rattlin' Rapala really come into their own! The loud rhythmic rattle of a Rattlin' Rapala will alert fish to the possibility of a meal, and the vibrations of those rattles will enable the fish to home in on the bait through the receptors in its lateral line. This tip is not used solely in freshwater. Fish will feed close to a rough shoreline in the sea, searching for food washed out of the sand or rocks by wave action.

- The more distance you can keep between you and the fish you want to catch, the better chance those fish are going to 'act naturally'. Too many anglers fail to realise how important it is to keep your distance. Always strive to at least make that first cast from a long way off. Try using planer boards or boat control tactics to keep your lure away from the influence of the boat. Sometimes, the fact that you put fish 'on guard' by giving away your presence is the only reason they don't bite.

- Even if a storm only skirts your fishing area, it can trigger a feeding frenzy. In other words, you may not have to get soaked by rain or bopped by hailstones in order to find fast action. Always avoid extreme weather – especially lightning – but if you can take advantage of the fish's response to rapidly changing light and pressure conditions, you can have a brief period of memorable fishing.

Rattlin' Rapala

Code: RNR   Freshwater – Sinking – Rattling

Main features:

- Multi purpose, long casting lure
- Works well in all conditions
- Can be fished at any depth
- Rapala's first plastic lure
- Incorporates two rattling chambers
- Balanced to fish either fast or slow

Fishing tips:

- Both jigging and countdown techniques work well with this lure
- Can be used for vertical jigging, even through a hole in the ice
- Use the rod tip to impart even more action and sound

Target predators:

Asp, perch, chub, black bass, zander (walleye), pike, panfish, snook

Technical features:

Code	Body length	Weight	Treble hooks	Swimming depth
RNR-04	4cm / 1 1/2in.	6g / 3/16 oz.	Two No. 7	Variable
RNR-05	5cm / 2in.	11g / 3/8 oz.	Two No. 6	Variable
RNR-07	7cm / 2 3/4in.	16g / 1/2 oz.	Two No. 4	Variable
RNR-08	8cm / 3 1/8in.	22g / 3/4 oz.	Two No. 3	Variable

Super Shad Rap

The history of the Super Shad Rap

1993 Super Shad Rap 14cm introduced.

2000 Stainless Steel (SS prefix) colours introduced:
Blue Mullet (SSBMU)
Gold Mullet (SSGMU)
Green Mullet (SSGRMU).

2002 New colours introduced:
Gold Mullet (GMU)
Hot Tiger (HT)
Yellow Tiger (YT)
Shad (SD)
Bluegill (BG).

2003 Walleye (W) colour introduced.

Fishing the Super Shad Rap

Cast out past suspected holding fish, and crank back through at a steady pace. Experiment to find the most suitable retrieval speed for the best action before you start your day's fishing.

Also try ripping the rod from a forward position to a backward position reeling in slack while returning the rod to the forward position. This 'stall' technique suspends the bait for a few seconds every cycle, much like an injured fish using its last reserves of energy.

Striper anglers like to retrieve extra slow with the rod tip up as high as possible to create a simulated surface feeding bait-fish. Be ready to set the hooks. Stripers are known to smash this bait when using this technique.

Be sure to use your wrists when casting this, and other, crank baits. For practice hold your hat under your armpit while casting. If it drops, you are using your arms, not your wrists.

Tips from the pros

• Did you know there are 'vertical' tuning options for Rapala lures? You can control the roll, or wobbling action, of a Rapala lure by bending the eye up or down with needle-nose pliers. By bending the eye down, towards the plastic diving lip, you get a more pronounced (aggressive) wobble, especially at slower speeds. By bending the eye upward, away from the lip, the swimming action becomes more subtle (less aggressive), and the lure will continue to track true even at higher speeds that might otherwise cause the lure to broach (turn on its side). All adjustments to a Rapala lure should be done gradually, and the results of each adjustment tested in the water, to make sure you don't go too far.

• 'Pay attention to how fast you crank when retrieving a Rapala lure,' suggests Ron Weber, founder of the Normark Corporation. 'I honestly think people used to catch more fish on the more traditionally styled Rapala lures when they had those old fashioned, slower reels. Now they have a high-speed reel, but they still crank at the same speed they did in the old days, so the lure is moving much faster. Some lures, like the Super Shad Rap, can be most effective when the delicate, wobbling action is allowed to come out. Reel too fast and you loose something. That's not true all the time, but it's at least something worth thinking about.'

• There's a growing trend among top trollers to try the latest generation 'super lines' to get extra running depth out of minnow plugs and crank baits. These lines have extremely thin diameters for their breaking strength, and that thin profile helps the lure attain up to 30 per cent greater diving depths than the same lure run on heavier line. If you're trying to get to deeper fish, it can make a difference.

Super Shad Rap

Code: SSR Freshwater – Saltwater – Floating

Main features:

- A robust, heavyweight lure made of balsa
- Shallow, wide swimming action
- Angled lip controls swimming depth
- Body shape imitates many bait-fish
- Designed for big fish and extreme conditions
- Fitted with VMC Perma Steel hooks

Fishing tips:

- Can be cast or trolled successfully
- Use a suitable line, a strong leader and snap swivel with this lure
- Use a slow retrieve to search around underwater features

Target predators:

Zander (walleye), pike, musky, bass, striper, blue fish, snook, tarpon, Nile perch, catfish

Technical features:

Code	Body length	Weight	Treble hooks	Swimming depth
SSR-14*	14cm / 5^1/2in.	45g / 1^5/8 oz.	Two No. 2/0	1.5–2.7m / 5–9ft.

* Fitted with VMC Perma Steel hooks

Husky Jerk

The history of the Husky Jerk

1995   Husky Jerk introduced in 12cm and 14cm sizes.

1996   8cm and 10cm sizes added to the range.

1997   6cm size introduced along with new colour CGH.

1999   Down Deep Husky Jerk 12cm developed from the Husky Jerk.

1999   New saltwater colours introduced:
Croaker (CR)
Pinfish (PF).

2000   10cm Down Deep Husky Jerk introduced. Baby Bass (BB) colour introduced. Shad (SD) colour introduced.

2001   Holographic colours introduced:
Blue Shad (HBSD)
Emerald Shad (HESD)
Shad (HSD).

2002   Glass colours introduced:
Glass Perch (GP)
Glass Minnow (GMN),
Glass Blue Minnow (GBM)
Glass Trout (GTR) and
Glass Copper Minnow (GCM).

2003   New colours introduced:
Glass Red Head (GRH)
Glass Fire Perch (GFP) and
Glass Purple Perch (GPP).

2004   New colours introduced:
Glass Black (GBK)
Glass Clown (GCL) and
Glass Muddler (GMD).

Fishing the Husky Jerk

The secret to Husky Jerk success is to crank-stop-crank to take advantage of the neutrally buoyant suspending action that this lure is known for.

There is one time of the year when the suspending Husky Jerk is so effective that it can literally produce a fish on every single cast.

That time is spring, when the water temperature reaches about 52 degrees F (11 degrees C) and the fish move into staging areas adjacent to spawning beds.

They are stacked up like cordwood, but normally they are hard to catch, the move has thrown them off their feed. When you suspend the Husky Jerk in front of them, their reflexes take over. The result is the kind of action fishermen constantly seek, but rarely experience – an absolute bonanza.

Tips from the pros

- In the cold to cool waters of spring, suspending minnow baits are powerful medicine on predator fish, especially bass. A Husky Jerk, for example, can be worked over shallow spots holding springtime fish. Cast the lure out, and work it back with a slow twitch-and-stop presentation. In prime areas, such as near a clump of weeds or woody cover, it can be effective to allow the bait to just sit there for an extended period. A minute might not be too long! Give those sluggish fish time to react, and they just might.

- Looking for a way to catch fish after a cold front comes through? Find a shallow flat that's being baked by the post-frontal sun, and it helps if it's a bit sheltered from the wind. Tie on a floating Rapala or Husky Jerk, and make long casts with it. Retrieve in aggressive pulls of the rod tip, letting it pause between pulls. It doesn't work every time, but it can stimulate inactive fish that are warming in the sunny water and ignoring other presentations.

- Zander (walleye) are sometimes attracted to lures with rattles, such as the Husky Jerk. In very muddy water, during heavy rains, thunderstorms, and in high winds with waves of two feet or more, it sometimes takes a little noise for your lure to get noticed over the commotion.

- Sometimes, the amount of time your lure spends in a critical spot can increase the number of fish you catch. For example, let's say you're casting crank baits for bass in shallow cover. You see a stump, or thick patch of weeds, and cast past it. On the first such cast, go ahead and reel quickly past the object. Aggressive fish are likely to pounce on it as it goes by. But if you get no response, don't hesitate to make the same cast again, to the exact same spot, and this time, fish the lure as slowly as possible as it nears the stump, or passes across the edge of the weeds. A Rapala Husky Jerk is a great lure for such a presentation, because you can almost 'hover' it in place as long as you want. On many days, a lot of fish need that extra 'reaction time'.

Husky Jerk

Code: HJ   Freshwater – Suspending

Main features:

- Neutral buoyancy suspending lure
- High-frequency internal rattle
- One of Rapala's best-selling lures
- Aerodynamic minnow shape
- Typical wounded minnow action
- Heavy weight and excellent balance

Fishing tips:

- Suitable for casting and trolling
- Stop the retrieve to let the lure suspend close to underwater features or weed beds
- Jerk the lure into motion to gain the fish's attention

Target predators:

Salmon, sea trout, pike, panfish, black bass, zander (walleye), snook

Technical features:

Code	Body length	Weight	Treble hooks	Swimming depth
HJ-06	6cm / 2^1/2in.	3g / ^{1}/8 oz.	Two No. 10	1.2–1.8m / 4–6ft.
HJ-08	8cm / 3^1/8in.	6g / ^{1}/4 oz.	Two No. 6	1.2–1.8m / 4–6ft.
HJ-10	10cm / 4in.	10g / ^{3}/8 oz.	Two No. 5	1.2–2.4m / 4–8ft.
HJ-12	12cm / 4^3/4in.	13g / ^{1}/3 oz.	Three No. 5	1.2–2.4m / 4–8ft.
HJ-14	14cm / 5^1/2in.	18g / ^{1}/2 oz.	Three No. 4	1.2–2.4m / 4–8ft.

Team Esko

The history of the Team Esko

1999 The Team Esko is introduced as a 7cm model only.

2003 New colours introduced:
Hot Tiger (HT)
Nordic Perch (NP)
Silver Foil (SF)
Gold Rainbow Foil (GRB)
Red Tiger (RDT)
Brown Tiger (BRT)
Blue Foil (BF)
Green Parrot (GPT).

Fishing the Team Esko

A floating lure designed by Esko Rapala. The Team Esko has the slightly bulkier body of the Countdown lure, but remains a very responsive floating lure.

Ideal for trout and sea trout, this lure will also take salmon. In still and slow moving waters it is suitable for small perch and small pike.

Fish the Team Esko just as you would fish an Original lure. Change your style of retrieve until you find one that works.

The Team Esko can be used with additional weights for searching the depths or longer casting.

Tips from the pros

* Lure speed, in some cases, is the 'forgotten variable' when it comes to catching fish on crank baits. Most crank baits will achieve their maximum diving depth at speeds ranging from 1–3 mph (1.5–4.5kph). But at what speed do the fish want the lure? That's another consideration, and the only way to discover the answer is by constantly experimenting until the fish 'tell you' by striking.

* Learn exactly how deep your crank baits run when you cast and retrieve them, and you'll catch more fish. You can even try to get your baits hung up. It sounds crazy, but if you can get your lure to snag on a brush pile or some other cover you're trying to fish, then use a lure retriever (tied to a rope, which is marked every foot (0.3m) to hook up your bait. Before you pull the bait loose, get right over the top of it, and you can tell (by reading the markings on the rope) exactly how many feet of rope are between you and the lure. *Voilà*! No more guessing how deep that lure runs when it's cast and retrieved.

* Colour is important! When you fish crank baits, have members of your party start out with lures of significantly different colour. Perhaps one will use silver and black, another a Firetiger, and another a gold, or blue, or chartreuse, or perch – you get the idea. Once a certain colour starts to produce, then have most or all people switch to that colour, to see if it will consistently produce. If the action slows, begin the experimentation all over.

* A slow moving, minnow-imitating plug can often be the key to catching fish in tough, post-cold front conditions. Try this proven set up: a small (5cm or 7cm) floating Rapala, attached with a smallish plain snap. About 18–24in. (46–61cm) in front of the lure, put enough split shot to get the lure down as deep as fish are holding (you can often spot fish signals on your depth finder under such conditions, even if they are not willing biters). *Very* slowly troll, perhaps just putting an electric motor in and out of gear, through the 'marks' on the depth finder. The slow, rolling flash of the lure can turn the trick on many days.

Team Esko

Code: TE   Freshwater – Floating

Main features:

- Extra light balsa lure designed by Esko Rapala
- L-shape lip provides a strong swimming action
- Larger body shape than the Original
- Aerodynamic extra-long casting shape
- Features VMC Cone Cut hooks
- Works well in fast water

Fishing tips:

- Tailor made for trout fishing in running water
- Use the rod tip to impart more action
- Do not retrieve too quickly in fast-flowing rivers

Target predators:

Asp, perch, chub, trout, salmon, black bass, sea trout

Technical features:

Code	Body length	Weight	Treble hooks	Swimming depth
TE-07	7cm / 2³/₄in.	6g / ⁵/₁₆ oz.	Two No. 6	1.2–1.8m / 4–6ft.

CELEBRITY BITES

John Wilson on his favourite Rapala lure

I dread to think how many years I've been using Rapala lures. What I do know is that without them, my catches would simply not be the same. If I were to be limited to just "one" lure for fishing in both fresh and saltwater around the world, I would have no hesitation in choosing a CD-18 Magnum in Silver Blue Mackerel (SM). On this lure alone, as seen on my television programmes over the last 20 years on both Anglia Television and Channel Four in the UK, I have accounted for giant lake trout in Canada's far north to 25 lb.-plus; sailfish out of Malindi along the East African coast to over 75 lb.; and from massive Lake Nasser in Egypt, which is of course the River Nile, dammed from Aswan all the way south for over 300 miles to Sudan, giant Nile perch to a staggering 150 lb.

I have learned to trust and rely on the design of Rapala lures to catch and hold big fish in the most testing conditions, and have little doubt that Rapala manufactures many of the strongest wooden fishing lures in the world. With trust comes confidence, so when I am planning a fishing safari wherever it might be in the world, I always pack a good selection of Rapala lures, and top of my personal list is the Rapala CD-18 Magnum (SM).

John's Lake Nasser guide Mohamed shares in the capture of yet another 100 lb.-plus Nile perch – fooled by the action of a 'Rapala lure, of course.

CHAPTER 5

International co-operation

1963–74

During the first meeting in Finland, Ron had explained to Lauri the need to expand the range of lures. The 'Original' floating lure was perfect as it was, but it did have limitations. Indeed the original letter written by Ray Ostrom to Rapala-Uistin in 1959 had even mentioned the need for a 'pimple' or jigging lure. The Scandinavians who had emigrated to Minnesota and Wisconsin had taken their winter fishing techniques with them, and there was a flourishing ice fishing business in the Midwest states. The idea of this lure was to jig it up and down to make it swim in either a circle or a figure-of-eight, attracting the fish that would eventually strike.

Lauri put his mind to the project and adapted the Original floating lure. The new, balanced jigging lure (called the Jigging Minnow) was manufactured from a combination of lead and balsawood. It had a single hook on each end of the lure whilst a treble hook was hung centrally from the belly. Esko Rapala remembers working on the development of the Jigging Minnow during 1960 and early 1961. Guided by his father, Esko eventually achieved the right combination of lead and balsawood to make the lure balance properly and flutter attractively as it was jigged up and down. The Original Finnish Jigging Minnow was introduced to the American market in 1961. The lure was initially made in two sizes, No. 5 and No. 7, and in two colours, silver and gold. Additional sizes No. 3 and No. 9 followed quickly. Ensio's records show that over 7,500 jigging lures were exported to the USA in that year.

Both Ron and Ray realised that there was a good opportunity to expand their business by importing ice drills. The renowned experts in ice drilling were without doubt the Finns; so, at Lauri's suggestion contact was made with a company called Mantere Brothers of Lahti who manufactured the Fin-Bore ice drill. The company did good business with Mantere Brothers, importing significant quantities of these. However, they eventually took the decision to stop selling the ice drills, as they were heavy and bulky, and did not fit into their warehousing and shipping programme.

- **The Original Finnish Jigging Minnow**
- **Tank-testing beats the competition**
- **The first contact with VMC**
- **A family tragedy**
- **Fish 'n Fillet knives**
- **Lauri visits America**

Competition and imitation

The Rapala business was now growing rapidly, and in 1963, just one year after the completion of their first factory, the family opened a second one at nearby Riihilahti. It was a constant race against time to keep production in pace with demand. The boom in lure fishing in the USA created a lure-manufacturing industry centred on Asikkala, based upon Lauri's knowledge that he had passed

Rapala's new factory at Riihilahti,
opened in 1963.
(Rapala company archive)

on to his employees. Naturally a parallel industry was spawned in the USA, but one of the most threatening competitive industries was based in Japan where copies of the Rapala lures were manufactured bearing names very similar to the Rapala product. At one time America had over 40 copies of the Rapala lures circulating throughout the tackle trade, including lures from Finland, Sweden, Japan, and of course lures manufactured in America.

One small manufacturer based on America's east coast took matters a little too far when he used a picture of a Rapala lure in one of his advertisements which also contained the words, 'As seen in *Life* magazine.' Ron and Ray had no option but to seek legal redress. Despite having to go to court in the manufacturer's home town, and regardless of the fact that the man regularly played golf with the local judge, Ron and Ray won the case, and the manufacturer was never heard of again.

Ray relates a story of a manufacturer who produced a copy of a Rapala lure made from an expanded foam product. The manufacturer left the lure samples in his car on a hot sunny day. When he returned, he found that the heat had caused all the lures to explode. 'Best thing that could happen to them,' said Ray.

Despite the threat posed by unscrupulous competitors, Lauri refused to lower his standards in order to increase production. His attention to detail and insistence that every lure should be tank-tested ensured that the Rapala lures were consistently superior to the lower priced copies that threatened to flood the market. In fact Nordic Enterprises in the USA frequently demonstrated Rapala lures against their competitors to prove that the Rapala product, whilst being more expensive, was significantly superior.

Lauri's insistence on tank-testing every lure was probably the main reason that Rapala lures saw off the vast majority of the competition. It was as true in 1963 as it is today that every lure is tested in a water tank to ensure that it swims both straight and upright. Trained staff attach the lure to a short length of monofilament, which in turn is attached to a short 'fishing rod'. The tester draws the lure through the water quickly then slowly watches the action. The lure can be fine-tuned by bending the nose wire left or right to correct a tracking problem, or up and down to correct the speed of the action. It is also possible to adjust the action by shaving a small amount of material from the plastic lip. However, this method is not recommended as a DIY option. The tank-testing is the last factory operation before the lures are dried and packed ready for shipping, and gives rise to the company's claim that, 'A Rapala lure swims straight out of the box.'

There was, however, one problem that tank-testing would never solve. Nordic Enterprises began to receive small packets from fishermen that contained the nose ring and two parallel lengths of brass wire that formed part of the hardware of a Rapala lure. The packets always contained a letter that told the same story. 'I was fishing and my lure either hit a snag or a fish. When I put some pressure on the line, it all came free, but all I retrieved was the nose ring and wires.' It was some time before the reason for the failures became apparent, and it required close inspection of the brass wire and the dissection of a number of lures to determine the cause. The brass wire at the front end of the lure appeared to be decomposing to a carbon material and therefore lost its strength.

The problem was in fact electrolysis, a common metallurgic reaction frequently experienced by users of outboard motors on boats. The brass wire, steel hook, aluminium foil and copper split ring were all reacting together to form an electrical charge, and the weakest component, the brass wire, was being burned during the reaction. Rapala's decision to use brass to avoid corrosion was a correct one in principle, but now the company changed to stainless steel, and the problem was solved.

1963 also saw important changes to Rapala distribution in Sweden. Victory Produkter AB, which had been the Rapala distributor since 1955, went into liquidation. Ensio and his father were aware that one of the assets of Victory Produkter was the Swedish registration of the Rapala name. The Rapala family were in touch with a Mr Bengtsson, a businessman with distribution companies in Sweden. Through his contacts the Rapala family managed to acquire the Swedish Rapala name registration, and once again they had control of their family name in one of their most important markets. The Swedish subsidiary of American lure manufacturer Heddon purchased the business of Victory Produkter AB.

In 1964–65 the Swedish distribution of Rapala lures eventually found its way to Fransk-Nordiska Handelskompaniet, a company owned by Mr Bengtsson. The literal translation of the name is 'French-Nordic', and the company's primary business was the importation of fishing tackle products from France. The company handled the distribution of Mouches-Ragot flies and VMC hooks; coincidentally some 35 years later both of these companies were to be members of the Rapala group of companies. Mr Bengtsson also maintained an interest in a Finnish company, and it was via this company that Rapala began its long association with the French hook producer VMC (Viellard Migeon et Cie).

The Original lure was difficult to cast in wind, and weight had to be added if it was to be used in deep water. The market desperately needed a weighted lure that would cast further and more accurately. Lauri and his sons used their Original model as a basis upon which to create a new design. Lauri was

Rapala's Countdown range in 1971.
(Rapala company archive)

adamant that the action of the new lure should be exactly the same as his Original model. After all, it was arguably the best wobbler in the world.

The lure was developed gradually on a trial and error basis. Esko Rapala was responsible for the design and production of the lure whilst his father offered advice and tested the prototypes. Two important factors eventually became apparent. If a lead weight were to be added to the lure to increase its weight, it would have to be placed directly on the lure's centre of gravity. This would minimise any effect the additional weight would have on the action of the lure. Secondly, the additional weight did affect the action of the lure, and a slightly larger body shape was required to maintain the wounded minnow action that had made the Original model so successful.

The prototypes were finally tested and approved by Lauri before being sent to the USA for Ron and Ray's approval. They voted the new lures an immediate success. For 1965 the new sinking lure was offered in 7cm (2.8in.), 9cm (3.6in.), and 11cm (4.5in.) models. The name 'Countdown' was invented by Ron, and came about from a method of fishing where the lure was cast, and the fisherman counted the number of seconds it took for the lure to reach the bottom. Once he knew how long it took, the fisherman could then fish the lure at the depth he wanted by casting and counting the number of seconds it took to reach the required depth. By using the countdown method an angler could in fact fish his Countdown lure from the bottom to the top of the water column thereby maximising his chances of finding the fish.

In addition to the new Countdown lure an 18cm (7in.) version of the Original lure was introduced, and a new 18cm (7in.) Saltwater lure was launched. The Finnish Saltwater Minnow was recommended for tarpon, striper, weakfish, redfish and snook in saltwater, plus both pike and musky in freshwater. It was in fact a standard lure fitted with two saltwater-resistant treble hooks. The cadmium plating on the hooks made them blunt, and a tag was attached suggesting that the purchaser should sharpen the hooks before the lure was used. Tarpon up to 150 lb. were taken on the Saltwater 18cm (7in.), but the balsawood lure was not robust enough to withstand a great deal of punishment.

Ray Ostrom and his brother-in-law Ramon Cronin took some gold Saltwater 18cm (7in.) lures to Florida to fish in the Keys with a guide called Rhodes. Ray cannot recall his Christian name, but does remember him approaching Ray,

The Rapala 18cm (7in.) Saltwater lure.
(Rapala company archive)

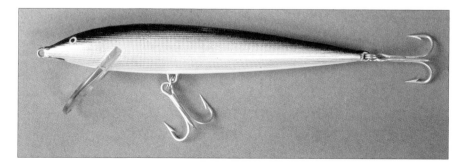

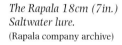

shouting, 'Why fish with the rest when you can fish with the best, and I'm the best!' Mr Rhodes suggested that it would be best to fish for tarpon at night near one of the long bridges that join the various islands in the Keys. They started fishing, and were using a powerful spotlight to see the fish jump, when suddenly a truck careened across the bridge. Ray could see flashes of light coming from the truck, and asked his brother-in-law, a Minneapolis police officer, 'What are those flashes from the truck?' Ramon replied, 'Those flashes

The extension to the first Rapala factory at Vääksy.
(Rapala company archive)

are gun fire! Get your head down!' It transpired that there had been a drugs bust in a nearby town, and the police were chasing the drug dealers. As the dealers drove across the bridge, they saw the boat with a powerful spotlight below them, and thought that the Coastguard was also chasing them, so they opened fire.

The Finnish Saltwater Minnow was introduced in the usual silver and gold colours. The silver coloured Saltwater, Countdown and Original lures were also given a coat of blue spray paint along the back during the production process; this was to make the famous Rapala Blue (B) colour that has been in constant production since its introduction in 1965. From a range of six lures in 1964, the company could now boast a total of 13 lures in 1965. Each lure was available in a choice of three colours – Blue (B), Gold (G) and Silver (S) – making a total range of 39 lures.

One immediate result of this increase in the product range was the expansion of the Vääksy factory that the family built in 1962. The Rapala brothers formed the opinion that they spent just as much time extending their factories as they did manufacturing and designing lures in the early 1960s.

The staff and sales statistics of the 1960s make interesting reading:

Year	Staff	Sales to USA of lures	Total sales of lures
1963	18	225,348	272,482 (1962–63)
1964	46	783,582	934,009 (1963–64)
1965	77	1,334,916	1,579,556 (1964–65)
1966	84	1,531,042	1,713,083 (1965–66)
1967	91	1,594,320	1,856,945 (1966–67)
1968	100	1,687,932	2,050,066 (1967–68)

These figures demonstrate that the Rapala-Uistin business was growing very steadily and very quickly. In fact the company was the largest employer in the Vääksy area.

Very few parts of the manufacturing process were mechanised in the early 1960s. The balsawood was sawn to size automatically, and lathes were used to shape the lures. Other than these two processes everything was completed by hand.

A family tragedy

The happiness of the Rapala family over the success of their business was to be cut short by a tragic event that even to this day saddens their hearts.

One July evening Lauri and Elma's youngest son, Kauko, was visiting some friends who lived on the banks of the Kalkkinen Canal. Kauko travelled to their house in his boat, a rowing boat with an outboard engine. His brother Ensio still maintains that the engine was a little too powerful for the boat.

Late in the evening, just as it was getting dark, Kauko started his journey home. No doubt the friends had enjoyed one or two drinks during the evening, and perhaps the effects of these and the failing light conspired for Kauko not to see a partly submerged log boom in the water. Kauko's boat hit the boom at some speed and Kauko lost control. He fell against the gunwale of the boat and into the water.

His body was recovered from the water the next day; his brother Ensio was there to witness it. Kauko always kept a fishing rod in his boat, fully rigged with a Rapala lure, and when his body was taken from the water the Rapala lure could be seen hooked into his trousers. The line still attached the lure to the reel and the broken rod.

A picture of Kauko Rapala taken just before his untimely death.
(Rapala company archive)

During the police investigation into Kauko's death, some neighbours reported hearing someone shouting from the direction of the canal. However, the shouting did not continue long enough for them to decide to investigate. It would appear that Kauko fought hard for his life before the deep water, powerful current, and the tangled rod, line and lure overcame him. To this day, Ensio keeps Kauko's broken rod in his summer cottage on the banks of the Kalkkinen Canal.

Kauko Rapala's friends and fellow workers remember him as a modest and sensitive person, much like his father. He was well liked and respected by his friends and neighbours in the village. His death devastated the Rapala family, but no-one more so than his father. Lauri had always enjoyed a drink, but his son Ensio believes that Kauko's death may have resulted in Lauri drinking more than was good for him. According to Finnish law, Kauko's share of the Rapala business, which he had received when he came of age, automatically reverted to his parents as Kauko had no wife or family of his own.

A few years before his death Kauko and his brother Esko had jointly purchased a summer cottage not far from their house. Lauri made an agreement with Esko to exchange Kauko's interest in the summer cottage with a share of the site where their house Noukkahonka was built. As a result of this exchange Esko became the sole owner of the summer cottage.

Normark's first offices in the USA, opened in 1965.
(Normark Corporation archive)

1965 was a busy year in the USA as well as in Finland. Ron and Ray decided to change the name of their company again. They were both native Minnesotans and they wanted to capture the spirit of northern Minnesota and Wisconsin. They eventually agreed on the name of 'Normark', which means 'north land'. All products sold by the company were branded either Normark or Rapala. 'We really liked the name. It had a good European sound,' says Ron Weber. The name of their Canadian company was changed to Normark Limited at the same time. Normark in Canada became the first of many overseas distribution companies to bear the Normark name. Ron and Ray also decided that they should move into more suitable premises. The new Normark company moved into an office and warehouse unit at 1710 East 78th Street, Minneapolis, which was to remain their home for many years.

It was in 1965 that Normark USA won its first Importer of the Year award, sponsored by *Sporting Goods Dealer*, a national trade magazine serving the sporting goods industry of the USA. The magazine surveyed more than 1,200 sporting goods dealers, wholesalers and sales representatives, who overwhelmingly selected Normark for its quality products. In addition the magazine named the Rapala lure 'The Hottest Selling Lure in the Country 1965'. The Rapala lure won the same award in 1966.

Not only was the Rapala lure outstripping the competion, it was also catching the most trophy fish. That same year, Rapala also dominated the annual Field and Stream Fishing Contest with eight winners, and the Sports Afield Big Fish Contest with 11 winners. At the time of writing, according to the International Game Fish Association no other lure has been responsible for more state, provincial, national and world records than the Rapala lure.

The tradition of fishing in the USA in the 1960s revolved around the dinner table. Catch and release policies were practised on some expensive game fisheries, but the general rule was to take home whatever you caught. Fishermen had little idea of how to preserve their fish for the journey home or of how to clean or fillet them ready for the freezer. Many fishermen, Ron Weber amongst them, took their fish to a local fish processing plant to be filleted because they had the correct knives for the job.

Ron noticed that the fish processors used very thin, flexible-blade knives to fillet the fish. The knives were not purchased in this condition. Years of use and constant resharpening had worn the blade into a state ideal for filleting the delicate flesh of fish. Ray and Ron discussed the possibilities of marketing such a specialist knife, and agreed that any fisherman would welcome a knife like this in his tackle box.

Aware that the best cutlery steel came from Scandinavia, Ron and Ray contacted Harald Brunou in Helsinki to ask his advice. Harald had no hesitation in recommending a small family business called J. Marttiinin Puukkotehdas Oy, which was situated in a town called Rovaniemi, right on the Arctic Circle in the north of Finland.

Normark contacted the Marttiini family in late 1965 and supplied details of the knife that the company required. Marttiini's expertise lay in the manufacture of traditional Lapland hunting knives: strong, sturdy, and designed to cut meat, tree branches, and anything else that the Lappish hunter required. They studied the request, but to Ron and Ray's frustration they answered Normark's enquiry with a definite 'No' because they thought the blade would be too lightweight and flimsy.

Ron and Ray decided to give Marttiini one last opportunity to make the knives. In 1966 Ron visited the factory at Rovaniemi and over lunch in a restaurant wrote an order for 20,000 knives on a paper napkin, subject to the company manufacturing the knives to the Normark specification. This was a huge order for the Marttiini family, and one that they could not refuse. They accepted. The Marttiini family still have the paper napkin in their files.

Prototype samples soon started to wing their way across the Atlantic. However, it was early in 1967 before the first production knives reached the USA. They featured the slim, flexible blade similar to the one that Ron had seen in the fish processing plant, with varnished birchwood handles and a leather sheath that incorporated a belt loop. The knives were marketed under the Rapala brand as the 'Rapala Fish 'n Fillet' knife. The Fish 'n Fillet range was gradually expanded to four knives of 4in., 6in., 7.5in., and 9in. models. The first knife was an immediate bestseller in the USA, and remains the most popular filleting knife in America today. Since its introduction it has been exported around the world. The total sales by Rapala and Normark companies are in excess of 30 million knives.

Ron and Ray launch the Rapala Fish 'n Fillet knife range in 1967. (Normark Corporation archive)

Ron and Ray can take some of the credit for teaching fishermen around the world how to fillet fish. In order to promote their new knives they published booklets and drawings showing the correct way to fillet the various shapes of fish commonly caught around America and Europe.

Back in Finland the death of Kauko resulted in some changes within the Rapala company. Gradually the three brothers took over more of the responsibility for running the business from their father. Ensio was responsible for the administration of the company, Risto looked after production, and Esko was in charge of purchasing and product development. In fact the changes were not at all difficult to make because the three brothers took responsibility for the jobs that they knew best.

Despite Kauko's death, the work of the Rapala company continued. In 1966 a 13cm (5.3in.) lure was added to the Saltwater range, and a Countdown 13cm (5.3in.) lure was introduced[13]. In 1967 the emphasis moved to smaller lures with the introduction of the Original and the Countdown 5cm (2in.) lures. Gradually the Rapala lures were reaching into niche markets as well as the mainstream in North America. It was North America, their largest market, that lead the development of new products.

A trip to America

The year of 1967 was without doubt one of the most important in the history of Rapala lures. It was the year when Lauri Rapala, with his son Risto, made his only trip to the USA. Risto and Lauri travelled to Minneapolis and fished for two weeks with Ron Weber and Ray Ostrom at Lake of the Woods along the US–Canadian border.

When Lauri and Risto arrived Ron told them that Lauri was more famous in America than Jean Sibelius or Paavo Nurmi. Lauri laughed, but Ron and Ray were to prove just how famous his name was in the USA. Their first stop on the journey north was at Duluth where they visited a Finnish owned café and boarding house for a coffee. Ron told the owner that Lauri Rapala was in his café. The rooms of the boarding house were rented to Finnish timber workers and the owner spread the word among them. In little less than an hour Lauri was surrounded by expatriate Finns, all of whom were proud to meet the maker of the famous Finnish lure. Just as they were about to leave Lauri visited the restroom. Ron and Ray waited patiently for him to return, but he did not reappear. Ron went to investigate, only to find Lauri surrounded by Finns, some of whom were in tears talking about their homeland. Their second stop was at International Falls. Ron also told the owner of another café who his guest was. In short order cars blocked the driveway, as more Finns and keen fishermen queued to meet Lauri.

They fished for walleye, northern pike and especially musky. For the first time Lauri and Risto could experience how their lures were used for species of fish not found in their native Finland.

Lauri and Risto Rapala, together with Harald Brunou, are welcomed to Normark by Ron and Ray.
(Rapala company archive)

---

[13] The 13cm (5.3in.) Countdown did not have a long life. It was first listed in Normark Corporation's catalogue in 1967 and continued until 1970, after which it was apparently discontinued.

Lauri aboard the boat the Lord Rapala, *that was named after him.*
(Normark Corporation archive)

A product development meeting aboard the Lord Rapala.
(Rapala company archive)

The American fishermen also used the lures in different ways. They used different rigs and different retrieves to make the lures more effective for specific species or fishing conditions. Lauri was not an experienced rod and line fisherman, and his casting was best described as adequate, but whatever he lacked in fishing technique he made up for in his knowledge and understanding of fish and their habits.

During their time at Lake of the Woods, the group stayed onboard Normark's houseboat the *Lord Rapala*, which was permanently moored on the lake. Ray and Ron used the boat to entertain writers and customers. It was an ideal base for fishing. A few years earlier they had found the boat for sale at Baudette, Minnesota for the sum of $10,000. Previously named *Reel 'em In*, Ron and Ray had no hesitation in renaming the boat.

One evening Lauri insisted on preparing the walleye they had caught for dinner. Ray in particular watched with interest as Lauri left the head on, then scaled and cleaned the fish. He carefully wrapped it in foil with some butter, and put it over the fire for a few minutes. When the fish was cooked, Lauri carefully selected the eyes and the cheeks as delicacies. Ray had never seen this before, as it was American custom to throw the head away. Even today he cannot bring himself to eat the eyes of a walleye, and to be truthful, he is not too keen on the cheeks either.

On the return trip to Minneapolis, Ray's car suffered an overheating problem so they pulled into a garage near Virginia, Minnesota. Ron told the owner who Lauri was, and without hesitation the owner went over to Lauri and started talking to him in perfect Finnish. Lauri was astounded, but he was beginning to understand just how much impact his lures were having in America, and what a good job Ron Weber and Ray Ostrom were doing in this important market. As he sat in the car he smiled, and said, 'Perhaps I am as famous as Sibelius.' The knowledge that Lauri and Risto gained from the trip returned to Finland with them, and was put to good use in the development of the next series of lures.

1968 was the year that Lauri Rapala was accorded the honorary title of 'Talousneuvos' by the President of Finland, Urho Kekkonen. The title was awarded in appreciation of Lauri's achievements in business, and the government recognised the contribution that the Rapala company made to both the national and regional economy. The Finnish people always address recipients of this award as 'Neuvos' in order to show their respect and appreciation towards the title holder.

In the same year Lauri was honoured with a Finnish National Entrepreneur award. Lauri was not comfortable being the centre of attention at ceremonies of this nature, so Ensio attended the event and was presented with the award on behalf of his father. All in all, not a bad year for the man who was born out of wedlock, could not read or write until he was in his twenties, and had spent a large part of his life in forestry and farming.

It was in 1968 that Ron and Ray decided to expand their business by purchasing a lure-manufacturing company based in Minneapolis. Bill Huntley had founded the National Expert Bait Company in 1932, and in 1968 he co-owned it with his son-in-law Dale Norton. The company's primary products were wide-bodied high quality spoons fitted with single, double or treble hooks via a split ring. Bill Huntley was ready to retire, so the deal was done. At the back of Ron and Ray's minds was the fear that something might happen to the Rapala company in Finland. With their new company, they could take up the production of the Rapala lures in the USA if need be. Fortunately nothing did happen to Rapala, and for the next ten years very little was heard of the National Expert Bait Company.

Esko Rapala made his first visit to America in 1969 and visited Ron and Ray in Minneapolis. During this visit the Mayor of Minneapolis, Charles Stenvig, conferred an Honorary Citizenship of Minneapolis upon Esko in recognition of the close association between the Rapala company and the city.

Yet another award was conferred upon Lauri Rapala in 1969 when the President of Finland personally awarded Lauri with an Export Prize in recognition of the company's achievements and its contribution to Finnish overseas trade.

Lauri and Harald Brunou take a walk on the deck of the Lord Rapala.
(Rapala company archive)

Lauri and Risto fish from the boat on Lake of the Woods.
(Normark Corporation archive)

*An American tackle dealer
describes fishing techniques
to Lauri and Risto.*
(Normark Corporation archive)

The Normark group of companies expanded again in 1969 with the formation of their UK company, initially called Loch Mer Ltd. The company was based in Buckfastleigh, Devon in south-west England, and its managing director was former British casting champion Omri Thomas. The company supplied a range of fishing tackle including Rapala lures and Fish 'n Fillet knives to the wholesale trade throughout England, Scotland and Wales. It was not until 1975 that the name Loch Mer was changed to Normark Sport Ltd.

In 1969 Ensio Rapala visited Sweden with the company's new international marketing manager Erkki Norell. They were not happy with their distribution arrangements in Sweden, and at the suggestion of Ron Weber and Ray Ostrom they visited Arjon, a fishing tackle manufacturer and distribution company based in Malung. Knekt Mats Olofsson was the vice-president of Arjon. He had known Ron and Ray since 1965 and had supplied them with blades for ice drills. As a result of the meeting the distribution of Rapala lures in Sweden was awarded to Arjon with effect from 1971.

The importance of Lauri's business to the Finnish economy was demonstrated in September 1970 when Lauri was invited to Helsinki on the

*Ensio receives the Finnish National
Entrepreneur Award 1968 on
behalf of his father.*
(Rapala company archive)

*Lauri receives the
honourary title of
'Talousneuvos'.*
(Rapala company archive)

occasion of an official visit by His Royal Highness Prince Philip, husband of Queen Elizabeth II of Great Britain. Prince Philip's visit was in connection with the British trade drive 'Britain in Finland 1970'. Prince Philip visited the Sokos department store in Helsinki as part of 'British Shopping Fortnight', and Lauri demonstrated his Rapala lures to the prince in a specially constructed testing tank. Prince Philip was a keen salmon angler himself, regularly fishing the famous River Dee in Scotland, and took great interest in the demonstration.

Enter the Magnum

In 1969 at the suggestion of Normark USA, Rapala started the design work for a lure that would move them to the forefront of saltwater lure technology. The Rapala Magnum series was launched in the USA to immediate acclaim. For 1970 the Magnum was available in 18cm (7in.) size only, but both Floating and Countdown models were launched simultaneously in the traditional silver and gold colours.

Ron Weber took the first two prototype samples with him on a fishing trip to Acapulco, Mexico. Ron and a friend chartered a fishing boat, and Ron dearly wanted to test the new Magnum. However, the skipper of the boat refused to troll the Magnum; his experience of trolling hard baits had always ended in failure, as the lures failed to track straight and became entangled with each other. Ron eventually got the skipper to fish four of his conventional feather and lead-head jigs on one side of the boat whilst Ron concentrated on trolling one of the new Magnums on the other side. An informal bet of a dollar a fish with his friend made the experiment that much more interesting.

The new Magnum did track straight, and at the end of the day Ron was 12 dollars better off. The skipper received one of the prototypes as a gift, and gave up charter fishing in favour of trolling commercially for yellowfin tuna. His new fishing venture only lasted a few days. The prototype Magnum was last seen heading for the horizon at great speed in the bill of a very large blue marlin.

The Magnum was the first Rapala lure not to use the traditional balsawood. Balsa was by no means tough enough to deal with saltwater predators that would include

Esko Rapala receives an honourary citizenship of Minneapolis.
(Rapala company archive)

Lauri Rapala demonstrates his lures to Prince Philip of Great Britain.
(Rapala company archive)

Roger Cannon with Marge and Ab Emby, the first managers of Normark Canada.
(Normark Corporation archive)

shark, tuna, wahoo and tarpon[14]. The wood chosen for the Magnum lures was abache, a wood related to mahogany and some three times heavier than balsa, but significantly lighter than the traditional plastics used in lure production. Abache wood is renowned for its dimensional stability and for its lack of knots or blemishes. It could withstand the attentions of the saltwater predators whilst maintaining the traditional Rapala wounded minnow action. It is used in all the Rapala wooden saltwater lures.

The introduction of the Magnum lure demonstrates the unique relationship between Normark in the USA and Rapala in Finland. Ron and Ray not only marketed and distributed Rapala lures; they astutely interpreted the future needs of the American anglers, and communicated those needs to the Rapala family. Because the Rapala brothers had never fished for largemouth bass, striped bass, redfish, crappie[15] or musky (species not found in Finland or other parts of Europe), they did not have an understanding of the equipment and lures required to catch these fish. Good communication, co-operation and a great deal of trust were required on both sides of the Atlantic in order to make this alliance of Finnish manufacturer and American distributor work.

In 1971 Ron and Ray together with Knekt Mats Olofsson, the vice-president, tried to purchase Arjon from its owner in order to incorporate the company into the Normark group. The negotiations were going well, when suddenly the owner suffered a heart attack. The heart attack was not fatal, but negotiations slowed in order to enable him to recover. The next that Ron, Ray and Mats knew was that the company had been sold to Astra-Walco. As a result of his heart attack the owner had panicked and sold the business as quickly as he could. The Rapala distribution was sold to Astra-Walco as an asset of Arjon.

Arjon was sold in November 1971, but by February 1972 a new company, Normark Scandinavia AB, had been established. Mats had 50 per cent of the

---

[14] Wahoo: a streamlined, large, fast-moving predator of the Scombridae family.
 Tarpon: a large, silvery fish with a bluish back of the Megalopidae family.
[15] Crappie: a freshwater sunfish of the genus Pomoxis.

company whilst Ron and Ray each had a 25 per cent interest. The new Normark company had a small but important range of products. It distributed Mitchell reels, Cortland fly lines and Normark branded knives from Marttiini and Fiskars. However, Rapala distribution in Sweden remained with Astra-Walco. In fact, in August 1972 Rapala signed an agreement with Astra-Walco extending its distribution of Rapala lures to Norway and Denmark as well. Normark Scandinavia would have to prove itself before it was awarded the Rapala distribution.

It was also in 1971 that Ron and Ray recruited a young salesman from the UK for their Canadian business. Roger Cannon worked for a company called Singlepoint that manufactured gun sights, a product distributed in the USA by Normark. Roger moved to Canada and set up a sales office in Toronto working from his home, and travelling around Eastern Canada to sell and promote Rapala lures, knives and accessories. Roger Cannon took over the management of the company in 1974 and remains in the position of president today.

A very important addition to the Rapala colour range was made in 1971. The standard gold foil lure was used as the base for the first brightly coloured Rapala lure. The back of the lure was spray-painted with a fluorescent red paint, and the Gold Fluorescent Red (GFR) colour was born. It has been in constant production since its introduction. The GFR was introduced in the Original, Countdown and Magnum lure ranges.

This brightly coloured lure had two distinct uses. Firstly, the fluorescent paint made use of low light, so the lure was more visible in dark or dirty water. Secondly the bright colour acted as a stimulant for wary or lazy predators to strike. Valuable lessons were learned from the introduction of the GFR; Rapala has been careful to produce a good balance of natural, neutral and stimulating colours since the early 1970s.

The Rapala family had always sent their products abroad to friends and to keen fishermen who often sent cash in advance in order to obtain a few lures. Their American and Canadian distribution was now well established, and their Scandinavian distribution appeared to be in order, so they were in a position to look to widen their export markets. Rapala signed a Japanese distribution contract with Shintoa Koeki Kaisha in April 1970, and this contract was to continue until Rapala opened its own distribution company in Osaka in 1999. As a result of their links with Mr Bengtsson of Fransk-Nordiska, Rapala signed a distribution agreement with Mouches-Ragot of France in November 1971. Mouches-Ragot was a family owned company run by André Ragot. The company was well known for its high-quality fishing flies and fly-fishing equipment. In this case the contract continued until Rapala purchased the company in 1991. The Ragot company continues to distribute Rapala products in France today – an unbroken run of 34 years.

A new home – and new ideas

It was during this time of rapid expansion that the Rapala family realised that they could not continue producing lures in small factory units for much longer. They required a modern, purpose-built factory in which they could manage their production more efficiently, increase output and maintain their high

The Deep Diver: Rapala's first deep-diving lure.
(Rapala company archive)

standards of quality. More importantly, the production process was becoming increasingly automated, and suitable premises had to be found for highly technical and very sensitive machinery that shaped the lure bodies to an accuracy of a fraction of a millimetre. The family was well settled in Vääksy, and their experienced home workers all lived in the surrounding area, so it was necessary to establish the new factory relatively close to their existing units. Eventually a site was found, financial arrangements were made and building work began on what was to become Rapala's permanent home.

The building was finished in early 1973, and the Rapala family were honoured when President Kekkonen of Finland officially opened the factory on 29 November that year. No doubt the fact that President Kekkonen was a keen fisherman himself had some influence on his decision to attend the opening ceremony. He had met Lauri and his sons before. But there is no doubt that Rapala's successful export business and the company's considerable contribution to Finland's export revenues made it a very important member of what was an elite group of Finnish international companies. In conjunction with the opening ceremony, the Finnish Central Federation of Handicrafts and Small Industries presented Lauri Rapala with a gold medal in recognition of his 35 years in business.

The Rapala headquarters building we see today is not the same as the factory built in 1972–73 although the original building is incorporated into the structure. An extension built in 1977–78 doubled the effective production area, and in 1983 a new section was built specifically for wood storage and handling, wood turning and metal work. Additional warehouse space was added some years later in an extension between the two original buildings.

1972 saw the introduction of yet another new lure to the Rapala range. Again at the suggestion of Ron and Ray, Rapala designed the Deep Diver. This was a radical departure from the existing Rapala lures. It was in fact the first of the 'fat-bodied' lures fitted with a large metal lip. The Deep Diver is best described as a thin version of the later Rapala Fat Rap lure (see Chapter 6). It was a brilliant trolling lure, but did not cast very well. The description of the lure in the catalogue read as follows:

> *The new Rapala with the 'new action' for huge trophy fish. The Rapala Deep Diver 90 floats at rest, dives almost vertically upon retrieve and will hold its depth at very fast or slow retrieve or troll. Effective when trolling for deep-schooled feeders or 'bottom bumping' for the very deep-water trophies. For a shallow or medium retrieve or troll, reduce speed of lure. The lure body is carved of iroko wood, with eyes, scales and other detail added with handcrafted care. All lures are carefully hand tank-tested and balanced – the finished product duplicating the true swimming action of live forage food.*

The Deep Diver 9cm (3.6in.) lure was introduced in four colours: Gold (G), Silver (S), Blue (B) and the new Gold Fluorescent Red (GFR). The new GFR colour was also included in the Balanced Jigging range of lures for 1972.

With effect from 1973 all production of Rapala lures was moved to their new factory at Vääksy. Initially the old factory units and workshops were rented out to other companies, but were eventually sold.

The first new lure to be produced in the factory in 1973 was the Deep Diver 7cm (2.8in.). This lure complemented the 9cm (3.6in.) model of the previous year. The size made it more attractive to smaller species, but did not detract from its big-fish catching potential.

In a total departure from its core business Rapala produced its first 'all metal' lure with the introduction of the 4.5cm (1.75in.) and 6.5cm (2.5in.) Vertical Jigging Pilkki. The Pilkki was a vertical jigging lure designed to be fished through a hole in the ice or from a boat. The lure was flat-sided and it had an eyelet in its tail to which the line was tied. A treble hook was fitted at the head end. The Pilkki was lowered to the bottom, then the rod was raised sharply, and lowered quickly in order to give the lure some slack line. The shape of the lure was designed to make it flutter as it sank back downwards, creating vibration waves in the water that attracted predatory fish. The new colours of Nickel Black and Copper Red did the rest. Normark Corporation sold the Pilkki in very good numbers, but the Rapala family eventually ceased its production in order to concentrate on their hard baits.

In 1974 the Rapala company made its first jointed lure. It had long been understood that jointed lures could be more productive in cold or cloudy water. The additional movement of the lure was a definite asset, which also produced attractive vibrations. These could cause a fish to strike at a jointed lure, but possibly ignore a standard model.

The Original Rapala floating lure formed the basis of the new Jointed design. It was not just a matter of

The current Rapala factory, opened in 1973.
(Rapala company archive)

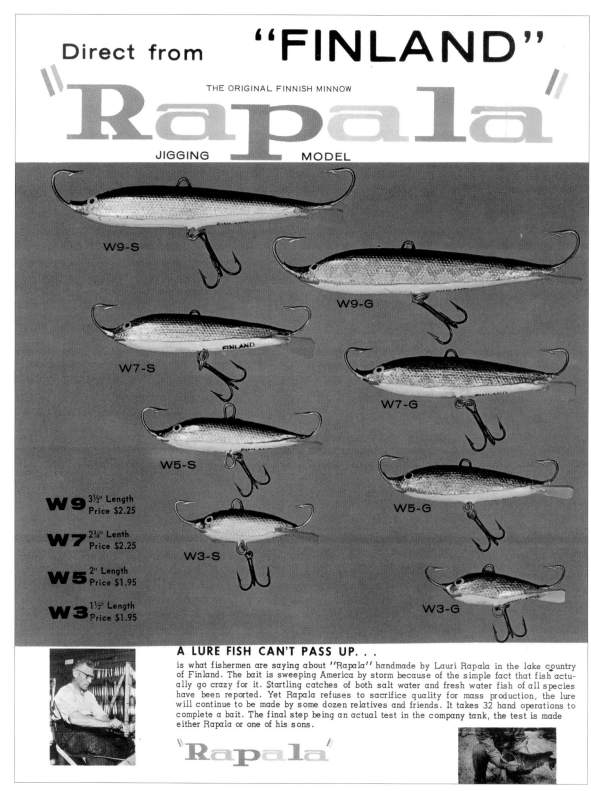

Direct from "FINLAND"

THE ORIGINAL FINNISH MINNOW

"Rapala"

JIGGING MODEL

W9-S

W9-G

W7-S

W7-G

W5-S

W5-G

W3-S

W3-G

W9 3½" Length
Price $2.25

W7 2¾" Lenth
Price $2.25

W5 2" Length
Price $1.95

W3 1½" Length
Price $1.95

A LURE FISH CAN'T PASS UP. . .

is what fishermen are saying about "Rapala" handmade by Lauri Rapala in the lake country of Finland. The bait is sweeping America by storm because of the simple fact that fish actually go crazy for it. Startling catches of both salt water and fresh water fish of all species have been reported. Yet Rapala refuses to sacrifice quality for mass production, the lure will continue to be made by some dozen relatives and friends. It takes 32 hand operations to complete a bait. The final step being an actual test in the company tank, the test is made either Rapala or one of his sons.

"Rapala"

Rapala jigging lures featured in Ron and Ray's first catalogue.
(Rapala company archive)

cutting a lure in half and creating a hinge. The 'wounded minnow' action of the lure had to be retained, but now both sections of the lure had to work together to provide that action. The Rapala brothers worked hard to get the action right, and eventually they discovered that the action of the front portion of the lure was absolutely critical. If they could preserve the traditional Rapala action in this area, then the rear portion would work in harmony. Eventually they achieved the desired result and the Rapala Jointed 9cm (3.6in.) lure was released.

On 20 October 1974, Lauri Rapala, the simple woodsman who became a legend in his own lifetime, died. Lauri had already suffered a heart attack in the 1950s when working hard to support his family and establish his fledgling company. The effects of this, coupled with Lauri's smoking and his love of a decent drink, culminated in him suffering from arteriosclerosis – the cause of his death at the comparatively early age of 69. Lauri was laid to rest in Kalkkinen Cemetery, close to his home. Just a few months prior to this, both Ron and Ray had been awarded bronze badges of merit by the Finnish Central Chamber of Commerce to commemorate Normark's contribution to Finnish international trade. They in turn recognised the immense contribution to their success made by Lauri Rapala. Both men travelled from America in order to pay their last respects to a business associate who became one of their closest friends.

Lauri's grave in Kalkkinen Cemetery.
(Rapala company archive)

Ray explained their close association with Lauri. 'Every time Ron and I met Lauri he had tears in his eyes, and every time we said goodbye to him he had tears in his eyes. Lauri took us in to his family. We were not just business associates, we were almost like adopted sons. If the relationship had not developed in this way our business would not have been such a success.'

Just one month after Lauri's death a young lady joined the staff of Rapala as a marketing secretary. Her name was Sirpa Glad. One of Sirpa's first jobs was to type a letter to Arjon of Sweden regarding the distribution of Rapala products. In a letter dated 2 December 1974 Arjon was informed that its contract for the distribution of Rapala lures was to cease with immediate effect. It appears that Astra-Walco had sold their distribution company Arjon to Abu, a famous Swedish manufacturer of fishing reels and lures. The Rapala brothers would not tolerate a competitor distributing their products and consequently terminated the Astra-Walco contract.

Just two days later, on 4 December, an agreement was sent to Normark Scandinavia informing them that they were the new Rapala distributors for Sweden. Normark Scandinavia was to purchase all the Rapala stock held by Astra-Walco or Arjon in order to avoid any cut-price disposal. The agreement was initially for one year with an option to extend it on a yearly basis. This is the core of the agreement that still exists between Normark Scandinavia and Rapala today.

In the meantime Normark Canada had increased Rapala sales to over half a million lures a year and the time had come to look for new premises. Unable to find what it wanted, the company built a 20,000ft.^{2} warehouse and office suite on an industrial park in Winnipeg. Marge and Ab Emby decided to retire from the business, and Roger Cannon moved to Winnipeg to take over as general manager. Rapala's distribution network around the world was beginning to take on a coherent and distinctive shape.

Down Deep Husky Jerk

The history of the Down Deep Husky Jerk

Fishing the Down Deep Husky Jerk

A great way to fish the Down Deep Husky Jerk is to fast-crank your lure down to the preferred depth, pause for a count of two or three, then do a 2–3ft. (0.6–1m) sweep forward, pause and reel up the slack to reset, then sweep again.

Watch your line for a strike as you are reeling slack; fish will often strike when you stop or just as you are beginning your next sweep.

Another little known crank-bait technique is the Carolina Rig with a 0.75–1 oz. (21–28g) bell sinker 18–24in. (45–61cm) in front of the lure.

Tips from the pros

• When you're working a suspending lure like the Husky Jerk, remember to pause after you twitch the lure. Make sure there is some slack in the line. Any tension in the line will cause the lure to continue moving towards you. You want the lure to sit motionless, at least part of the time. Watch your slack line for movement, which would indicate a strike.

• A secret of good crank-bait anglers is to experiment with baits that run deeper than the water you're fishing. Let's say that you are in 8ft., and the lure you choose can get down to 12ft. Simply fish it slowly, feeling closely for when the lure is bumping bottom. You can 'finesse fish' right on or near the bottom this way with great control. It's a super way to attract bites from reluctant fish that 'have seen it all'.

• In some situations you need a crank bait that gets down fast. In all situations, a crank bait that digs down fast is an advantage, because the lure spends more time in a productive depth zone during the retrieve. The Down Deep Husky Jerk has a specially designed lip that causes it to dig down immediately. In just a few cranks of the reel handle, you can be bumping bottom in many situations, which can make a huge difference in how many fish you catch.

• Get serious about 'super tuning' crank baits for trolling. Let out your lure at boatside, a short distance back, then crank up the engine to 5mph (8kmh), much faster than most people ever fish. If the lure is going to 'blow out' to one side, the high speed will make it obvious. Carefully bend the lure's eyelet a little at a time, in the direction the lure is tending to drift. If it runs true at 5mph, it'll dig hard and straight, no matter how much line you let out or how far you cast.

• Even in what seems to be fairly clear water, sediment can block most of the penetrating light after just a few feet. So fluorescent colours become important in many waters. In stained water, include colours like Fluorescent Red, Orange, Chartreuse and Firetiger in your collection.

Down Deep Husky Jerk

Code: DHJ   Freshwater – Deep Diving – Suspending

Main features:

- Fast, deep-diving lure
- A very tough lure
- Strong, aggressive swimming action
- Neutral buoyancy suspending lure
- Heavy weight and excellent balance

Fishing tips:

- Excellent casting lure that can be trolled
- Use this lure to get down to the fish fast
- Stop the retrieve to let the lure suspend, then start it again with a jerk

Target predators:

Asp, perch, chub, trout, black bass, salmon, sea trout, zander (walleye), pike

Technical features:

Code	Body length	Weight	Treble hooks	Swimming depth
DHJ-10	10cm / 4in.	11g / 3/8 oz.	Two No. 5	2.1–4.8m / 7–16ft.
DHJ-12	12cm / 4³/4in.	15g / 1/2 oz.	Three No. 5	2.4–5.7m / 8–19ft.

Shad Rap RS

The history of the Shad Rap RS

1982 The Shad Rap 7cm lure is introduced.

1999 The Shad Rap RS is introduced in 5cm and 7cm sizes.

2000 4cm size is introduced.

Fishing the Shad Rap RS

This lure can be cast and trolled, but its special 'suspending' feature can only be used when the lure is cast. Remember to let the lure suspend near any likely underwater obstructions or features where predatory fish may hide.

Fish can be attracted by vibration, but the type of vibration can be crucial. Change the speed and type of retrieve to alter the vibrations emitted by the lure. Without doubt, one type of retrieve will be found to be more successful than another.

Use this lure's long casting ability to search shallow water at distance to avoid spooking the fish.

Tips from the pros

• A secret of top anglers is to use larger baits when fish are on the bite. On those days when fish are 'hitting,' you can actively fish for bigger fish by tempting them with bigger lures. In a way, what you are doing is deterring more of the smaller fish.

• Here's a trick used by musky hunters, shared by the experts at Rapala. If a big fish follows your lure but won't hit, try moving away and coming back at another angle. It also helps if you position the sun at your back, so the fish has to look into it while approaching your boat. This lighting condition makes it harder for the fish to see your movement.

• When you're trolling and you get a strike, but the fish doesn't get hooked, keep that lure in the water. If the rod is in a rod holder, take it out and begin to manually pump it, then let it stall out. Frequently 20 or 30 yards down the line, they'll come back and crush it.

• The diameter of your line can make a tremendous difference to the trolling depth of your lure. The greater the diameter of the line, the more resistance it creates, which pulls the lure towards the surface. If additional depth is a critical factor then try one of the new 'super lines' or select a monofilament with a reduced diameter.

• Plan ahead when you are fishing. 'Chuck and chance' fishing just won't bring the results of a well-planned day. Systematically work through your selection of lures, and remember to search the water from top to bottom. Figure out where the fish are likely to be, bearing in mind water temperature, wind direction and the time of the year. A few minutes thought will save a wasted day on the water.

Shad Rap RS

Code: **SRRS**   Freshwater – Suspending – Rattling

Main features:

- Plastic body with rattling cavity
- Heavier than balsa Shad Raps
- Casts well into wind
- Suspending, neutral density lure
- Fitted with a deep-diving lip
- Complete with Rapala VMC hooks

Fishing tips:

- Remember to stop the retrieve near underwater obstructions to let the lure 'suspend'
- Vary the speed of the retrieve to change the rhythm of the built-in rattle
- Concentrate around both surface floating and submerged features for the best action

Target predators:

Zander (walleye), pike, bass, salmon, perch

Technical features:

Code	Body length	Weight	Treble hooks	Swimming depth
SRRS-04	4cm / 1 1/2in.	5.3g / 3/16 oz.	Two No. 6	1.5–4.5m / 5–15ft.
SRRS-05	5cm / 2in.	8.8g / 5/16 oz.	Two No. 5	1.5–4.5m / 5–15ft.
SRRS-07	7cm / 2 3/4in.	12.4g / 7/16 oz.	Two No. 3	1.5–4.5m / 5–15ft.

Skitter Pop

The history of the Skitter Pop

1998 Skitter Pop introduced in 7cm and 9cm models with new colours Frog (F) and Hot Clown (HCL).

1999 Skitter Pop 5cm model introduced.

2000 Skitter Pop 12cm model introduced.

2000 New colours introduced:
Lime Frog (LF)
Silver (S).

2000 Stainless Steel colours (SS prefix) introduced in sizes 9cm and 12cm:
Blue Mullet (SSBMU)
Gold Mullet (SSGMU)
Green Mullet (SSGRMU).

Fishing the Skitter Pop

When fish are aggressive or busting bait, use the 'skitter technique'. This is a retrieve with a steady cadence (either slow or fast) while pumping the rod tip, creating a stop and start motion imitating a fleeing or wounded bait-fish.

Another technique is 'popping the lure'. This is done by giving the lure a sharp jerk, then letting the lure rest whilst reeling in the slack. The lure will spit water quite a way using this approach.

The third technique is 'twitching' which was made famous by the Original floating Rapala. Fish the Skitter Pop in the same fashion, casting it out, letting the water calm, then twitching the lure on the surface. This will imitate a wounded bait-fish or frog struggling on the surface.

Tips from the pros

• Give the fish exactly what they want, and they will show their appreciation by rewarding you with some great sport. There is nothing more exciting than surface fishing in the summer months with a popping lure like the Rapala Skitter Pop. But to be successful, you have to master a number of different presentations. Some days you can make a long cast and rip the lure back as fast as you like, but on another day, the same fish will want the lure twitched back slowly with hardly any disturbance. Mostly, the weather is the major factor in determining how the fish will react; but get it wrong and you will swear that there is not a fish for miles around. On the other hand, get it right and you will have a memorable day's fishing.

• Under sunny conditions, generally speaking fish hold tight to cover. That makes it more important to make accurate casts. And while it's not always true, it can be important to place your lure on the shady side of cover too.

• Finding fish will always be the most important factor in your success. But don't downplay the importance of lure colour. In big-time bass and walleye tournaments, as an example, lure colour is almost always a significant factor by the time the event is over. One colour usually produces better than others. Find the fish, but then make sure you give them what they want!

• For those anglers who glue their eyes to sonar when searching for fish, take a look up every once in a while and search the sky and water's surface for clues of activity. The pros remind us that birds chasing bait-fish can often mean predator fish pushing those bait-fish to the surface. And any time you see the tell-tale skittering of bait being chased, it's worth working the area.

• Keep your movements to a minimum when fish are likely to see you. Many anglers don't realise how far fish can see, and how wary they are of movements, especially overhead activity. Standing up high in a boat or bank, waving your rod high in the air as you make a cast, and other movements will put fish on guard even if it doesn't completely spook them away.

Skitter Pop

Code: SP   Freshwater – Floating – Top Water

Main features:

- Famous balsa bodied popping lure
- Unique cup-shaped swimming lip
- Imitates small fish frightened to the surface
- Creates loud splash in front of the lure
- Can zigzag, bubble and splash
- Tail dressing simulates natural tail movement

Fishing tips:

- Use the 'walk the dog' retrieve by pumping the rod tip during a steady retrieve
- Twitch the lure on the surface to imitate an injured bait-fish
- Try slow and fast retrieves; they both work well, but the fish decide which one is best on the day

Target predators:

Pike, black bass, musky, striper, snook

Technical features:

Code	Body length	Weight	Treble hooks	Swimming depth
SP-05	5cm / 2in.	7g / 1/4 oz.	Two No. 6	Top water
SP-07	7cm / 2 3/4in.	7g / 1/4 oz.	Two No. 5	Top water
SP-09	9cm / 3 1/2in.	14g / 1/2 oz.	Two No. 3	Top water

Tail Dancer

The history of the Tail Dancer

2000 The Tail Dancer is introduced in 7cm and 9cm models.
Colour range comprises:
  Blue (B)
  Chub (C)
  Emerald Shiner (ESH)
  Gold Chub (GC)
  Hot Chub (HC)
  Perch (P)
  Red Tail Chub (RC)
  Rainbow Trout (RT)
  Silver (S)
  Shad (SD)

2001 The Tail Dancer 5cm is introduced.

2002 New colours introduced:
  Firetiger (FT)
  Gold Fluorescent Red (GFR).

2003 The Deep Tail Dancer 11cm is introduced.

2004 New colours introduced:
  Brown Tiger (BRT)
  Green Parrot (GPT).

Fishing the Tail Dancer

The 'stop and go' technique works wonders with the Tail Dancer. Crank your bait down, then pause for a one or two count, then crank ahead, then stop. During the 'stop' the lure actually backs up, simulating a fish actually riding the currents present in all waters.

Another sure-fire technique is to simulate a feeding bait-fish by bottom bouncing the Tail Dancer whilst either trolling or retrieving.

Trolling the weed line with the Tail Dancer has also proved to be an extremely effective technique. Fishing professionals attribute the success to the wide tail action with a relatively stationary head. A close resemblance to real minnows.

Tips from the pros

- There is something about balsawood that makes it the ideal material for lure production. Jarmo Rapala, grandson of Lauri, the founder of the Rapala dynasty puts it down to weight. Balsawood is far lighter than the lightest plastic available. The lighter the lure, the better it responds in the water. If you compare a balsa lure with an identically sized and shaped plastic lure, the balsa model will respond to the slightest twitch of the rod tip, whilst the plastic lure will hardly move. Couple the balsawood action with a built-in rattle system and you have the best of both worlds. That is what the Tail Dancer offers fishermen today, a wide tail action and a rattle. Practice your retrieves with the Tail Dancer and it won't let you down.

- Willy-nilly casting without regard to how deep your crank bait is running may be one of the biggest blunders made by anglers. It might seem like a lot of trouble to 'get to know' your baits well enough to predict their running depth on the average cast and retrieve, but at least try this trick. If your lure is not contacting cover or the bottom at all, either get closer to the cover or put on a deeper running lure, or both. Keep going with deeper running lures until you at least occasionally kick bottom. A lure swimming along in the open water will trigger some fish, but by contacting objects your catch will improve a lot.

- How fast is too fast when it comes to a trolling pass? According to the experts, it can depend on several factors, including water temperature, time of year, and recent weather changes. But at midsummer and into early autumn, it's astounding how fast you can troll crank baits and trigger tons of strikes. Speeds of up to 5mph (8kph) and beyond can do the trick when other presentations get ignored.

- Approaching a spot from a variety of angles can really help you catch more fish. It's hard to say why this works, but if you use your motor to purposely change the direction you travel across an area, experience says you'll get more bites.

Tail Dancer

Code: TD   Freshwater – Floating – Deep Diving

Main features:

- Balsa body with high frequency rattle
- Long swimming lip makes it dive deep
- The first rattling balsawood lure
- 'Banana body' provides wide swimming action
- Special VMC Vanadium hooks
- Maintains its action at slow speed

Fishing tips:

- Vary the speed of the retrieve to let the action of the lure change
- Can be successfully fished at all depths and speeds
- Stop the retrieve to let the lure float upwards for a few seconds

Target predators:

Zander (walleye), pike, trout, black bass, salmon, panfish

Technical features:

Code	Body length	Weight	Treble hooks	Swimming depth
TD-05	5cm / 2in.	6g / $^3/_{16}$ oz.	Two No. 7	1.0–1.8m / 3–6ft.
TD-07	7cm / 2$^3/_4$in.	9g / $^5/_{16}$ oz.	Two No. 6	1.8–2.7m / 3–9ft.
TD-09	9cm / 3$^1/_2$in.	13g / $^7/_{16}$ oz.	Two No. 4	2.7–3.6m / 9–12ft.

Jointed Shad Rap

The history of the Jointed Shad Rap

2001 Jointed Shad Rap introduced in 5cm size.
Colour range comprises:
Baby Bass (BB)
Brown Crawdad (BCW)
Blue Shad (BSD)
Crawdad (CW)
Fire Crawdad (FCW)
Firetiger (FT)
Perch (P)
Red Crawdad (RCW)
Silver Baby Bass (SBB)
Shad (SD) and
Silver Shad (SSD).

2002 4cm model is introduced.

2003 Jointed Shad Rap 7cm is introduced.
New colours introduced:
Hot Perch (HTP)
Walleye (W).

Fishing the Jointed Shad Rap

Seasoned anglers know that sometimes it takes a slight exaggeration of the lure's unique 'bait-fish in distress' behaviour to get the undivided attention of an otherwise disinterested game fish. The Jointed Shad Rap is ideally suited to the slowest possible rate of retrieve and therefore is extremely successful in capturing the attention of finicky feeding and warier species.

The Jointed Shad Rap can be fished in the same manner as the original Shad Rap. Any extra weight should be placed well ahead of the lure.

Pull this lure out after a cold front passes or when fishing shallow, extremely clear water.

Tips from the pros

• When it's cold and the fish are sluggish, it takes something extra to stimulate them into action. Often the added stimulus can be provided by a jointed lure. The exaggerated action and the added vibration can turn a totally disinterested fish into a rod-wrenching monster. Be careful if the water is very cold. Don't speed up your retrieve to get more action and vibration. Keep the retrieve slow, but use the rod tip to make the lure jerk and flash.

• Occasionally, try using a lure that runs 'too deep' for the water you're fishing. For example, if you're casting along an area full of shallow rocks, tie on a lure that can easily run deeper than the bottom. Cast it out and crank down until it bumps bottom. Stop a second, then reel again until it bumps bottom. Continue in this manner, making the lure scoot along and kick up an underwater dust storm. Many predator fish can't resist this type of presentation.

• When retrieving or trolling a crank bait, pauses are the built-in opportunities for fish to inhale your lure. Sometimes, in their zeal to 'cover a lot of water' searching for active fish, anglers might unwittingly become robot-like in their presentation. If you catch yourself being too 'steady' with retrieve speed, make yourself build in more pauses, and changes of speed. You can't get the benefit of a suspending lure without letting it pause for a few seconds now and again.

• If you want to catch more fish on crank baits, concentrate on depths from 6–12ft. (2–4m) an often productive range on many waters. And get out and away from the shoreline, where many plug casters spend most of their time. Find ridge edges, mid-depth flats, drop-offs, humps and cover – and break out of your bank-clinging rut.

• When fishing a suspending bait like the Rapala Jointed Shad Rap, keep it moving when you see a following fish. When you see a fish following the lure try to take the lure away from the fish by speeding up or changing direction. That's when they'll crush it. When a fish is chasing an injured minnow, the minnow is not going to stop to be eaten, so don't stop your lure either.

Jointed Shad Rap

Code: JSR   Freshwater – Suspending – Deep Diving

Main features:

- A jointed version of the famous Shad Rap
- Fitted with VMC Pyramid Point hooks
- Large lip ensures fast, deep dives
- Rattling
- Unique jointed tail imparts fast, tight action
- A neutral buoyancy suspending lure
- Maintains its action at low speed

Fishing tips:

- Move the rod tip during the retrieve to make lure jerk
- Stop the retrieve to let the lure suspend near underwater features or weed beds
- A good lure for cold-water fishing

Target predators:

Black bass, chub, salmon, trout, perch, pike, zander (walleye)

Technical features:

Code	Body length	Weight	Treble hooks	Swimming depth
JSR-04	4cm / 1 1/2in.	5g / 3/16 oz.	One No.8 and 10	1.2–1.8m / 4–6ft.
JSR-05	5cm / 2in.	8g / 1/4 oz.	One No. 6 and 7	1.8–3.9m / 6–13ft.
JSR-07	7cm / 2 3/4in.	13g / 7/16 oz.	Two No. 4	2.1–4.5m / 7–15ft.

CELEBRITY BITES

Italo Labignan on Rapala 'confidence'

Over the last 20 years I have been fortunate enough to produce hundreds of trophy sport-fishing TV programmes and specials from around the world. Over these two decades I have learnt that there is one word that summarises why I use Rapala lures: confidence.

Confidence to catch fish in any fishing conditions, no matter where I fish in Canada – from the Pacific coastal rivers and streams for Pacific salmon and steelhead, the Northwest Territories for monster lake trout, the Prairies for trophy pike, or eastern Canada for big walleye and bass – or indeed anywhere else in the world. I have the confidence that I can always depend on Rapala to make fish strike.

I choose Rapala because I know the quality, fish-tantalising action, and wide variety of sizes and colours can make any game-fish hit; from pan-size trout and panfish, to giant char and saltwater fish.

If I could fish with only one Rapala, it would be the Husky Jerk series. Cast and retrieved, trolled, or 'twitched', they can swim at any desired depth, and they produce a tantalising action that even the most in-active fish will strike.

CHAPTER 6

A family business

1975–88

T he untimely death of Lauri Rapala marked the end of an era. No longer was the inventor of the Rapala lure there to offer advice or encouragement. His quiet voice, always welcomed by every member of the Rapala staff, was no longer to be heard. However, Lauri's spirit lived on in his sons Risto, Esko and Ensio, who proved themselves to be the driving force of the Rapala business.

Lauri's wife Elma continued to live at Noukkahonka near Kalkkinen for some years after Lauri's death. In the early 1980s she suffered a stroke, but recovered in hospital. However, it was obvious that she could no longer cope well on her own. The children purchased an apartment in Vääksy for Elma so that she was close by in case she required help. Later she moved to another apartment in the centre of Vääksy. Elma continued to spend some time at Lyyranmäki during the summer months. The family had built a small cottage there after the original home was demolished. Elma died in 1986 and is buried in Kalkkinen Cemetery next to her husband.

As a direct result of Lauri's death the structure of the Rapala company was changed. The company was reformed into a limited company, Rapala Oy. Ensio Rapala was appointed managing director of the new company, Risto production director, and Esko purchasing director. The three brothers were members of the board. Basically these appointments changed very little. The brothers had assumed responsibility for various sections of the business over a period of years, and they were well used to dealing with the day-to-day running of the company.

1975 marked the creation of the 25 millionth Rapala lure since production began in such an informal way in 1936. In order to mark the event Risto, Esko and Ensio designed and manufactured a special plaque, which they presented to Ron and Ray on one of their visits to Finland. The plaque featured an Original Floating Rapala, which continued to be the best-selling fishing lure 15 years after its introduction to American and Canadian anglers by Normark. It continues to be displayed on the wall of Normark's headquarters today.

The new Rapala 9cm (3.6in.) Jointed lure introduced in 1974 was proving to be a great success, and following Rapala's established principles, 1975 saw the introduction of the Jointed 11cm (4.5in.) lure. The number of employees working both at the factory and at home now totalled 163, in order to cope with a production total of over three million lures for the second year in succession. Normark Corporation in the USA continued to be the largest

- **The Rapala sons take up the reigns**
- **20 years of Rapala–Normark co-operation**
- **Ron and Ray are knighted by the Finnish government**
- **A fire in the factory**
- **Marketing and promotion in the USA**
- **Rapala introduces four-colour printing technology**

The Rapala Silver Mackerel (SM).
(Rapala company archive)

customer, and took over 66 per cent of the factory's production, but Rapala's new export markets in France, Japan and Italy were beginning to contribute significant numbers to the production total. The company was now actively searching for new export markets as confidence grew that Rapala lures were effective in all fishing conditions around the world.

However in 1975 there was to be a significant interruption in lure production at the Rapala factory. On 4 July a workman was repairing valves in the extraction plant that removed paint dust from the factory area. The electric drill he used created a spark that ignited acetone vapour in the extraction system, and a serious fire broke out. Luckily the factory staff were at lunch and no-one was injured, but the painting and lacquering plants were completely destroyed. Three months' production was lost as a result of the fire as the unit was rebuilt and new machinery installed. The first installation in the new unit was an efficient sprinkler system. Ron Weber was heard to comment, 'What a way to celebrate Independence Day!'

1976 saw the introduction of the Jointed 7cm (2.8in.) lure, but more importantly it also saw the introduction of one of the most important saltwater colours that Rapala has ever produced. Silver Blue Mackerel (SM) was introduced to the Magnum range of lures and remains one of the most accurate bait-fish representations that Rapala has designed. More importantly, however, it caught fish in almost every ocean and sea around the world.

The manufacturing process of the Silver Blue Mackerel colour took Rapala's production process forward by one more stage. The lures were first dipped in a pearl pigment; then they were transferred to a spray-painting booth and were mounted upright on spikes in long rows with their backs facing forwards. The painter sat on a chair that was mounted on wheels, which were in turn mounted onto a short 'railway track'. The painter would select the spray gun with the special blue paint. He would hold the spray gun in front of him and using his feet, he would push himself in the chair along the railway track whilst spray-painting the lures. Then he would propel himself back again, giving the lures a second coat. This ensured that each lure was accurately sprayed iridescent blue across the back, and not along the sides. The next stage used exactly the same process, but this time a template was lowered in front of the lures. The template had the pattern of the black stripes cut in it. This time the painter selected the spray gun containing the black paint. Keeping the spray gun in front of him and at 90 degrees to the lures he repeated the process again. When the lures were finished they had a blue back with the characteristic black tiger markings. The mackerel colour pattern has also been used in green and gold (GM) and, surprisingly, in purple (PM). The spray-painting method of application continues to be used for the 'Mackerel' colours today.

In the USA Ron and Ray had launched an education programme for anglers. Paperback books with titles such as *How to Fish a Rapala by the Book* and *How to Clean a Mess of Fish Without Making a Mess of the Fish* were

Spray-painting lures in a specially designed spray booth.
(Rapala company archive)

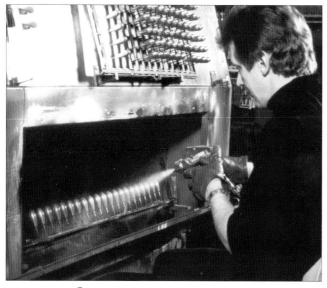

published with the primary intention of educating fishermen in how to use Rapala-branded products. The books were written by acknowledged outdoor writers, and many thousands were printed and used as a promotional tool to increase the public's awareness of Rapala lures and Fish 'n Fillet knives.

They also took the decision to diversify into other outdoor sports areas. In 1974 the company entered the cross-country ski business, importing skis initially from Madhus of Lillehammer in Norway, and later from another Norwegian company, Troll Ski of Rindahl. The business did well, but two winters with little snow and increasing competition from established ski manufacturers lead Normark to pull out of the sector some seven years later.

In 1975 Ron and Ray took the decision to appoint Carmichael Lynch, a well-respected Minneapolis advertising agency, to handle their advertising and marketing. Their brief was wide-ranging, and the company was involved in product launches, brand-name promotion and Normark's educational advertisement design. In one of its first advertisements produced for Normark, the agency photographed a silver Rapala Original next to a real minnow in order to demonstrate that the Rapala minnow 'out-minnows the minnow'. Later advertisements featured full-colour, double-page spreads with superb colour drawings of the major predatory fish, and plenty of educational copy for the readers. The association with Carmichael Lynch continues to this day.

The famous 'Rapala out-minnows the minnow' advertisement.
(Normark Corporation archive)

Ron and Ray also understood the value of trade shows. In America the major show was run by the American Fishing Tackle Manufacturer's Association (AFTMA). Normark applied for membership, but was refused on the grounds that it did not actually manufacture anything. The AFTMA show was held in the Hilton Hotel at Chicago for many years, so Normark, along with Mepps and Garcia, set up a rival show in the Bismark Hotel across the street. Eventually the number of companies exhibiting at the Bismark Hotel grew to a level that concerned AFTMA to such a degree that they rescinded their earlier decision and admitted Normark and the other 'Bismark' companies to the Association.

Ray and Ron also had a good way of dealing with customers upset at not receiving their full allocation of lures. When a customer started to complain, they would pin a badge on the complainant's lapel that read, 'I Gave Rapala Hell Club'. The result was an immediate easing of the tension, and a good business discussion could follow.

One customer got into the habit of placing orders for three times the number of lures he required in the hope of receiving enough lures to see him through the season. When supplies eventually matched demand, the customer contacted Normark complaining, 'Why the hell are you sending me all these lures? I will never be able to sell them all.' He was told that he had placed orders for all the lures. 'Oh, I know that,' came the reply, 'but you are usually only able to deliver 30 per cent of what I order.'

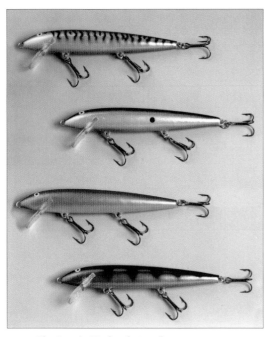

The Rapala Husky, designed to cast into strong winds.
(Rapala company archive)

The first Perch (P) coloured lures.
(Rapala company archive)

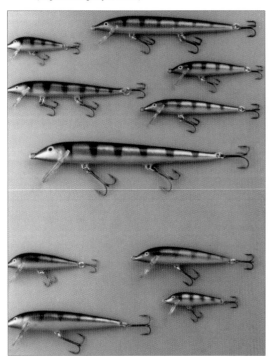

Technology brings progress

The development of the Rapala lure programme was now gaining pace rapidly. As Risto, Esko and Ensio introduced more state of the art machinery at their Vääksy factory, the production levels rose accordingly. Just as importantly, however, the quality of the product improved as the machinery reduced tolerances to a bare minimum. The brothers took the decision to build the first of three extensions to the factory in 1977, and in effect doubled the manufacturing space.

In 1977 two new lures were launched. The Husky 13cm (5.3in.) was a floating lure with a larger body profile than the Rapala Original. It was designed at the request of fishermen from Texas, where strong winds are a regular handicap to good casting. The extra weight of the Husky made it suitable for use with heavier lines, or in adverse weather conditions. Whilst the Original imitated a slim, delicate bait-fish, the Husky copied the rounder, more heavily built profiles of larger fish. The Husky was used in the same way as the Original, but now the fisherman had a choice of lure shapes to help him imitate the bait-fish present in the water that he was fishing.

The second lure launched in 1977 was the Fat Rap, Rapala's first proper 'round-bodied' lure, designed to dive very deep and to impart a frenetic wobble. The Fat Rap was introduced in both 5cm (2in.) and 7cm (2.8in.) models. It was Rapala's answer to the American fashion in fat-bodied lures that lasted for about ten years. The main lure in the category was the 'Big O' but this was an expensive hand-made lure, and Normark's customers wanted something just as effective, but at a lower price. The Fat Rap had some characteristics that made it a valuable lure. For instance, the fisherman could retrieve hard in order to make the lure dive deep, then stop winding and let the lure float upwards. This type of retrieve was a well-kept secret for a number of years, and it worked very well. The shape of the lure and its fast, tight action also emitted increased vibrations, so the lure was useful in dark or cloudy water. To this day the Fat Rap is regarded as one of the classical bass crank baits in the USA.

With the introduction of the Fat Rap new colour patterns were required. The Fat Rap was a deep-running lure primarily used to bounce along the bottom, so one of the new patterns to be introduced was the Crawdad (CW). The Crawdad colour imitated the crayfish, which was found in many lakes and rivers of the USA and Canada.

Following on from the introduction of the Silver Blue Mackerel colour of the previous year, Rapala used the same technology (but on a much smaller scale) to produce their first accurate freshwater imitation of the perch. The new Perch (P) colour was introduced on the Original and Countdown lures for the 1977 season. It had long been known that European predatory fish such as perch, pike and zander (walleye) were happy to feed on young perch. The perch is a meaty fish and the dorsal spines are no problem to a hungry predator. Now Rapala was to specifically target perch-feeding predators for the first time. However, it was not long before they established that their new perch-specific colour was successful in waters that contained no perch at all. The combination of black, green and orange was sufficient to lure some predators into striking regardless of whether they had ever seen a perch before.

Having established that accurate imitation was successful in its own right, but not vital to the success of a lure, both Normark and Rapala moved forward with confidence to produce a wide variation of patterns for both salt and freshwater. Some patterns were imitative, some were suggestive, while others can be best described as stimulative.

1977 was also the year when Ray Ostrom and Ron Weber decided that they had to do something with the National Expert Bait Company that Normark had purchased back in 1968. Since the takeover, the company had performed well below the level expected of it, and it needed new life breathing into it. Additionally, the likelihood of Finland being invaded by Russia had receded, so the manufacture of Rapala lures was going to stay where it was.

During the mid seventies the art of fishing had begun to change. Gone were the days of 'chuck and chance'. Fishermen were beginning to think seriously about catching fish. This quest for knowledge and the need to solve problems was promoted in the USA by magazines such as *In-Fisherman*, which promoted a more scientific and analytical perspective toward fishing. Fishing was becoming a craft and the craftiest animal that Ron and Ray had ever seen was the fox. In fact the animal to beat all others was undoubtedly the arctic fox.

The decision was made. The National Expert Bait Company was renamed Blue Fox, and Carmichael Lynch were tasked with designing the logo.

The Blue Fox name and logo were introduced at the AFTMA sport-fishing show in August 1977. As well as giving the company a new image Ron and Ray also gave it a new address. Blue Fox was moved from its outdated premises in south Minneapolis to a more suitable site in the town of Cambridge in rural Minnesota. It was from these premises that Blue Fox was to design and produce some of the most radical lures ever seen in the USA. They were crafty – just like a fox.

The Fat Rap Shallow Runner.
(Rapala company archive)

Following on from the 1977 success of the Fat Rap, 1978 saw the introduction of the Fat Rap Shallow Runner in both 5cm (2in.) and 7cm (2.8in.) versions. The original Fat Rap was now named the Fat Rap Deep Runner. The new Fat Rap was designed to work in shallow water, over weed beds or submerged obstructions. It could be used to run sub-surface, creating an exciting wake behind it.

The Perch colour was extended to the Jointed series of lures, making them extremely attractive to pike and musky fishermen, and an exciting new colour called Silver Fluorescent Chartreuse (SFC) was introduced, which featured a silver belly with a fluorescent chartreuse back. It was Rapala's second stimulative colour, joining the already popular Gold Fluorescent Red, which had been available for some time. The SFC colour was designed for dark or dirty water. The highly reflective silver belly and bright fluorescent back picked up and used the available light well, making the lure highly visible.

With production reaching almost 5 million lures a year and the company employing almost 300 workers, Ensio Rapala was awarded the Asikkala Entrepreneur of the Year award in 1978 in recognition of the employment and prosperity that Rapala Oy had brought to the Asikkala region of Finland.

1979 saw the introduction of just one new lure – the smallest one that Rapala had ever produced. The 3cm (1.2in.) Mini Fat Rap could dive to 5ft. (1.5m) and was designed to coax shy predators out of weed beds and underwater cover. It also proved to be an excellent lure for trout and sea trout in rivers and fast-flowing streams. With fishing tackle becoming increasingly lighter and more delicate the Mini Fat Rap was ideally suited to the rapidly growing ultra-light sector of the market.

However, the most important introduction was of a new Rainbow Trout (RT) colour. In order to produce an accurate representation of the rainbow trout, new technology was required. Rapala purchased special four-colour plate printing machines from Germany, and for the first time printed the pattern onto the lures. Making full use of this new colour process, the designers at Rapala produced a superb imitation. The Rainbow Trout was introduced in the Original and Countdown series of lures. Since its introduction in 1979 it has been in continuous production in several lure ranges.

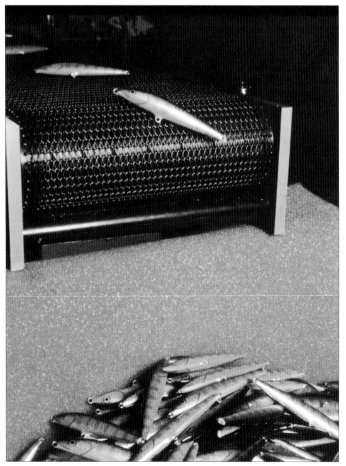

Rainbow Trout (RT) lures after the printing process.
(Normark Corporation archive)

In order to develop colours for lures of different shapes and sizes it was necessary for an artist to produce a watercolour painting. This would be photographed and processed to produce a set of four-colour separations from which the printing plates were produced. Each lure, and each size of lure, would require a separate watercolour painting for each pattern. It was not until the late 1990s that computer software became available that would help the designers to enlarge, reduce or re-shape a design to suit a range of lures in various sizes. Rapala continually invested in updating their computer software to make the most of the new printing machines. The other advantage of using the four-colour plate process was of course a vast saving in production time. Now that all the colours were printed during one pass through the printing machine there was no drying time and no necessity to move the lure bodies from one painting section to another. Printing the colour schemes also omitted any colour or design errors that might creep into a painting process.

Whilst 1979 was perhaps a less active year in Europe, Blue Fox was making headway in the USA. A fisherman called Roland Martin joined the staff as a fishing consultant. Roland was one of the best-known bass anglers of all time, and he designed a range of five signature spinner baits that immediately moved the Blue Fox company up the league table from a small regional lure company to a truly national player. The launch of the Roland Martin Spinner Baits introduced Blue Fox to the anglers of the Deep South of America, who focus their attention on large-mouth bass and panfish. Blue Fox was on the way up.

A change of scenery

1980 was a year of further expansion for the Rapala company. The decision was taken to move some of the assembly, tank-testing and packaging away from the Vääksy factory in order to make more room available for production. The total number of Rapala lures produced had now reached over 50 million pieces. As a consequence of this decision the first Rapala overseas factory was established at Inverin, County Galway, in Ireland. The company, Rapire Teoranta, was registered there in 1980. The decision to establish a factory in Ireland was purely financial. The west coast of Ireland was very underdeveloped. The costs of living were low, and wages were much lower than in Finland. Coupled with that was the fact that very generous grants, tax incentives and extremely low rents were available to companies setting up business in the area.

The west coast of Ireland remains one of the few areas where the native Irish language of Gaelic is still spoken as the language of choice, and one of the conditions placed upon Rapala was that their employees should be permitted to speak Gaelic amongst themselves. The preservation of Gaelic is quite rightly of great importance to the Irish. However, the company found that the speaking of Gaelic was not a problem; it was the English language spoken with a broad Irish accent that caused the Finnish factory managers severe headaches. The Finnish people have always studied languages. It is accepted that Finnish is a difficult language to learn, so they have learned Swedish and English at school. The Finnish staff based at Rapire Teo were partly selected because of their good English-speaking skills, but the Irish accent sometimes defeated them. Martin Lydon was appointed factory manager and the Finnish management team soon learned to give any necessary instructions to Martin who would pass them on to the production staff. Martin continues to be the factory manager there today, and his attention to detail has ensured that over the years the Rapala lures produced in Ireland are manufactured exactly to the standards of those created in Finland.

The plaque commemorating 20 years of Rapala–Normark co-operation.
(John Mitchell)

With more production space in their Vääksy factory, the Rapala brothers extended their product range with the introduction of the Countdown Jointed lure. The floating Jointed lure was selling well in all markets, but a Countdown model would make the Jointed series more versatile. Its ability to cast well in a wind and dive deeper than its floating counterpart made it a valuable addition to the range. The Countdown Jointed was introduced in 7cm (2.8in.), 9cm (3.6in.) and 11cm (4.5in.) models.

At this time Normark Corporation in the USA was purchasing over five million lures a year from Rapala out of a total production of just under seven million. In fact the company was purchasing over 75 per cent of Rapala's output. In order to mark this achievement, and to recognise the contribution that both Ron Weber and Ray Ostrom had made to the economy and culture of Finland, the Finnish Government awarded both men Knights First Class of the Order of the Lion of Finland at a special ceremony in Minneapolis. Harald Brunou had made a specially detailed application to the Finnish Government requesting that consideration be given to making an award to Ron and Ray. The Finnish Consul made a special trip from New York to attend the ceremony.

North of the border in Canada, Roger Cannon was rapidly developing Normark's business. The company was importing three quarters of a million lures each year from Finland. Normark's premises in Winnipeg were proving to be too small, and the decision was made to move the company east, closer to its major markets. Normark moved to a purpose-built office and warehouse facility outside of Toronto. Ron and Ray made the decision to purchase three acres of land, about twice as much as they required. The new Normark premises were of course much larger than the Winnipeg facility, so much so that part of the building was leased to another company. The rent income paid the mortgage. Normark occupies the same site today and the building was extended in 2004.

1981 saw Rapala's emphasis centre upon their saltwater lures. Both Floating and Countdown Magnums were introduced in 11cm (4.5in.) and 14cm (5.7in.) sizes. It was 12 years since the Magnum 18cm (7in.) lure had been introduced, so it was time that attention was paid to this sector of the market. Additionally, Rapala's largest lure to date, the Magnum 26cm (10.6in.), was also launched. Many anglers just could not believe that a lure of this size could catch fish, but the Rapala 26cm was produced at the request of Rapala's French distributor Ragot, which had excellent contacts with European big-game fishermen who often travelled to the African continent to fish for large saltwater species. The Rapala Magnum 26cm (initially named 'Concorde' by the French) is now frequently listed in the record books as the captor of tuna, marlin and numerous species of shark.

In addition to the two new sizes, two important new colours were introduced. Rapala's spray-painting technique was applied to the new Green Mackerel (GM) colour. Based on a gold body, the iridescent green back crisscrossed with bold black

The Countdown Jointed range of lures.
(Rapala company archive)

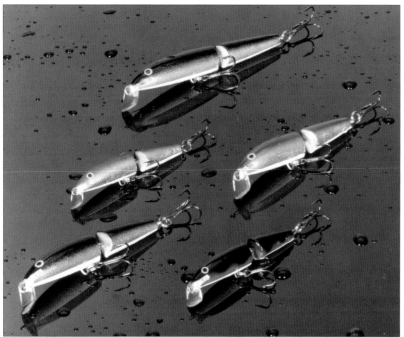

Ron and Ray are knighted for their contributions to the economy of Finland.
(Normark Corporation archive)

tiger stripes was a hit from the moment it was launched. However, the second new colour, whilst not so striking in appearance proved to be an all-time saltwater winner.

The Red Head (RH) was added to the Rapala range at the insistence of the French, who actually named it 'Tropic' because it was used off the African coasts. The Red Head was simply a pearl-bodied lure with a red head. There was nothing complicated or fancy about it, but it worked. In fact it worked so well that the Red Head colour is now present in every one of the Rapala saltwater lure ranges. It might be the reflective flash of the pearl sides, or it might be the contrast between the vivid red head and the pearl body; no-one can be absolutely sure why this colour combination is so successful. It is a fact that over 25 years on the Red Head colour remains the most popular saltwater colour amongst Rapala fishermen around the world.

New Success

During the middle and late seventies, the American fishing-tackle industry raced from one fad to another. Many different lure designs were introduced. Some were lucky enough to last for one season, but many did not last even that long. As a result, by the early 1980s the market was rather flat. It needed something new and dynamic to kick start it again. Back in 1978, Ron and Ray had suggested to the Rapala brothers that they work on a shad[16] project. 'We weren't sure how

Normark's office near Toronto.
(Action picture library)

---

[16] A name given to various migratory fish, similar to herring, of the genus Alosa.

successful the shad imitation would be, perhaps as successful as other Rapala lures such as the Countdown or the Jointed, but we thought that it had the potential to turn a few heads,' comments Ron Weber.

Rapala produced three prototypes for Ron and Ray to choose from. They produced a shad, a baby bass and a crawfish lure. The shad pattern was selected for further testing. The project was completed in 1981 when the final samples of the prototype deep runner 7cm (2.8in.) model from Finland were successfully and secretly tested in the USA. Ray undertook a lot of the testing, and used the prototypes in a number of walleye tournaments. He recalls one incident a few days prior to a tournament when both he and his fishing partner Jack Maciosek were using the 7cm (2.8in.) prototype. 'We were catching walleye in the five to eight pound range. They were good fish. Another boat containing a local fishing guide and his customer came to fish close to us, and they were catching fish of between one and two pounds. The guide called to us, 'What the hell are you using. I've seen it and it's not a Rapala.' I didn't say a word. The guy shouted across again, 'Can I see it?' My answer was just one word, 'No.'

Ray was so impressed with the new lure that he phoned Roger Cannon in Canada. 'Can I have your prototype samples?' Sure enough Roger sent them in the post. Ray also did the same to Mats Olofsson in Sweden, and more lures arrived by mail. Ray now had 17 prototype lures, virtually the total world availability. Ray won quite a few walleye tournaments before the lure was introduced to the market.

The new lure was called 'Shad Rap'. However, there was bad news from Finland. With production at the factory nearing its maximum capacity, the Rapala brothers told Ron and Ray that they would only be able to produce 350,000 Shad Raps in 1982. A simple calculation said it all: 50 million anglers and only 350,000 lures equalled potential disaster. In actual fact, the factory managed to produce about 600,000 Shad Raps, but despite almost doubling their estimated production, demand for this fantastic new lure was overwhelming.

A marlin taken on a CD Magnum Red Head (RH) lure.
(Rapala Media Service)

It was obvious that if the new Shad Rap was a success, Normark would have problems with their retail customers. Ron and Ray decided immediately that their advertising had to emphasise the importance of getting a Shad Rap right away, before they were all gone. They briefed Carmichael Lynch, who designed one of the most memorable double-page advertisements in American fishing tackle history: 'Beg One, Borrow One or Steal One'. Bill Carrera, Normark's sales agent in the New England states recalls, 'That ad was unlike anything the industry had seen. It bowled people over.'

It did not take long for the word to spread about the Shad Rap's fish-catching ability, and the industry was already aware of the lure's limited stock. The Normark offices were besieged with phone calls from dealers trying to obtain Shad Raps or attempting to increase their orders for them. Normark staff spent their days on the phone trying to allocate the limited stocks fairly, whilst their dealers tried to get as many of them as they could. Angry dealers demanding deliveries of Shad Raps confronted members of the Normark sales force, in spite of the warnings about ordering early. In turn, angry fishermen confronted dealers who had either sold their stock, or had not ordered in time and had no stock to sell.

Normark Corporation soon found itself with back orders of over one million lures, and there was no way that the Rapala family could increase their production. The thoughts of Ron and Ray went back to 1962 when the Rapala Original lure first made its impact upon the USA.

As news of the Shad Rap spread, fishing and hunting journalists such as the *Minneapolis Tribune*'s Ron Schara, reported the overwhelming demand for the lure. He reported that the already poor situation was being compounded by resort owners and small bait shops renting out their stocks of Shad Raps on an hourly basis. Some dealers even required a substantial deposit because they knew that a lost Shad Rap could not be replaced until the following season. Ron Schara also reported incidents of Shad Raps being sold on the black market for as much as $45. It was accepted practice for tackle dealers to limit their customers to no more than two Shad Raps at a time.

Normark ended their advertising campaign with a double-page spread on a blue background. However, the picture of the Shad Rap that had originally been featured on the advertisement had disappeared. The advertisement copy was very simple; 'They are all gone.'

Ron and Ray were aware that the shortage of Shad Raps coupled with the lure's undoubted success was likely to lead to copies of the lure invading the market. In order to avoid this, new packaging was introduced that included a 'Seal of Excellence'. A small drawing of Lauri Rapala carving a lure with the words 'Hand Tuned, tank-tested.' was introduced in 1982 on all Rapala boxes to assure customers that, indeed, they were buying the real thing. Copies of the Shad Rap were soon to be found in the USA – and not only did the manufacturers try to copy the lure, they also tried to copy Normark's advertising campaign!

The runaway success of the new Shad Rap lead in 1983 to a second extension to Rapala's Vääksy factory. This time the extension was designed to handle the importation, storage and handling of the balsawood. More wood was held at the factory and more wood-turning machines were installed in an effort to meet the demand for the Shad Rap.

In 1983 Esko's son Jarmo joined the staff at Rapala after completing his university degree. Jarmo had worked in the factory during his school holidays since the age of 15, and was well acquainted with the way the company worked. He was appointed regional sales manager.

A Scandinavian perch taken on a Deep Shad Rap nears the net.
(Rapala Media Service)

To follow up the success of the Shad Rap Deep Runner 7cm (2.8in.) lure, the company introduced a 5cm (2in.) version. This established policy had always worked well in the past, and there was no reason to change tack now. However, in the case of the Shad Rap another alternative was to be launched. The 7cm (2.8in.) Deep Runner could dive to about 6ft. (1.8m), which made it an ideal lure for searching deep water or underwater gullies. What the fishermen wanted now was a lure of the same shape and action that they could use effectively in shallower water. Therefore in 1983 the Shad Rap Shallow Runner was introduced in both 5cm (2in.) and 7cm (2.8in.) versions. Whilst the Deep Runner featured a long, straight diving lip, its shallow-running brethren were fitted with a short, angled lip. The 7cm (2.8in.) Shad Rap Shallow Runner had exactly the same action as the Deep Runner, but would dive to less than 4ft. (1.2m). Now Shad Rap fishermen could effectively search the water from top to bottom.

Leaving aside the Fat Rap, the Shad Rap was the first Rapala lure to move away from the typical cylindrical minnow shape. It featured a deeper yet more slender body shape, more of an oval pattern with contours to match gill covers. The Shad Rap shape demonstrated just how far the Rapala brothers had developed their wood-turning techniques on the new machines installed in the Vääksy factory.

The excitement of launching the new Shad Rap Shallow Runner somehat overshadowed another introduction that year – the Countdown Magnum 9cm (3.6in.) model.

Compared to 1983, the following year was relatively uneventful. Perhaps it was time to sit back and evaluate the progress that Rapala had made in recent years. It was certainly time to study the fishing-tackle industry and make plans for the years to come. The only new lure to be launched was the Jointed 13cm (5.3in.); however, this was to be an important model because it made Rapala's Jointed range of interest to saltwater fishermen. The Jointed 13cm, especially in Blue (B), was found to be the ideal lure for the European sea bass. Sport fishermen were not the only ones to purchase the lure. Professional bass fishermen based in the Channel Islands and the south-west of England purchased these lures 100 at a time, and it was not long before the 'J-13 B' became Normark UK's best-selling lure.

In 1984 the product development department of Rapala received a significant boost when Jarmo Rapala was appointed to lead the team. Now, with a dedicated manager, the research and development of new lures would form a more integral part of Rapala Oy's business development plans.

Ray Ostrom, always a fisherman at heart.
(Normark Corporation archive)

Ray calls it a day

Ray Ostrom, one of the founders of Normark Corporation, was best described as a reluctant businessman. In 1984 he decided that it was time to retire. He could see that Normark

The 1983 extension to the current Rapala factory at Vääksy.
(Rapala company archive)

was getting larger, and that his leisure time would in fact diminish as his responsibilities within the company increased. This was not a situation that suited him at all. He loved his fishing and hunting, and now that he and his family were financially secure he could spend his leisure time doing what he loved best. Ray's share of Normark Corporation, Normark Limited in Canada and Normark Sport in the UK was purchased by Ron Weber in a cash deal, making Ron the sole owner of Normark Corporation. The Normark Scandinavia side of the business was not included in this deal, and Ray continued to maintain his shareholding in that company and its subsidiaries.

You may recall that Normark Corporation owned a houseboat on the Lake of the Woods named the *Lord Rapala*, where Lauri and Risto stayed during their trip to America. Ray purchased the houseboat from the company with the intention of restoring it. Unfortunately, as the boat was gradually stripped down, it became clear that it was in too poor a state to be saved, so it was dismantled. Years later he was to complete the building of a new houseboat, which is still moored at the Lake of the Woods. Parts of the original *Lord Rapala* are incorporated into the new boat, which is named the *Norma Ray*.

Ron used to travel to Finland twice a year to discuss product development and pricing with the Rapala family. Roger Cannon was a frequent travelling companion, and recalls an incident that occurred during some delicate pricing negotiations. 'We had just about concluded our negotiations for the next year's pricing of the lures when the matter of currency conversion was raised. We always tried to hedge against taking currency losses, but there was an inherent risk. Sometimes you won, and sometimes you lost. The same applied to the Rapala family who negotiated their prices in either Finnish marks or dollars.

'At the time the dollar was very weak, and conversion into Finnish marks was costing the family money. They therefore decided that it would be a good idea to negotiate the prices in dollars, but to actually invoice us in German Deutschmarks!'

Naturally this idea did not get past the discussion stage, but it did result in a unique agreement between Rapala and Normark Corporation regarding currency conversions. It was agreed that each company would calculate its profits or losses on currency conversion on an annual basis. Normally one company would make a profit whilst the other made a loss as they were at opposite ends of the currency conversion process. The company that made the profit on the conversion would pay half of it to the company that made the loss thereby reducing the currency conversion risk.

1985 saw the introduction of the largest Shad Rap to date when the 9cm (3.6in.) model in both Deep Runner and Shallow Runner versions was launched. This introduction brought the Shad Rap range in to the 'big fish' league where pike and musky fishermen were taking a healthy interest in Rapala's new offerings.

Rapala also extended their saltwater range with a slightly unlikely lure called the Sliver. Rapala's Italian distributors suggested its design to imitate the long, slender garfish (or needlefish) found in the Mediterranean around the Italian coast. It also imitated sand eels, launce, pipefish and many other species. The Sliver was made of hardwood, and it featured a metal lip just like a Countdown Magnum, but here the similarity ended. The Sliver was a jointed lure with the hinge two-thirds of the way back along the body. The action was very tight. Introduced initially in the 20cm (8.15in.) size, the Sliver immediately caught the attention of saltwater lure anglers. In some ways it was a pity that it took a further two years to introduce the 13cm (5.3in.) version, which met with universal acclaim. The Sliver continues in production today in four of its original range of colours. The introduction of the Sliver marked a change in Rapala's research and development strategy. Now they were prepared to look at ideas from around the world in saltwater as well as freshwater to broaden their range of lures.

In Finland the Rapala brothers had strengthened their board of directors with the addition of two well-known local business consultants. It was at this time, when the Rapala business was extremely profitable, that the advice from the consultants was to diversify in order to protect the interests of the company should something drastic happen to the fishing-tackle industry. There were definite signals from the USA that the fishing-tackle industry was going through a difficult time with declining angler numbers and a lacklustre industry. The consultants advised that the company was too dependent upon Normark Corporation and the American market. The Rapala brothers were extremely hesitant, but the opportunity to diversify by purchasing another business was also attractive due to the substantial tax savings that could be made. Rapala therefore acquired the business of Matkaaja Oy, a caravan manufacturing company. At the time, caravanning was one of Finland's fastest growing leisure pursuits.

Remembering Lauri

On 30 August 1985 in a simple ceremony at Hayward, Wisconsin, Lauri Rapala was posthumously enshrined in the American National Freshwater Fishing Hall of Fame. Enshrinement is the highest honour accorded by this organisation, which requires recipients of this award to:

- Be recognised as a pioneer in an essential aspect of freshwater sport fishing;
- Have contributed a lasting and significant national or international impact to the benefit of freshwater sport fishing;
- Be recognised for excellence and innovation of contributions to freshwater sport fishing;
- Have achieved magnitude or importance of endeavours, which stands out among contemporaries as being avant-garde, unparalleled, unprecedented, transcendent, and having served as an inspiration to others;
- Be recognised for contributions which are singular and distinct, and without which some critical aspect of freshwater sport fishing, as it is currently known, would most likely not have existed.

Without doubt, the woodsman from Finland who carved his first lure from pine bark in 1936 was a worthy recipient of such an honour. Subsequently both Ron Weber and Ray Ostrom were also enshrined in the National Freshwater Fishing Hall Of Fame, a fitting tribute to the two men who were so instrumental in developing America's lure-fishing tradition.

In 1986, the year that marked a half-century of Rapala lure production, the Magnum range was enhanced by the introduction of the Countdown Magnum 7cm (2.8in.). This was the smallest Magnum produced by Rapala, but its bulky hardwood body and strong hardware made it a favourite of pike anglers as well as inshore sea fishermen. Initially designed for the Mediterranean market, Jarmo Rapala and a team of top saltwater fishermen took the 'CD-7' Magnum prototypes to Brindisi, Italy, and entered a tuna-fishing competition. The Rapala team technically won the competition with a superb catch of longfin tuna, but decided to disqualify themselves because the lures that they were using were prototypes not yet available in European tackle stores. Almost 8.5 million lures were produced in the year 1985–86, and the workforce increased to over 300 for the first time.

In the USA, Ron appointed Jerry Calengor as vice-president of marketing. Jerry was a marketing and advertising executive with a great deal of senior management experience. Earlier in his career Jerry had sold Skidoos to Ray Ostrom when Ray was still running his shop. He became the company's art director with special responsibilities for catalogues, booth design and packaging. Jerry was a very gifted commercial artist. His skill and imagination moved Normark forward into the major league of packaging design. He later played a key role as both general manager and president of Normark Corporation.

1987 saw the long-awaited introduction of the Sliver 13cm (5.3in.) lure. Whilst the inspiration for this lure undoubtedly came from the Mediterranean, especially Italy, this smaller Sliver proved to be an absolute winner on the Atlantic coasts of Europe where the bass are to be found close to rocky shorelines.

Having produced the smallest Magnum the previous year, 1987 saw the popular 18cm (7in.) model revamped. Designed primarily for saltwater use, this Magnum also found its way into pike and musky fishermen's tackle boxes.

In Finland the Rapala board of directors continued their policy of diversification and acquisition with the purchase of the Finnish luxury boat manufacturer Flipper Boats Oy. The thousands of lakes in central Finland together with the comparatively safe waters of the Gulf of Finland and the Baltic Sea make boating (together with fishing) one of Finland's major leisure pursuits. It appeared a natural progression to link their fishing business with a boating one. Flipper Boats Oy was a manufacturer of high-quality motor cruisers that could sleep as many as six people depending upon the size and configuration of the boat.

With hindsight, it is safe to say that diversification of this nature was not a good idea. The sales of both the caravan and boat businesses were concentrated 100 per cent in Finland and Sweden, making them liable to regional swings in the economy. Both businesses were capital intensive, involving the purchase of expensive raw materials, and the storage of very high value inventory. The high sales price of both caravans and boats resulted in equally high receivables that incurred additional costs in markets with already low margins. Perhaps the major problem was the lack of Rapala's management experience in these new industries, and their lack of management resources. This resulted in the businesses being left to run themselves with little control from the new parent company.

Plastic fantastic

Rapala's biggest break from tradition came in 1988 when for the very first time they produced a plastic lure. The company had always remained devoted to wood because its natural buoyancy made it so responsive to every movement of the rod tip and line. However there was now a new requirement that needed addressing, and that requirement was sound. It had long been established that the movement of a lure in the water created vibrations that fish could pick up in the sensory organs along their lateral line. However, until the late 1980s the importance of these vibrations was not fully realised.

The need now was for more vibrations to attract fish from a wider area, and to attract them in dark or dirty water. The immediate answer was to implant small metal balls inside a plastic shell. As the lure wobbled through the water the metal balls would click against the shell and emit both noise and vibration.

Rapala's answer to these demands was the Rattlin' Rapala, a lipless plastic lure containing not one but two chambers that held metal balls of different sizes. Each chamber emitted sound on a different wavelength to entice a wide variety of predators to the lure. The body of the Rattlin' Rapala was made in two halves, the metal balls were inserted in the cavities, and the hardware was installed before the two sides were sonically welded together. The use of plastic also permitted the Rapala designers a greater degree of freedom when it came to colour design, and the Rattlin' Rapala has always lead the way in colour development since its introduction. The Rattlin' Rapala was obviously a marked departure from Rapala's core business, but success in both fresh and saltwater ensured its future, and indeed Rapala's further development of plastic-bodied lures.

Jarmo Rapala travelled to Florida where he met Roland Martin, Ron Weber and his son Craig, to spend some time fishing for bass with the prototypes of the Rattlin' Rapala. They fished Lake Okeechobee, one of the very best bass waters in the state. Jarmo remembers, 'We must have caught a hundred bass a day, and we were convinced that the Rattlin' Rapala out-fished other similar lures.'

The introduction of the Rattlin' Rapala to the USA made the lipless, rattling crank bait a nationally popular lure. Before the Rattlin' Rapala was introduced, this type of lure was limited to a few small regions of the USA. The Rattlin' Rapala was the largest ever volume introduction for Rapala, and the long production runs made it possible for Rapala to consider more automated production lines for plastic lures.

A very important milestone was reached on 5 February 1988 when the 100 millionth Rapala lure was produced. The actual lure, a Shad Rap, is mounted on a plaque in Rapala's headquarters in Vääksy, whilst lure number 100,000,001 is on an identical plaque on the wall of Normark Corporation's headquarters in Minneapolis.

In America, Normark Corporation, together with their advertisement agency Carmichael Lynch and Fiola Marketing, launched the Rapala Fishing Club. Fishermen throughout the USA were invited to share their lure-fishing secrets and to field-test the new Rapala lures before they reached the general consumer. The Rapala Fishing Club brought Normark closer to their ultimate customers, the fishermen, and the knowledge of potential traits in fishing that Normark gained was used to good effect in the development of future Rapala lures. Recently the Rapala Fishing Club has undergone a makeover and it is now managed by North American Outdoor Group. Its 50,000 members now receive their own magazine within the pages of *North American Fisherman*, a premier American fishing magazine with a subscriber base of some 525,000 anglers.

Now at the end of the 1980s it was time for the next generation to take up the reigns of management at Rapala Oy, and a new chapter in the history of the company was about to begin.

The 100 millionth lure produced by Rapala is contained within a plaque in their offices at Vääksy.
(John Mitchell)

'Dives To'

The history of the 'Dives To'

2002 Designed by David Fritts and the Rapala Research and Development team, the 'Dives To' is introduced in two models, the DT-10 (6cm) and the DT-16 (7cm).
The original colours are:
  Silver Foil (S)
  Firetiger (FT)
  Shad (SD)
  Blue Shad (BSD)
  Red Crawdad (RCW)
  Dark Brown Crawdad (DCW)
  Green Tiger (GTR)
  Bluegill (BG),
  Baby Bass (BB)
  Perch (P).

2003 The DT-6 (5cm) is introduced.

2004 The DT-4 (5cm) is introduced.

Fishing the 'Dives To'

The 'Dives To' is a unique Rapala lure in that its code (e.g. DT-10) does not refer to the length of the lure. The number following the DT designation refers to the depth at which the lure is designed to work. You will see that there is little difference in size between the lures. It is their weight and design that determines just how deep they will dive.

To get the best out of the 'Dives To' cast it just as far as you can. As soon as you start the retrieve, the lure will dive to around its predetermined depth, and it will stay there until the angle of the line forces it upwards at the end of the retrieve.

The 'Dives To' is an ideal lure for searching the water. It stays in the strike zone longer, making every cast more effective.

If you know the depth of the water that you are fishing, select the 'Dives To' that suits the conditions. The lure has a side-to-side action and emits a special rattle that can only be emitted by a balsawood lure.

Tips from the pros

- Try using crank baits designed to run deeper than the water you're fishing in. It's one of the secrets of the tournament-winning pros: reel down quickly so the lure bumps hard off the bottom, let it rise, then maybe retrieve it in slowly, so it ticks bottom occasionally. Vary the speed of your retrieve, and how often you twitch the rod tip. The main thing is this: whenever your lure hits bottom, it stirs up sediments and makes noises and vibrations that attract the attention of bigger fish – the ones you want to catch.

- When casting deep-diving crank baits, point the tip of your rod toward the lure as you retrieve, says Rapala pro David Fritts. 'The Crank bait King' winds his favourite baits, like the 'Dives To', with the line coming straight into the guides, rod pointed directly at the lure. 'You can really feel what the bait's doing that way,' he says. 'I can tell when a fish hits and pushes forward, which takes away the pull of the lure. I can even tell when a fish turns on the bait, and maybe its tail pushes up the water, which causes the bait to skip a beat. Then I can be ready for the strike.'

- To get the best results from the 'Dives To' lure use the thinnest diameter line that you can. The lures were tested on a standard 10 lb. line. Thicker lines will reduce diving depth, and thinner lines will increase it. Use a long cast all the time; it makes sure that the bait gets down to its proper depth, then it keeps it there, and it searches the water more quickly.

- Don't just fire away when you are casting crank baits. Make mental notes at all times of where your lure hit the water, so that you systematically cover new ground with each cast. If you bump cover, consider it a clue that you've found a potential hot spot, and put your lure 'down that same path' at least twice. Thorough anglers catch more fish.

'Dives To'

Code: DT   Freshwater – Deep Diving – Rattling

Main features:

- A balsa crank bait with an internal rattle
- Thin tail design
- Pulls easily through the water
- Quick dive resting position
- Extra-thin curved polycarbonate lip
- Perfectly balanced and long casting

Fishing tips:

- Designed to dive faster, to hit the strike zone sooner, and to stay in the strike zone longer
- Designed to cast like an arrow, the DT can be cast over 45m
- The further the cast, the longer the lure is in the strike zone

Target predators:

Black bass, zander (walleye), pike, striper

Technical features:

Code	Body length	Weight	Treble hooks	Swimming depth
DT-04	5cm / 2in.	9g / 5/16 oz.	Two No. 6	0–1.2m / 0–4ft.
DT-06	5cm / 2in.	12g / 3/8 oz.	Two No. 5, 6	0–1.8m / 0–6ft.
DT-10	6cm / 2 1/4in.	17g / 3/5 oz.	Two No. 4	0–3m / 0–10ft.
DT-16	7cm / 2 3/4in.	22g / 3/4 oz.	Two No. 3	0–5m / 0–16ft.

Long Cast Minnow

The history of the Long Cast Minnow

2001 First introduced in the 10cm size.
Colour range comprises:
Blue (B)
Chub (C)
Gold Chub (GC)
Hot Chub (HC)
Perch (P)
Red Tail Chub (RC)
Rainbow Trout (RT)
Silver (S)
Shad (SD)
Trout (TR).

2002 8cm and 12cm (saltwater) sizes introduced.
New colours introduced:
Fire Sardine (FSRD)
Spotted Minnow (SPM)
Head Bleeding Minnow (HBM)
Gold Fluorescent Red (GFR)
Red Head (RH)
Firetiger (FT).

Fishing the Long Cast Minnow

Fishing the Long Cast Minnow from Rapala opens up some new territories to anglers.

When fishing shoaling predatory fish like stripers look out for birds over schooling fish. Generally these schooling fish will be skittish, and sound when spooked. Stop well short of the school, working the edges of the school. First cast in to the outside and twitch your minnow past the school. Keep casting to the school working your way into the middle over a number of casts.

When boat fishing and approaching a point, cast out across the point and draw the lure back across the point. This technique allows you to work both sides of the point's drop offs, typical locations that can hold fish.

Be sure to test the action of your lure before you start fishing, experimenting to find the optimum speed that gives you the best swimming action.

Tips from the pros

• The 'Weight Transfer System' is the magic behind the LC Minnow. Patent pending weight transfer design uses the angler's casting power to rocket the lure beyond previous casting distances. Once in the water, gravity resets the assembly for an unhampered retrieve. The locking system also makes it possible to twitch the lure on the retrieve without causing the weight to shift or move to the back of the lure, which would destroy the lure's swimming action.

• Cast past your intended target when fishing shallow cover. Many times, anglers are proud of their ability to place pinpoint casts tight to logs, brush, or weeds. What they don't realise is that – especially if they begin their retrieve as soon as the lure hits the water – the splashing bait can spook even big fish from the spot. The lure is pulled away before the frightened fish turns to see it, and an opportunity is lost.

• You have to start somewhere! Most top anglers begin their search for fish in relatively shallow water. If you can find and catch fish in the shallows, it makes everything easier: it's easier to present a lure, you can often see the strikes, you get to watch the fight, and the fish are easier to release alive. But if you don't get any bites in the shallow water, systematically work your way deeper.

• Don't always use all the speed at your disposal! With today's high-speed reels, many anglers move their lures through the water at two speeds – fast, and faster. Sometimes, especially with crank baits that have a delicate wobbling action, you'll catch more fish if you work slowly.

• Make your first cast in a new spot a long one. Too many anglers don't approach a new spot quietly. If you're in a boat, slow way down, long before you get within fishing distance. Let your wake settle down, and make a long cast into the spot. Land the cast on the 'near' side of the spot, so that if you hook a fish, you can fight it out away from the spot without spooking other fish in the vicinity. By making that first cast a long one, you have a better chance of getting a natural reaction from the most aggressive fish in the area.

Long Cast Minnow

Code: LC   Freshwater – Saltwater – Floating – Shallow Runner

Main features:

- Long casting lure
- Shallow runner
- Patented weight transfer system
- Balsa body
- Rolling swimming action
- VMC Pyramid Point/Perma Steel (LC-12) hooks

Fishing tips:

- A long distance, shallow-running lure
- Suitable for fishing over rocky outcrops and weed beds
- A brilliant sub-surface lure

Target predators:

Sea bass, bass, pike, tarpon, salmon, zander (walleye), stripers

Technical features:

Code	Body length	Weight	Treble hooks	Swimming depth
LC-08	8cm / 3¹/₈in.	7g / ¹/₄oz	Two No. 6	0.3–0.9m / 1–3ft.
LC-10	10cm / 4in.	11g / ³/₈oz	Two No. 3	0.3–0.9m / 1–3ft.
LC-12	12cm / 4³/4 in.	19g / ¹¹/₁₆ oz.	Two No. 3 Perma Steel	0.3–1.2m / 1–4ft.

Skitter Walk

The history of the Skitter Walk

2001 The Skitter Walk 11cm model is introduced.
Colour range comprises:
Blue Mullet (BMU)
Bone (BN)
Gold Mullet (GMU)
Green Mullet (GRMU)
Red Fish (RF)
Red Head (RH)
Silver Mullet (SMU)
Speckled Trout (ST).

2002 8cm model introduced.

2003 New colours introduced:
Fire Shad (FSD)
Translucent Shad (SDT)
Blue/Silver Translucent (BT)
Black/Silver Translucent (BST).

2004 New colours introduced:
Holographic Blue (HB)
Holographic Silver (HS).

Fishing the Skitter Walk

Imitating a swimming mullet or fleeing bait-fish, the Skitter Walk is designed to 'walk the dog' with ease.

Change the action of the lure by either keeping the rod tip up or down.

Jerk the lure then wind in the slack. The lure will first move to one side, then the other, each time emitting a loud rattle.

Adjust the rhythm of your retrieve, the speed of the jerk, and the distance you move the rod tip in order to tune your retrieve to the requirements of the fish. One day it will be fast and furious and the next day it will be slow and smooth.

Cast to likely fish holding areas, to schooling fish, or in to schools of frightened bait-fish.

Tips from the pros

• Here's a hint that can help you determine whether a fish truly hits your lure. If the fish has the front hooks in its mouth – that is, if it attacked the lure aggressively enough to get hooked on the front hooks – you probably had everything right (lure colour, presentation, depth etc.) But, even if you're catching fish, if every fish is barely hooked on the back hooks, consider changing something – try another colour, run it deeper or shallower, slow it down, or speed it up.

• If you fish waters that have weeds, you know that the outside and inside edge of the weeds can be a great place to catch fish. But did you realise that weed growth can vary from month to month during the summer and autumn? The pros stress that a deep weed line can change dramatically, even in just a few weeks, so each time you fish a lake, study it closely with your sonar to see at what depth the weeds stop growing, how thick the weeds are, and how close they come to the surface.

• Take the close ones first! Resist the temptation to cast deep into a spot, or all the way to the shore, on the first presentation in an area. Thoroughly present your lure to the 'close' spots first, so if you hook a fish you can fight it without disrupting the entire spot. If you cast all the way into the spot and hook a fish 'way in there', you have to drag it, kicking and screaming, past the other fish in the area – which can spoil your chances of catching them.

• When working a spot for bass, try concentrating your efforts into the wind. Hold your boat in position with the electric motor, and deal with the frustrations inherent in casting into the wind. When you hook a fish, you can simply shut down the electric motor and let the wind turn you out and away from the spot. That way, you can fight the fish without spooking the others in the area.

Skitter Walk

Code: SW   Freshwater – Top Water

Main features:

- The ultimate 'walk the dog' lure
- Integral weight improves casting distance
- Very tough plastic body
- Rolls from side to side creating flash
- Easy to use in all kinds of conditions
- A great surface lure

Fishing tips:

- Fish fast or slow and raise or lower the rod tip to control the swimming action
- A variety of retrieves can easily be mastered with this lure
- Use a tight knot to get the best action from this lure

Target predators:

Pike, black bass, musky, striper

Technical features:

Code	Body length	Weight	Treble hooks	Swimming depth
SW-08	8cm / 3¹/8in.	12g / ⁷/16 oz.	Two No. 3	Top water

Deep Tail Dancer

The history of the Deep Tail Dancer

2000 The Tail Dancer is initially introduced in 7cm and 9cm models.

2001 The Tail Dancer 5cm is introduced.

2003 The Deep Tail Dancer 11cm is introduced:
Silver Foil (SF)
Blue Foil (BF)
Green Parrot (GPT)
Gold Rainbow Foil (GRB)
Hot Tiger (HT)
Nordic Perch (NP)
Brown Tiger (BTR)
Red Tiger (RDT).

2004 New colours introduced to the Deep Tail Dancer range:
Flash Perch (FLP)
Purpledescent (PD)
Rainbow Trout (RTF)
Hot Flash (HFL).

Fishing the Deep Tail Dancer

The 'stop and go' technique works wonders with the Deep Tail Dancer. Crank your bait down, then pause for a one or two count, then crank ahead, then stop. During the 'stop' the lure actually backs up simulating a fish riding the currents present in all waters.

Another sure-fire technique is to simulate a feeding bait-fish by bottom bouncing the Deep Tail Dancer whilst either trolling or retrieving. The Deep Tail Dancer can get down to 30ft. (9m), and will bounce the bottoms that other lures cannot reach.

Trolling the weed line with the Deep Tail Dancer has also proved to be an extremely effective technique. Fishing professionals attribute the success to the wide tail action with a relatively stationary head. A close resemblance to real minnows.

Tips from the pros

- A secret of good crank bait anglers is to experiment with baits that run deeper than the water you're fishing. Let's say that you are in 8ft., and the lure you choose can get down to 12ft. Simply fish it slowly, feeling closely for when the lure is bumping bottom. You can 'finesse fish' right on or near the bottom this way with great control. It's a super way to attract bites from reluctant fish that 'have seen it all'.

- Put emotion in to your presentation with fish-imitating baits. One of the things that triggers a response in bigger fish is signs of panic in a particular bait-fish. Try using stop-and-go, bursts of speed, and slow struggling motions. Sell the idea that your lure is on its 'last legs' and you may be fast to a big fish!

- If you're having a problem with floating weeds and other debris travelling down your line and snagging on your crank baits, try this trick: put a small split shot on, a few feet up the line. The sinker can be used to help the lure attain a greater depth – and if you're happy with the depth the lure achieves on its own, a tiny sinker won't add much. The sinker will collect much of the wayward material that would otherwise impair the action of your lures, and you'll catch more fish. (Note: a ball bearing swivel, tied into the line a few feet above the lure, performs much the same job, without adding any weight.)

- High-speed retrieves may trigger strikes at times, especially from saltwater fish. But the pros tend to agree that more fish are caught by changes in speed and direction than they are by sheer speed alone. The pros rarely 'burn' a crank bait fast. They prefer relatively slow-speed reels (about a 4.3:1 gear ratio), and usually maintain what they call a 'medium pace', building in the strike-provoking action by pauses and jerks and changes in speed.

Deep Tail Dancer

Code: TDD   Freshwater – Floating – Very Deep Diving

Main features:

- Balsa body with high frequency rattle
- Extra long lip makes it dive very deep
- The first rattling balsawood lure
- Very wide tail action
- Front red Pyramid Point hooks
- Maintains its action at slow speed

Fishing tips:

- Keep the rod tip down to obtain the maximum diving effect
- Can be successfully cast or trolled
- Stop the retrieve to let the lure float upwards for a few seconds

Target predators:

Zander (walleye), pike, trout, black bass, salmon

Technical features:

Code	Body length	Weight	Treble hooks	Swimming depth
TDD-11	11cm / 4^3/8in.	21.3g / ^{3}/4 oz.	Two No. 3	7.5–9.0m / 25–30ft.

Saltwater Skitter Walk

The history of the Saltwater Skitter Walk

2001 Skitter Walk is introduced in 11cm size.

2002 8cm model introduced.
New colours introduced:
Fire Shad (FSD)
Translucent Shad (SDT)
Blue/Silver Translucent (BT)
Black/Silver Translucent (BST).

2003 New colours introduced:
Hot Chartreuse (HCH)
Hot Pink (HP).

2004 New colours introduced:
Black Chartreuse Head (BKCH)
Holographic Blue (HB)
Holographic Bone Chartreuse
(HBNC)
Holographic Orange
Gold (HOG)
Holographic Silver (HS).

Fishing the Saltwater Skitter Walk

Imitating a swimming mullet or fleeing bait-fish, the Skitter Walk is designed to 'walk the dog' with ease.

Change the action of the lure by either keeping the rod tip up or down.

Jerk the lure then wind in the slack. The lure will first move to one side, then the other, each time emitting a loud rattle.

Adjust the rhythm of your retrieve, the speed of the jerk, and the distance you move the rod tip in order to tune your retrieve to the requirements of the fish. One day it will be fast and furious and the next day it will be slow and smooth.

Cast to likely fish-holding areas, to schooling fish, or in to schools of frightened bait-fish.

Tips from the pros

• When the fish are feeding at the surface, don't cast a lure into the middle of the shoal. Cast slightly short, or to one side, and try to take fish from the outside of the shoal. In this way you can take a number of fish before the shoal gets spooked. The Skitter Walk will help you cast a long way so that you can keep a good distance from the fish.

• If you are casting to a target like floating rubbish, try casting past the target and slightly to one side. Then you can work your lure right past the fish that are sheltering underneath. Don't forget to search all round by moving the boat into ideal casting positions. Above all, do it quietly.

• Fish don't just hold under surface matter. You will find them holding above submerged features. Look for rock piles, sea grass meadows where they hunt for food, and kelp beds near the surface.

• Get the most out of the Skitter Walk by experimenting with different actions. The Skitter Walk is a great 'walk the dog' lure. Cast a long way off, then start the retrieve with the rod tip up. Jerk-pause-rewind, jerk-pause-rewind. Each time you jerk, the Skitter Walk will move either left or right, and the internal bearing will emit a very audible 'click'. Vary the speed and length of the jerk, then vary the length of the pause. As the Skitter Walk gets closer to you, drop the rod tip and continue the retrieve right up to the bank or the boat. Fish will follow the lure right close in so don't lift the lure out until you can check that there is nothing following on behind.

• Don't be in too much of a hurry to strike a fish that takes a surface lure. Give the fish time to turn down and away before you set the hooks. In most cases the fish will do it for you, but tighten up as much as the line will allow just to make sure that the hooks are set before you start the fight. And keep that line tight! A slack line often means a lost fish.

Saltwater Skitter Walk

Code: SSW   Saltwater – Top Water – Rattling

Main features:

- A tough saltwater surface lure
- Ideal 'walk the dog' lure in calm conditions
- Fitted with VMC Perma Steel hooks
- Rolls from side to side emitting flash
- An excellent long casting lure
- Large internal rattle creates cadence rattle

Fishing tips:

- Fish it with a slow jerking action over likely fish holding spots
- Raise or lower the rod tip to change the lure's action
- Learn the various types of retrieve possible with this lure

Target predators:

Sea bass, bonito, tarpon, barramundi, redfish, snook, tuna

Technical features:

Code	Body length	Weight	Treble hooks	Swimming depth
SSW-11	11cm / 4¹/₃in.	19g / ⁵/₈ oz.	Two No. 2	Top water

CELEBRITY BITES

Ally Gowans on his Rapala 'friends'

There are hundreds of types of fishing lures: spoons, spinners, minnows, plugs, and of course Rapalas. Strangely I never call a Rapala a plug or a minnow. It's different, it's distinct – it's a Rapala. My favourites are the original balsa lures. Somehow they are more than just a lure; they are friends that go fishing with me. I think of them as people, and I can remember where I bought the old ones over 30 years ago.

In the intervening years they have, like me, lost some of their gloss; they have had bits replaced; and they are showing signs of age due to countless days on the river. Each one brings back special memories, but these old warriors, scarred by fish teeth, bruised by rocks, and rescued from trees, instill me with great confidence.

Each one has been re-tuned to flutter and vibrate to suit different conditions many times, and their once-shiny coats are scratched and worn through where the hook points glance against them. Most importantly they still catch lots of fish. I know when they are working well; I can feel the vibrations through the rod and visualise the seductive underwater dance that will drive the fish into a crazy bite.

Suddenly the rod arches, almost pulled from my hands, and a frenzied monster-fish fights and flashes beneath the rippling waves. Thanks to my Rapalas, the friends that go fishing with me.

CHAPTER 7

A time of change

1989–97

In 1989 the Rapala company celebrated its official 40th anniversary. Towards the end of the previous year a number of board members had proposed that Jarmo Rapala, the son of Esko and grandson of Lauri, should take over the running of the company. Jarmo had a good track record. He had been working at the factory since his adolescence and had proved his skills in regional sales management, product development, and sales and marketing. Jarmo had overseen the shift in company focus from solely America to a global vision, and the distributors around the world appreciated his communication skills.

Before his official appointment to the board, Jarmo Rapala already attended its meetings. He remembers well a meeting in November 1988 when he informed its members that he would consider leaving the company if they did not make dramatic changes to the caravan business. Jarmo was afraid that the company was heading for trouble, and its requests for additional funding and finance were depleting the Rapala assets. Perhaps Jarmo was sufficiently detached from the top tier of management to be in a position to see exactly what was happening.

When the board unanimously voted that Jarmo should become president of Rapala Oy they also decided to recruit a person with proven business experience and manufacturing knowledge to assist Jarmo with the running of the caravan and boat businesses in particular. A young managing director of a company that produced equipment for the manufacture of prefabricated houses was recommended to the board – Jorma Kasslin.

Jorma first met Jarmo Rapala at a meeting at Helsinki airport along with the two outside members of the Rapala board. Further meetings followed between Jarmo and Jorma, and they began to get to know each other. Jorma Kasslin made it clear that he would only join Rapala if Jarmo were given overall control. It appeared pointless to him to go into a company as deputy managing director if the senior management did not change.

Eventually, on 1 January 1989 Jarmo Rapala was appointed president of Rapala Oy. Jorma Kasslin joined the business as managing director of their caravan company and a director of Flipper Boats Oy. He also became deputy managing director of Rapala Oy.

In early June, Jarmo and Jorma went to Germany to visit a caravan manufacturing company that was potentially for sale. What they saw there opened their eyes regarding the structure and performance of their own

- **Lauri's statue erected in Vääksy**
- **Normark Corporation's new offices**
- **150 million Rapala lures**
- **Jarmo Rapala takes control**
- **Jorma Kasslin joins the Rapala company**
- **Rapala enters the distribution business**
- **Rapala–Shimano co-operation**

caravan company. Instead of purchasing the German business, the pair returned to Finland resolved to sell their caravan company as quickly as they could.

In the summer of 1989, at the AFTMA show in Las Vegas, Ron Weber invited Jarmo Rapala to a secret meeting. Ron informed Jarmo that he was ready to sell his shares in Normark Corporation in the USA, Normark Limited in Canada and Normark Sport Limited in the United Kingdom. Furthermore, Ron informed Jarmo that he had a potential buyer in place that was also interested in purchasing Rapala itself. The potential buyers were present at the meeting.

Ron's decision to sell his shares was potentially disastrous news to Rapala. The Rapala name was registered in the USA by Normark, and could well be sold with the company. This was the second time in its history that Rapala risked losing control of its brand name in a major export market. The company that had worked so hard to establish itself as the foremost lure-manufacturing company in the world risked competing against lures made by another manufacturer branded 'Rapala' in the USA. However, Jarmo and Jorma saw the matter in a different light. This was the opportunity that they wanted to regain ownership of the brand name in the USA, and to take control of their major distribution companies. Jarmo began negotiations with Ron Weber and with two Finnish banks that were asked to make the capital available for Rapala Oy to purchase Ron's shares. One bank refused the deal, stating that in their view the company could not execute an acquisition of this nature, and that Rapala could not run a company in the USA. They made comments about how the USA was 'far away from the fields of Asikkala', and how different it was to run an international company. Obviously they had no faith in the Rapala management whatsoever. However, Jarmo and Jorma's negotiations with the other bank were more successful despite its insistence that each of the Rapala brothers should make a financial guarantee of several million Finnish marks.

There was also the matter of the Rapala board of directors to consider. It was not an easy matter to convince all of them that the purchase of distribution companies in the USA, Canada and the UK was a good idea, especially as it would result in the company being heavily laden with debt. Whilst some members were very much in favour of the scheme, other members were less keen, and voiced doubts similar to those of the bank that turned down Jarmo's idea. However, the board finally agreed, and in May 1990 Rapala Oy completed the purchase of Ron's shares.

Timing was not a critical issue as far as the possible purchase of the Normark companies was concerned. Ron Weber was prepared to give Rapala as much time as the company required to raise the cash to buy his interests. He wanted Rapala to purchase his shares, but at the same time he wished to continue his association with the companies that he and Ray Ostrom had formed. From Rapala's point of view, the company was happy to delay the final purchase in order to ensure that there were no 'financial surprises', and that the purchase terms were the best that they could possibly achieve. It was however critical from another aspect. The year 1990–91 marked the beginning of a major economic recession around the world. Markets collapsed in one day (Black Monday) and millions of people found themselves out of work, and just as importantly, without money. One of the first industries to suffer was the leisure industry. In Finland the boating and caravan businesses saw demand for their products drop by 90 per cent in less than a year.

Whilst the negotiations with Ron Weber were taking place, both Jorma and Jarmo were trying to sell the boat and caravan businesses together with the real estates related to them. Both were eventually sold in the summer of 1990. Jarmo recalls that he was criticised for accepting a low price, but he and Jorma had agreed that they would take the capital out of the businesses, and would accept whatever they could get. If Jarmo and Jorma had not sold the two companies when they did – and it was a matter of only a few weeks as far as the critical timing was concerned – there is no doubt that the recession would have claimed not only the caravan and boating businesses, but Rapala itself.

On 25 November 1989, in a touching tribute to Lauri Rapala, and on the anniversary of his birthday, a bronze statue of the founder of the Rapala company holding a trout was unveiled on the banks of the Vääksy Canal, not far from the company's headquarters. Many of his friends from Normark were present at the ceremony including Ron Weber from the USA.

The changes in the management structure of Rapala did not hinder the product development programme, and 1989 saw the introduction of two new lures. The Rattlin' Rapala 5cm (2in.) was introduced to support the previous year's launch of the 7cm (2.8in.) model, and a brand new 3cm (1.2in.) Countdown lure was added to the range. The 'CD 3' was the idea of Browning in Italy, the distributors of Rapala lures at the time. It was intended for trout in the fast-flowing streams of northern Italy, but it eventually made its mark in many countries around the world.

The unveiling of Lauri Rapala's statue.
(Normark Corporation archive)

In their financial year 1988–89 the company sold over 9.5 million lures, and employed 374 people in Vääksy and 36 in Galway, Ireland.

Rapala Oy was now in a unique position. As far as the international fishing-tackle trade was concerned, Rapala was the only company to control both its production and its major distribution network. The advantages of this are clear to see. Manufacturers generally rely on independent distributors to sell their products into overseas markets. They have to rely on the distributor to do a good job for them, and to devote sufficient time, energy and cash to the sale, promotion and marketing of the products. Rapala, however, owned their distributors in America and Canada, their two largest markets, and had a controlling interest in their UK distributor. The company could therefore totally control the sales and marketing policies of its distributors in order to ensure that every sales opportunity was maximised.

The benefits of Rapala's distributor ownership did not stop there. The company now enjoyed direct access to its major markets. No longer did the Rapala team have to rely on second-hand information about market trends, demands and requirements; they could find out for themselves. The availability of good-quality information made the job of the Rapala research and development division so much easier, and for the first time Rapala could make 'species specific' lures for niche markets as well as the general markets that they had previously supplied so successfully. In fact, this opportunity was so important that Jarmo Rapala based himself in the USA for most of 1991, whilst Jorma Kasslin moved to Normark Sport in the UK, where he started to work on the establishment of a European distribution network for the Rapala company. Rapala was now on the way to becoming one of the major fishing-tackle companies in the world.

As early as 1989 negotiations had begun with Knekt Mats Olofsson regarding the purchase of Normark Scandinavia and its associate companies. Normark Scandinavia had been set up independently of the Normark companies in America and Canada, and therefore was dealt with as a strictly separate matter. The shareholding of Normark Scandinavia was also far different from the USA companies that had been purchased the year before. Ron Weber owned 25 per cent of the shares, and was prepared to sell them to Rapala. However, Ray Ostrom also owned 25 per cent, and Mats Olofsson owned the remaining 50 per cent. Mats did not want to sell his shares to Rapala, and Ray Ostrom was content to retain his shareholding. A stalemate ensued.

Eventually Mats Olofsson phoned Jarmo in January or February of 1991 and told him that he was prepared to sell Normark Scandinavia and its subsidiary companies. A deal was struck in mid 1991 to purchase the shareholdings of Ron Weber, Ray Ostrom and Mats Olofsson.

The purchase of Normark Scandinavia by Rapala included the following subsidiary companies and assets.

• Normark Norway, a company that was making substantial losses and was closed about a year later.

• Normark Denmark, a one-man operation that was also closed about a year later.

• Normark Spain, a one-man operation that had no sales. The company was relocated from Seville to Madrid and restructured. Hannu Murtonen was appointed managing director, and it was Hannu who laid the foundations that resulted in Normark Spain becoming the premier fishing-tackle distributor in the country within 12 years.

• Normark Holland, a Dutch distribution company that had also been opened as a European gateway company where goods from the American and European manufacturers were imported in bulk then broken down and shipped to distributors around the Middle East and Europe. This company was closed a year after the purchase, and the bulk storage and distribution business was taken over by Normark Sport in the UK.

• Normark Finland, a distribution company jointly owned by Normark Scandinavia and Rapala that was proving to be very successful with a good market share.

- The remaining 8 per cent of shares in Normark Sport Limited, the distribution company in the UK.

Between 1991 and 1992, Jorma and Jarmo concentrated their efforts on strengthening the vital distribution channels for the Rapala business. Among their key achievements in this period were the following:

- The purchase of Rapala's long-time French distributor Ragot S.A. in July 1991. Along with Ragot, Rapala purchased its manufacturing subsidiary SIPP, which made sea-fishing jigs and lures. France was always considered an important export market for the company.

- The encouragement of cross-distribution of products among those fishing-tackle manufacturing companies in the USA and Europe formerly distributed by Normark. The addition of other important brands to each company's portfolio at once made them important domestic distributors, and also contributed significantly to their profitability.

- The selection and appointment of new Rapala distributors in Denmark (Steen Yde, subsequently purchased by Rapala in 1995) and Norway (initially Solvkroken, then Elbe, which was purchased in 1999).

Rapala lure 150,000,001.
(John Mitchell)

Jarmo Rapala and Ron Weber cut the first turf on the site of Normark Corporation's new offices.
(Normark Corporation archive)

151

Normark Corporation's headquarters at Minnetonka.
(Normark Corporation archive)

• The refocusing of Normark Scandinavia AB as a domestic distributor, as opposed to an international one. Its hunting division was established in 1996.

• The establishment of the Rapala–Shimano Distribution Agreement. Rapala's Normark distribution companies would distribute Shimano products in Finland, Sweden, France and Spain, whilst Shimano companies would distribute Rapala products, and the products of other manufacturers distributed by the Normark companies in Italy, Germany, Belgium, Holland and Luxembourg.

By the end of 1992, Rapala had a basic worldwide distribution network. Jarmo and Jorma adopted a forward-thinking policy to emphasise the local management structure, and to respect the local management concerns and legal requirements.

Another Rapala milestone was reached on 6 September 1993 when the company manufactured its 150 millionth lure. The lure is mounted on a plaque that hangs in Rapala's headquarters. Meanwhile in America, the building of Normark Corporation's new office and warehouse complex at Minnetonka began. Jarmo Rapala and Ron Weber cut the first turf to signal the start of building operations. It was also in 1993 that a new board of directors was formed, consisting of Esko Rapala (Chairman), Eero Makkonen, Jarmo Rapala and Jorma Kasslin. The old board of directors remained in place as a supervisory board, but Jarmo and Jorma felt that their style of management was not geared to a modern business environment. They needed the ability to move quickly when necessary, and the new board made it possible for them to get faster decisions whilst maintaining proper control.

New lures for the early nineties

A Countdown Magnum in CG colour accounts for a small tuna.
(Rapala Media Service)

1990 was marked by a significant increase in the number of new lures produced. The first Rapala Squid lure was introduced in 9cm (3.6in.) and 11cm (4.5in.) models. An 8cm (3.25in.) model of both the Deep and Shallow Running Shad Rap was launched. A larger 8cm (3.25in.) Rattlin' Rapala was seen for the first time, and a new Countdown Magnum 13cm (5.3in.) model was launched. In addition a new colour, Constant Guigo (CG), was added to the saltwater range of lures[17]. The orange mackerel-type stripes over a mother of pearl base has consistently taken saltwater fish since its introduction.

1991 saw the launch of Rapala's second rattling lure in the form of the Rattlin' Fat Rap, which was introduced in 4cm (1.6in.) and 5cm (2in.) models. The Rattlin' Fat Rap was a true rattling crank bait, adapted from the 1978 Fat Rap. Attention

---

[17] The CG colour was designed by the French big-game fisherman Constant Guigo as a result of his years of experience in big-game fishing.

was again devoted to the Magnum series of lures with the introduction of the Countdown Magnum 10cm (4in.) model. Rapala's experience in four-colour printing lead to the introduction of the new Trout (TR) colour. The Rainbow Trout (RT) colour, introduced in 1979, had proved so successful that a brown trout imitation was a logical step forward.

As far as Rapala was concerned, 1992 was a year of consolidation. The company had grown very quickly in the previous two years. The purchase of the various distribution companies through 1990 and 1991 had drained the company's cash reserves, and built up a significant amount of debt, so it was time to reduce the debt and improve the cashflow situation. The new product introductions for 1992 reflect this attitude. A smaller 4cm (1.6in.) Rattlin' Rapala was introduced alongside a larger 7cm (2.8in.) Rattlin' Fat Rap. The Shad Rap range reverted to the original Rapala concept when the Blue (B) colour was revised. Instead of using a mother of pearl base colour, the lures were covered in silver foil before being sealed with lacquer and spray-painted with a blue back. The reflective properties of the silver foil were found to be superior to that of paint. A new stimulating colour, Firetiger (FT), was introduced to the Magnum range. Firetiger was a combination of a dark green back with black mackerel strips, light green/yellow flanks and an orange belly. The actual design varies according to the lure shape. Since its introduction in 1992 Firetiger has been used in almost all lures in the Rapala range, and is without doubt one of the best-selling colours that Rapala has ever designed.

1993 saw the introduction of a unique lure as far as Rapala was concerned. The 7cm (2.8in.) Minnow Spoon was not a fish-shaped lure. Indeed it was a spoon, but shaped in such a way as to imitate the body shape of a fish as it was retrieved. The Minnow Spoon did not spin like traditional spoons, nor did it wobble from side to side like a traditional Rapala lure. The Minnow Spoon twisted from side to side along its horizontal axis as it was retrieved, without actually spinning at all. The outside or convex side of the lure was painted in a selection of fish-imitating colours whilst the inner or concave surface was finished in highly reflective silver. The lure was available with either a treble hook or a fixed single hook incorporating a weed guard. The lure made an immediate impact, especially in the UK; Normark's sales manager actually caught a pike on his very first cast whilst demonstrating the lure to Normark's team of salesmen at their annual sales meeting.

A pike taken on a Super Shad Rap Walleye (W) colour is beaten.
(Rapala Media Service)

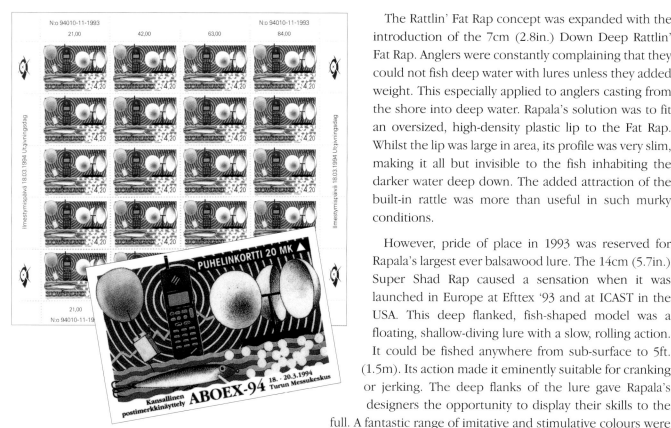

The Finnish postage stamp and phonecard depicting successful exports, featuring a Rapala lure.
(Rapala company archive)

The Rattlin' Fat Rap concept was expanded with the introduction of the 7cm (2.8in.) Down Deep Rattlin' Fat Rap. Anglers were constantly complaining that they could not fish deep water with lures unless they added weight. This especially applied to anglers casting from the shore into deep water. Rapala's solution was to fit an oversized, high-density plastic lip to the Fat Rap. Whilst the lip was large in area, its profile was very slim, making it all but invisible to the fish inhabiting the darker water deep down. The added attraction of the built-in rattle was more than useful in such murky conditions.

However, pride of place in 1993 was reserved for Rapala's largest ever balsawood lure. The 14cm (5.7in.) Super Shad Rap caused a sensation when it was launched in Europe at Efttex '93 and at ICAST in the USA. This deep flanked, fish-shaped model was a floating, shallow-diving lure with a slow, rolling action. It could be fished anywhere from sub-surface to 5ft. (1.5m). Its action made it eminently suitable for cranking or jerking. The deep flanks of the lure gave Rapala's designers the opportunity to display their skills to the full. A fantastic range of imitative and stimulative colours were introduced, and the colour range is continually refined today. The Super Shad Rap was a European pike lure without equal, and it quickly established itself as a best seller in the major markets of the world. Indeed, it was not long before Rapala began to receive stories of the lure's success in the sea as well as in freshwater. The Super Shad Rap range has never been extended past 14cm (5.7in.), but saltwater versions are now a permanent part of the range, and the lure was subsequently redesigned in order to offer a Countdown version.

On 18 March 1994 a Finnish postage stamp was introduced into circulation, which recognised the value of exports to the country's economy. There, amongst the mobile phones, electronic equipment and radio waves, was a Rapala lure. The company commissioned the printing of a special post card and sent samples of this with the postage stamp to their clients and friends around the world.

The success in 1993 of the new Minnow Spoon resulted in new 6cm (2.45in.) and 8cm (3.25in.) sizes being launched in 1994. Again, as per the previous year, they were available in either a treble-hook or a single-hook pattern with weed guard version. The Down Deep Rattlin' Fat Rap range was extended to include a new 5cm (2in.) version. The Countdown Magnum range was again extended to include new 8cm (3.25in.) and 22cm (8.95in.) versions.

The new lure for 1994 was the 3cm (1.2in.) Blue Fox Minnow Spin. This lure formed a link between the Vibrax spinner and the Rapala lure. A Vibrax blade was mounted on a wire that formed part of the structure of a lipless Rapala Countdown body. The result was a lure that flashed as the spinner blade rotated ahead of the wobbling Rapala body. A single treble hook was fitted at the tail of the lure. The blade colours of Gold, Silver and Firetiger were carefully matched to the colours of the lure bodies. The lure was branded Blue Fox, as Blue Fox was a spinner and spoon manufacturer whereas Rapala produced wobblers. The company was very careful to maintain its reputation in specific areas of the fishing-tackle market, and did not wish to create any confusion regarding the areas of expertise enjoyed by its various manufacturing arms.

The family bows out

1995 was to be a revolutionary year for Rapala. Jarmo and Jorma's plans for the development of the company began to take shape late in 1994 when some of the 13 Rapala family shareholders requested them to explore the possibility of selling Rapala to a Finnish conglomerate. Perhaps they felt they were no longer in control of the company, or perhaps they realised that the company was working its way out of its debts, was financially secure and was again worth a reasonable price per share. Jarmo Rapala believes that some of the family shareholders had realised afterwards how close they came to losing everything in the caravan and boat ventures, and wanted to cash their chips in now. The popular view is that some of the Rapala brothers felt rather uncomfortable and did not 'fit in' with the current management structure. The sale of shares by the family members would also avoid complications in future years when the third family generation came to inherit their parents' shares. It would not be possible for seven cousins to run the business in the same way as their fathers, with all of them being involved in key decision making on a day-to-day basis. The company was much larger now with a number of international subsidiaries.

Jarmo held meetings with the Finnish conglomerate, and an offer was made for Rapala. Jarmo and Jorma, however, considered that the offer was on the low side, and turned it down. They recommended that the Rapala board refuse the offer, and undertook to look for other potential buyers.

Some time afterwards, Jarmo and Jorma presented another option to the Rapala board: private equity investment. Late in 1994 Jarmo, with the approval of the board, approached Bankers Trust via a contact of Eero Makkonen's. Jarmo, Jorma and Eero's negotiations resulted in Bankers Trust making an offer some 30 per cent higher than that of the Finnish conglomerate with the additional opportunity for the shareholders to reinvest up to 10 per cent of the company's purchase value. Bankers Trust in turn laid off part of the risk to City Venture Capital. Jarmo, Jorma and Eero Makkonen were expected to make a significant investment in the company in order to prove their commitment to its future. At the end of months of negotiations, the

Rapala's Deputy CEO and Chief Financial Officer, Steve Greer, addresses a business conference in 2002.
(Lars Ollberg)

family shareholders finally accepted the offer, although some of them would rather not have sold at all.

Jarmo Rapala was appointed chief executive officer (CEO) of the Rapala Normark Corporation, and Jorma Kasslin was appointed chief operating officer (COO). A particularly gifted accountant, Steve Greer, who had handled the due diligence investigation and report on behalf of the two banks, was invited to join the company as its chief financial officer (CFO).

For the first time in its history, Rapala was no longer a family company. Now investment banks, which had their representatives on the board of directors, owned the majority of the shares. Provided that the company continued to produce a decent return on their investments the bankers were happy, and it was the job of Jarmo, Jorma and Steve to ensure that the company performed to their owners' satisfaction. For many of the managing directors of the Normark distribution companies this was their first experience of international finance management, and the reporting requirements and financial controls that were imposed came as something of a shock. However their own business experience and the guidance of the new Rapala management team quickly established the new financial policies required to run the companies effectively and efficiently.

A Husky Jerk suspends in front of an obviously interested bass.
(Rapala Media Service)

Another significant landmark was reached in 1995 when the worldwide sales of filleting knives designed by Ron Weber and manufactured by Marttiini reached in excess of 25 million pieces. No doubt Marttiini were pleased that they eventually decided to make a knife to Ron's specifications.

In 1995 Rapala launched some of their most successful lures. The 12cm (4.9in.) and 14cm (5.7in.) Husky Jerks were plastic bodied, minnow-shaped lures with an in-built rattling chamber. Nothing too unusual in that specification, but there was one very important added factor that made the Husky Jerk stand out from its competitors. It was a suspending lure; in other words it had neutral buoyancy, and if the retrieve were stopped, the lure would 'suspend' and hang quite still in the water. It took some time to explain to fishermen who were used to continuously retrieving their lures that the Husky Jerk would take fish whilst it was stationery, but this was indeed the case. The Husky Jerk could be cranked down to the right depth, and then left to suspend near an underwater obstruction or weed bed. The resident predators would think that lunch was served, and the rods would almost be jerked from the fisherman's grasp. If the lure did not take a fish whilst it was stationary the chances were that a predator would take it as soon as the retrieve recommenced.

In the USA the Husky Jerk was targeted at southern bass anglers, but it also found support among walleye, pike and in-shore saltwater anglers. Cabela's, one of North America's largest mail order fishing-tackle companies, named the lure the 'Number one new product'. It was even featured in the *Wall Street Journal*. It immediately became the number-one best-selling lure in America when it was launched in 1996.

The plastic, minnow-shaped body of the Husky Jerk again gave Rapala's designers the opportunity to demonstrate their skills, and the lure was launched in a colour range that included a number of never-before-seen patterns, such as the Tennessee Shad.

In addition to the new Husky Jerk, Rapala extended the Minnow Spin range to include 2cm (0.8in.) and 5cm (2in.) models. A new 3cm (1.2in.) Original floating Rapala was also launched. Colour additions also extended the Blue Fox Vibrax selection of spinners.

Rapala's research and development department had been very busy the previous year developing a new silver-plating technique, and the results of their hard work were launched in 1995. Rapala was the first company to electro-plate real silver onto wood. Even today the process is not discussed outside of the company, but the results were phenomenal. Where previously silver foil and lacquer were thought to be the ultimate answer, the new silver-plated finish offered increased reflective brilliance. The silver-plating of the basic lure and over-painting with specially selected paints resulted in a new range of colours being made available in selected patterns.

Such innovations continued to fuel the sales and growth of the business. During Rapala's 1994–95 financial year, almost 14 million lures were sold to over 80 export countries, and the number of employees rose to 470.

After the runaway success of the Husky Jerk in 1995, the 8cm (3.25in.) and 10cm (4in.) models were launched in 1996, and quickly followed in the footsteps of the larger models. The new lure for 1996 was the Countdown Shad Rap, which was introduced in 5cm (2in.), 7cm (2.8in.) and 8cm (3.25in.) models. The Countdown Shad Rap could be cast further and more accurately, and of course it could be fished at a greater depth than the floating model. Its introduction opened up great opportunities for fishermen to cover water previously not fishable with the Shad Rap series of lures.

Rapala's new silver-plating process also offered their designers opportunities to produce more lifelike colours. The Roach series of colours was introduced to the Shad Rap and Super Shad Rap families of lures. The range was made up of Blue Roach (BRO), Green Roach (GRO), Orange Roach (ORO) and Roach (RO). A new colour, Silver Gold (SG), was also introduced to the Shad Rap range, and Dorado (D) was added to the Magnum range.

A new 7cm (2.8in.) Minnow Spin lure complemented the Blue Fox range, and a new Orange Shad (SDO) colour was added to the Minnow Spoon selection.

The new lures for 1996 were the 7cm (2.8in.) and 9cm (3.6in.) Risto Rap, named in honour of Lauri's eldest son Risto Rapala. The Risto Rap was a balsawood lure (Risto would have nothing else), and was a success in America even before it hit the shelves. Several months prior to its formal introduction, the American Sportfishing Association named it the 'best new freshwater hard bait of the year.' The lure was also instrumental in helping Minneapolis angler Jim Moynagh to win the $1 million Forest L. Wood Minnetonka Tournament. Retailers responded, and promptly gobbled up Normark Corporation's first-year allocation of 500,000 lures. Ron Weber commented, 'Over time, I realised that very little really changes if the proper principles are in place. Every year we try to top the previous year. It all boils down to this: we're fishermen first, and we just try to bring out lures, knives or other outdoor products that our fellow anglers simply can't live without.' In addition, the Husky Jerk range was complemented by the addition of the 6cm (2.45in.) version.

1997 was the year for exotic new colours as well as new lures. Hot Mustard (HM), Plum Shad (PSD) and even Parrot (PRT) were new colours amongst the more regular patterns. Black Red Head (BRH), Clown (CLN), Gold Shiner (GSH), Purple Mackerel (PM), Silver Blue (SB), Silver Green Mackerel (SGM), Silver Green Shad (SGSD) and Shiner (SH) were added to Magnums and Shad lures.

During the company's 1996–97 financial year a record of almost 17 million Rapala lures were sold around the world, and the number of employees remained at just under 470 people.

A different kind of float

During 1997 the plans were laid to move the Rapala company forward into its next stage of development. The Rapala family agreed to sell its remaining 10 per cent of Rapala shares, and Rapala Normark NV was set up in The Netherlands to act as a holding company for the growing Rapala Normark Group of companies. New investors joined Bankers Trust and C.V.C. The plan was to make a placing of Rapala shares on the Helsinki Stock Exchange. Jarmo Rapala announced his retirement from the presidency of the company at a meeting in Monte Carlo. After years of travelling the world he wanted to spend more time with his young family; however, he was to continue his link with the company by heading the product development division. Jarmo recommended that Jorma Kasslin should replace him as CEO, and the investment banks were pleased to endorse his proposal. Jorma Kasslin was appointed president of the company in preparation for the placement of the shares on the stock exchange. However, timing was critical, as the markets were particularly volatile throughout 1997, and the year ended without the placement being made.

Throughout the 1990s Rapala's factory in Ireland had become increasingly important. Rapire was producing very high-quality products, and its labour costs were low; however, there were signs that the cost of labour in Ireland was about to rise. The production process of Rapala lures is labour intensive. Despite the introduction of many automated systems, the production of wooden lures to very close tolerances demands a large amount of supervision, maintenance and control. Labour costs in Finland had been rising throughout the 1990s, and Rapala was forced to make a decision that Finland was no longer economically suited to this form of manufacturing.

Rapala devised a plan that all the key operations involving strict quality control and unique expertise were to remain in Finland whilst labour intensive operations should be performed elsewhere. By adopting this policy, Rapala would be in a position to combine high-quality production with a competitive cost structure to compete against competition from Asia, and especially China.

Now, at the end of 1997 everything was ready to move the company forward again. Rapala had a new manufacturing plan that would require considerable financial investment, and the policy to partly move the company into public ownership was in place. This was a matter of correct timing and accurate pricing that required much patience and impeccably good judgement.

Saltwater Skitter Pop

The history of the Saltwater Skitter Pop

1998 Skitter Pop is introduced. Colours include:
Frog (F)
Hot Clown (HCL).

1999 5cm size introduced.

2000 12cm size introduced. New Lime Frog (LF) and Silver (S) colours added.

2000 Saltwater Skitter Pop introduced in Stainless Steel (SS prefix) colours:
Blue Mullet (SSBMU)
Gold Mullet (SSGMU)
Green Mullet (SSGRMU).

2003 New colours introduced:
Blue Mullet (BMU)
Pearl Orange (CG)
Silver Mackerel (SM)
Green Mackerel (GM)
Chartreuse Mackerel (CM).

Fishing the Saltwater Skitter Pop

The number of saltwater fish that are attracted to a surface lure is amazing. In fact, all seas have their compliment of surface-feeding predators.

Cast the lure into likely areas and use the same retrieves described for the freshwater version of the Skitter Pop.

Cast at schooling surface fish, but be careful to cast to the outside of the school so as not to spook them.

You can troll the Skitter Pop for small tuna, bonito and wahoo, but it helps to put the occasional jerk into this lure just to make it change direction for a second or two.

Tips from the pros

- The lure that catches lots of fish for you in early morning and late evening might not trigger strikes at midday. It's common, for example, for fish to go for larger lures at 'prime time' and stop striking them at midday. Try using smaller lures, and/or lures with actions different from the ones that work best for you early and late.

- Don't forget to watch and wait! A surface lure like the Skitter Pop can trigger strikes in many different ways. Learn all the different retrieves, and perhaps invent a few of your own. Most importantly, learn whether the fish want the lure ripped across the top, or jerked and twitched then left alone. Work this lure too fast and you will pull the lure away from a triggered fish without knowing it. It's all a matter of finding out just how the fish are feeling today!

- In the sea, a few miles from the nearest coastline, there is little to attract fish to any particular location. However, find some floating rubbish and you can be in business. Anything from the branch of a tree to discarded rubbish will attract fish looking for both food and shelter. Keep well away in the clear water and use a long cast, gradually working towards the target. Don't be in too much of a hurry to start the retrieve, and keep things nice and quiet. If the fish are there, you will soon get to know, then you can start taking them from the outside of the shoal, and work towards the centre.

- After every fishing trip, make sure that you don't have water build-up in the trays holding your expensive lures. Open your tackle box at home and dry them out. Hooks sitting in water, especially saltwater can rust in a matter of days. It doesn't take much decay to weaken the hooks and erode their ability to hold fish.

- Do you take vacations to ocean-front destinations and wonder whether you could catch a few fish from shore? Pack a rod next time, and plan to fish the surf as the tide is rising, or at high tide. That's when in-shore flats fish are as close to the beach as they can get.

Saltwater Skitter Pop

Code: SSP   Saltwater – Top Water

Main features:

- Can be cast from either shore or boat
- Very effective for many saltwater species
- Special range of saltwater colours
- Creates large splash in front of the lure
- Fitted with VMC Perma Steel hooks
- Special internal rattle in balsa body (12cm)

Fishing tips:

- Try all types of retrieve to find the one that the fish prefer on the day
- In calm water twitch the lure to imitate a wounded bait-fish
- Fish this lure around surface debris and shallow reefs for good results

Target predators:

Sea bass, tarpon, tuna, bonito, wahoo, redfish, snook

Technical features:

Code	Body length	Weight	Treble hooks	Swimming depth
SSP-09	9cm / 3^1/2in.	14g / ^{1}/2 oz.	Two No. 3	Top water
SSP-12*	12cm / 4^3/4in.	40g / 1^7/16 oz.	Two No. 2/0	Top water

* Equipped with special internal rattle.

Glass Shad Rap

The history of the Glass Shad Rap

2003 Introduced in 4cm, 5cm and 7cm sizes. A special range of 'glass colours' added:
Glass Fire Perch (GFP)
Glass Gold Red (GGR)
Glass Perch (GP)
Glass Black (GBK)
Glass Blue Shad (GBSD).

2004 New colours introduced:
Glass Brown Crawdad (GBCW)
Glass Citrus Shad (GCS)
Glass Purple Shad (GPS)
Glass Purple Sunfire (GPSF).

Fishing the Glass Shad Rap

The legendary Shad Rap has evolved. New technology has created a prismatic 'glass' three-dimensional look that is unique and innovative.

When the light hits the lure it reflects in hundreds of directions at once. It's the same principle behind facets on a diamond. The chameleon-like Glass Shad Rap actually picks up the colour of its surroundings and bounces the same colour back in an iridescent glow.

Fish the Glass Shad Rap just as you would the Deep Running Shad Rap. It can be extremely effective where there are a lot of small bait-fish that tend to have the same kind of colouration as the Glass Shad Rap.

Tips from the pros

- One of the most common mistakes anglers make when fishing crank baits is to use a snap swivel. Those gadgets are wonderful for use with line-twisting lures such as spinners, but not only are they unnecessary with most crank baits, they often detract from the lure's action.

- Anglers who fish from the shore often aren't careful enough when approaching a spot. It isn't good enough just to duck down low, or to wear drab or even camo clothing – although those things are important. You also have to walk softly – more softly than you can imagine when on soft, boggy ground. Fish can feel the vibrations of your footsteps, and even if they don't move away, they grow cautious.

- When bass fishing is really tough, here's a trick used by the top tournament pros to trigger strikes. Grab a spinning rod rigged with 6 lb. line and tie on a Shad Rap (shallow or deep diver depending on the water depth). Make relatively long casts and reel it slowly, steadily, around cover or over fish holding flats. Believe it or not, it can turn the trick on days when nothing else works!

- Big fish tend to be more wary than smaller individuals. If you're casting a crank bait, try pitching it softly with an underhand motion. The lure will land much more softly on the water, which means more quietly, and the stealth of the entry will spook fish less.

- High-speed retrieves may trigger strikes at times, especially from saltwater fish. But the pros tend to agree that more fish are caught by changes in speed and direction than they are by sheer speed alone. The pros rarely 'burn' a crank bait fast. They prefer relatively slow-speed reels (about a 4.3:1 gear ratio), and usually maintain what they call a 'medium pace', building in the strike-provoking action by pauses and jerks and changes in speed.

Glass Shad Rap

Code: GSR   Freshwater – Deep Diving

Main features:

- New 'Glass Technology'
- Deep-diving lure
- Heavier than balsa, this lure casts well
- New range of special colours
- Neutral buoyancy suspending lure
- Loud rhythmic rattle for intense fish attraction

Fishing tips:

- Search deep holes slowly with this lure
- Use a 'stop and go' retrieve or move the rod tip to impart more action
- Stop the retrieve and let the lure suspend near underwater cover

Target predators:

Perch, pike, zander (walleye), trout, chub, salmon, bass

Technical features:

Code	Body length	Weight	Treble hooks	Swimming depth
GSR-04	4cm / 1 1/2in.	5g / 3/16 oz.	Two No. 6	1.5–3.3m / 5–11ft.
GSR-05	5cm / 2in.	9g / 5/16 oz.	Two No. 5	2.1–3.3m / 7–11ft.
GSR-07	7cm / 2 3/4in.	12g / 7/16 oz.	Two No. 3	2.1–4.5m / 7–15ft.

Countdown Super Shad Rap

The history of the Countdown Super Shad Rap

1993 The Super Shad Rap introduced in 14cm size only.

2000 Rapala receives reports from British and continental pike anglers that the lure is being adapted to either suspending or countdown use with great success.

2003 Rapala completes its research and produces the Countdown Super Shad Rap for the first time in:
  Blue Shad (BSD)
  Nordic Perch (NP)
  Hot Perch (HTP)
  Silver Shad (SSD).

Fishing the Countdown Super Shad Rap

Use the 'countdown method' to get the best out of this lure. It imitates good-sized bait-fish that don't dart about like their smaller cousins, so you have to make the Countdown Super Shad Rap behave just like a decent sized meal for a large predator.

Establish the depth, or the water cover over a weed bed, then slowly fish your lure over the bottom or the weeds letting it roll lazily from side to side.

Imitate a feeding fish by occasionally giving the lure a quick jerk to make it move quickly to one side and flash its broad flanks.

Occasionally stop the retrieve and let the lure sink for a second or two before starting the retrieve again.

Tips from the pros

• During the spring, and in the evenings and early mornings in hot summer weather, the fish will congregate in the shallower water that is either cooler, more oxygenated, or in the spring, the right depth for spawning. Long casting, shallow-diving lures can be used with great success, as there is less chance of the fish being spooked by noise from a boat close in or vibration from the shore.

• Following fish can often be triggered into striking with erratic stop-and-go, surge-and-pause movements. If you see a fish coming behind your lure – and even when you don't – build some of these actions into your retrieve at some point during the cast. You don't have to do it on every cast, but make sure you experiment with it each time out.

• Due to its specially angled lip the Countdown Super Shad Rap is very responsive to rod tip action. Slow down or stop the retrieve for a few seconds before jerking the lure back into life. If you do this around submerged obstructions where the big predators are likely to hang out you will be rewarded with some exceptional strikes.

• Get back in the saddle! Saddles (deeper water connecting two shallow structures) are great holding spots for fish. They take many forms, but if it seems the connection between a shallow structure and shore, or two shallow structures, has weeds or other cover in it, all the better. You can figure this 'highway' between the two shallow zones will hold fish many times. Fish it often and it will pay off.

• Put emotion into your presentation with fish imitating baits. One of the things that triggers a response in bigger fish is signs of panic in a particular bait-fish. Try using stop-and-go, bursts of speed, and slow struggling motions. Sell the idea that your lure is on its 'last legs' and you may be fast to a big fish!

Countdown Super Shad Rap

Code: CDSR   Freshwater – Saltwater – Sinking

Main features:

- A superb long casting lure
- New sinking and diving capabilities
- Fitted with VMC Perma Steel hooks
- Countdown depth control
- Perfectly balanced for a slow, wide action

Fishing tips:

- Search slow and deep for the large predators
- Use the Countdown method to systematically search the water column
- Stop the retrieve and let the lure 'hang' near underwater cover

Target predators:

Pike, zander (walleye), catfish, snook, tarpon, redfish, striper, Nile perch

Technical features:

Code	Body length	Weight	Treble hooks	Swimming depth
CDSR-14	14cm / 5¹/₂in.	71g / 2¹/₂ oz.	Two No. 2/0	1.5–4.0m / 5–13ft.

Glass Fat Rap

Fishing the Glass Fat Rap

The Fat Rap has a well-earned reputation for taking finicky fish. When crank-bait anglers encounter open water and weary fish they reach for their lightweight outfit, and tie on a Fat Rap. The tight swimming action of this lure is perfect for these conditions.

The Glass Fat Rap works great using the 'bump the stump' method, based on the fact that big bass and often smallmouth will be concealed near the shelter of an ambush point. Hunt out these ambush points (lily pads, log pilings, submerged vegetation, docks, boat houses and of course stumps), and cast to them literally bumping against them on retrieve.

The lure's strong, square plastic lip should fend off most hang-ups, but if you pick up a weed, give your rod tip a strong backward sweep.

Another technique that really benefits from the Glass Fat Rap's swimming action is cranking. When over points, rock piles or sloping weed beds, cast to the shallow area of the structure and retrieve down the slope bumping the bottom.

Tips from the pros

• When fishing is tough – you've tried every spot you can think of and every presentation you know – try this tip from Rapala pro Larry Dahlberg: take a Glass Fat Rap or Down Deep Rattlin' Fat Rap, which dives at a steep angle, and troll it at high speed – up to 5mph (8kmh) and even faster – along spots that you know should hold fish. Hit the very tips of the points, the little boulder piles, the spot-on-the-spot type of thing. That lure will dive deep while it's still close to the boat, and very much under control, so you can make it go anywhere you want it to go. Make repeated, fast trolling passes over the same spot at a lot of different angles. You can move the boat very fast and catch fish, even in cold water, and even in spring and autumn.

• Strive to develop your sense of feel when retrieving crank baits, suggests bass-pro David Fritts. By paying more attention to the subtle feel of any given crank bait coming through the water (the Down Deep Rattlin' Fat Rap and Glass Fat Rap are favourites) you will just 'know' when something interrupts the normal action. It can mean the lure is out of tune, that it has caught a bit of weed, or that a fish has 'turned on it' and is following the lure. In all cases, valuable information that can help you catch more fish.

• Here's a great method to catch big-river steelhead, Pacific salmon, Atlantic salmon and pike; tie on a 5cm or 7cm Glass Fat Rap. Play out about 75ft. (23m) of line, and face your boat into the current. Run the motor in forward gear, but only enough so that the current still washes the boat slowly downstream (the opposite direction you are facing). Steer the boat so it slowly wanders back and forth across the stream as it gets pushed down. The best stretches are long, uniform flows or moderate current; slicks above rapids (be careful); and over submerged rocks and ledges. This is the traditional Scottish method of 'harling' for salmon.

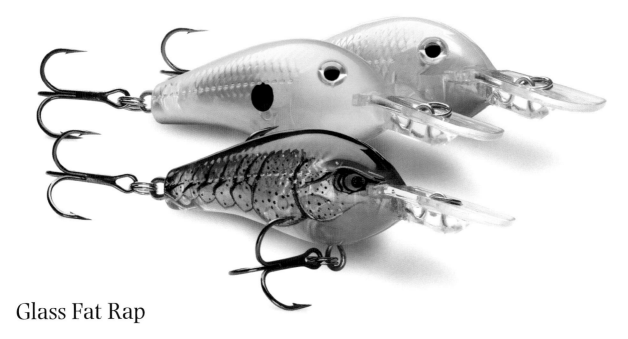

Glass Fat Rap

Code: GFR   Freshwater – Floating

Main features:

- All the action of the Fat Rap
- Added rattling effect
- New 'glass colours'
- Square lip makes it bounce off an obstruction
- A deep-diving lure
- Performs long, accurate casts

Fishing tips:

- A good crank bait for searching water quickly
- The more this lure contacts the bottom, the better it will perform
- Use the rod tip to impart action and change the rhythm of the rattle

Target predators:

American bass species, pike, perch, chub, walleye (zander)

Technical features:

Code	Body length	Weight	Treble hooks	Swimming depth
GFR-05	5cm / 2in.	11g / 3/8 oz.	One No. 4 and one No. 5	1.5–2.1m / 5–7ft.
GFR-07	7cm / 2 3/4 in.	18g / 5/8 oz.	Two No. 3	2.1–2.7m / 7–9ft.

X-Rap

The history of the X-Rap

2004 Introduced in 10cm model for fresh and saltwater use.

Freshwater colour range:
Clown (CLN)
Gold (G)
Glass Ghost (GGH)
Hot Head (HH)
Hot Pink (HP)
Hot Steel (HS)
Olive Green (OG)
Perch (P)
Purple Gold (PG)
Purple Ghost (PGH)
Silver (S)
Silver Blue (SB)

Saltwater colour range:
Ayu (AYU)
Blue Sardine (BSRD)
Clown (CLN)
Gold (G)
Glass Ghost (GGH)
Hot Head (HH)
Hot Steel (HS)
Olive Green (OG)
Purple Ghost (PGH)
Silver (S)
Silver Blue (SB)
Silver Blue Mackerel (SBM)
Silver Green Mackerel (SGM)
Spotted Minnow (SPM)

Fishing the X-Rap

The 'X' of X-Rap stands for 'extreme action'. The lure has a high intensity flash, a hard vibration, and an erratic side-to-side darting action. Learn how to use it well.

The teaser tail on the freshwater version continues to move long after the lure has stopped. Remember to give this suspending lure plenty of time to entice a wary predator from its lair.

Use the rod tip to change the sound and action of the lure. You can jerk it hard, twitch it, or use a steady retrieve. Just remember to vary the speed and direction of the retrieve all the time.

Get this lure to hang near underwater features and obstructions for best results, and always start its retrieve with a quick jerk, just in case a predator is close at hand.

Tips from the pros

• One of the 'secrets' top anglers use to consistently catch fish is to change their approach often. Average anglers who struggle to catch fish are often in a rut. They spend too much time in the same types of spots, or fishing the same type of presentation. The best anglers, by contrast, treat their fishing day as a huge experiment, always, in effect, 'asking the fish what they want' by offering them different things until they bite on something.

• Spend part of every fishing trip practising some form of presentation you consider a personal weakness. It's the only way to become a versatile angler. If you spend all your time fishing with a certain type of lure, using a method you've already mastered, what do you do on the days it doesn't work?

• If one of your crank baits comes out of tune, don't toss it back in the box. Put it aside, then tune it up before you quit, or before you begin fishing next time. That way, you don't waste valuable time trying to figure out which lures got knocked out of tune by over-zealous fish, or send them back down after you've forgotten which one needed attention.

• Slow and steady is the way to go when fighting fish. You'll see top anglers pumping their rods to gain line, then reeling quickly to make up the ground gained. But notice that they never allow slack to form in the line. No matter what you do to bring that hooked fish to boat or shore, don't do it in a jerky manner. Slack line often means a missed fish.

• Depth can be a real key to finding active fish. Casual anglers might not realise that they're doing all their searching at one general depth level, ignoring other possibilities. Systematically search different spots, and different depths, until you find biters. Once you find a productive depth, it can be important to stay there – at least for that day.

Saltwater X-Rap

Freshwater X-Rap

X-Rap

Code: **XR / SXR**   Freshwater – Saltwater

Main features:

- Super long casting lure
- Rattles, but not too loud
- Scale and lateral line detail
- Teaser tail moves with the slightest twitch
- A neutral density suspending lure
- Classic Rapala action with a wider roll

Fishing tips:

- Remember that this is a suspending lure and give it time to work round good cover
- Vary the retrieve from a steady pace to an occasional twitch or a hard jerk
- Use long casts when you approach a new fishing area in order to avoid spooking the fish

Target predators:

Black bass, perch, pike, walleye (zander), salmon

Technical features:

Code	Body length	Weight	Treble hooks	Swimming depth
XR-10	10cm / 4in.	13g / 7/16 oz.	One No. 4 and one No. 5	1.2–1.8m / 4–6ft.
SXR-10	10cm / 4in.	13g / 7/16 oz.	Two No. 3	1.2–1.8m / 4–6ft.

Jigging Shad Rap

The history of the Jigging Shad Rap

2004 Jigging Shad Rap 5cm introduced initially to the USA in the following colours:
Glow (GL)
Blue (B) with red centre treble
Glow Blue (GB)
Glow Fire Tiger (GFT)
Perch (P)
Glow Red (GR) with red centre treble
Silver (S)
Glow Clown (CGLN) with red centre treble
Shad (SD) with red centre treble
Glow Green (GG)
Pearl (PRL) with red centre treble.

Fishing the Jigging Shad Rap

Developed for ice fishing, the Jigging Shad Rap has a more pronounced action, with a slow circle down action. Raising in a sharp 'snapping' motion will cause the bait to circle faster. A quick 'vibrating' motion can also be used at fixed depths.

The central treble hook can be tipped with bait to entice fish on those cold winter days when they don't really want to feed.

Find underwater structure to gain maximum benefit from the Jigging Shad Rap. Fish congregate around structure at all times of the year, and in order for a jigging lure to be successful, you have to use it directly amongst the fish.

Tips from the pros

• The Jigging Shad Rap isn't a straight-up-and-down jigging lure, but you've got to get the timing right for it to work well. The trick is to lower the rod tip quickly so that there is slack line between the Jigging Shad Rap and the rod tip. When there is slack line, the lure picks up speed and the flow of water past the special tail makes the lure move forward. Because the lure is fished vertically, this forward movement is translated into a circular swimming pattern, which can be irresistible to predators.

• A secret of west-coast bass chasers – using the 'winter' jigging Rapala in open water, is producing huge fish for anglers everywhere. The 'Jigging Rap' as it's known in some circles, has a unique action, a sliding, circling movement that flashes and really pulls the trigger on predator fish. It's not just for ice fishing any more. The Jigging Shad Rap will do the same.

• The fishing pros have learned to make a jigging lure swim in circles. Don't lift the rod tip in the usual way; just jig it continuously and very softly – no more than an inch up and down movement. This is enough to make the water move past the lure's tail and impart a slow forward movement that is translated into a circular swimming action. The constant jigging helps the lure to emit a subtle vibration that will attract fish from a distance.

Jigging Shad Rap

Code: WSR   Freshwater – Saltwater – Jigging

Main features:

- Zinc weighted jigging lure
- Fixed nose and tail hooks with belly treble
- Suitable for summer and winter use
- Specially shaped shad body
- Large range of colours and sizes
- Balanced design allows for deep jigging

Fishing tips:

- Designed primarily for fishing through the ice for perch and pike
- Find an underwater structure and concentrate your jigging around it
- Change the speed you jig the rod to alter the circle down speed of the Jigging Shad Rap

Target predators:

Perch, pike, zander (walleye), black bass, lake trout

Technical features:

Code	Body length	Weight	Treble hooks	Swimming depth
WSR-05	5cm. / 2in.	3.5g / 1/8 oz.	Belly treble	Variable jigging lure

CELEBRITY BITES

Rex Hunt on his farewell catch

Throughout my 14 years on television I have travelled the world, and I have used Rapala lures in many different countries. One memorable catch was on the mighty Zambezi River at Victoria Falls. Casting and retrieving a CD-9 GFR (Gold Fluorescent Red) I hooked and landed a 4kg tigerfish. It still remains one of my top catches today.

To emphasise how much confidence I have in Rapala lures, I caught a 34 lb. Barramundi recently on a new Rapala Taildancer.

This capture was special. It was my last show. I relied on my gut feeling that the Taildancer would do the trick, and it did. After a great struggle I gently removed the lure from this magnificent fish. I gave her a kiss on the cheek and sent her on her way.

With my eyes filled with tears I turned to the camera and said goodbye. That memory will last me a lifetime.

Now I will be spending much more time on the water without the pressure of the cameras. It goes without saying that I will again be relying on my collection of Rapala lures. When I want to give myself the best possible shot I choose Rapala lures. I love them.

Rex Hunt, Rex Hunt Fishing Adventures, Australia.

CHAPTER 8

Expansion and diversification

1998–2005

W hat was to be Lauri Rapala's greatest angling honour was posthumously awarded to him in 1998 when he was inducted into the International Game Fish Association Hall of Fame[18]. Today there are a little over 50 inductees including Isaak Walton, Dame Juliana Berners, Zane Grey and Ernest Hemingway, so Lauri is in good company. Lauri's commentary in the IGFA Hall of Fame reads as follows.

Lauri Rapala (1905–1974) 1998 Inductee

Lauri Rapala invented the first Rapala lure, the fishing lure that would become an international success and would be the first product of the Normark Company, one of the most familiar names in angling equipment. Born into poverty on the island of Sysmä, in the village of Rapala, Finland, Lauri Saarinen grew up fishing the many lakes and streams for pike, perch, trout, and whitefish. When his family moved to the parish of Asikkala, the clergyman writing in the parish register forgot Lauri's surname and substituted the name of the island from which he had come. Thus, Lauri Rapala. As a young man, Lauri fished to help his impoverished family survive. During this time, he created a lure that moved through the water like a wounded minnow. The lure was amazingly effective. Word of Rapala's lure spread, and soon gained popularity with anglers throughout Finland. Demand grew and Lauri began to employ friends and family to help whittle the lures. Large-scale export of the Rapala lures to the United States began in the early 1960s and quickly created a sensation. The Rapala attracted bass, stripers, salmon, muskie, and trout. A *Life* magazine article in 1962 featured Lauri Rapala and his lures, and demand shot through the roof. (The issue of *Life* happened to be the same one that covered the death of Marilyn Monroe, the all-time best-selling issue of the magazine.) The original Rapala lure, its many variations and dozens of other products bearing the Rapala name, are now in use worldwide.

In January 1998 Jorma Kasslin appointed Juhani Pehkonen, whom he had known since their time at university, as head of the company's lure production

- **The IGFA Hall of Fame**
- **Rapala becomes a public company**
- **Rapala purchases Storm lures**
- **The purchase of VMC Pêche**
- **Development of the distribution business**
- **Advanced manufacturing in new factories**
- **The Storm soft plastic baits**
- **Diversification within the fishing tackle industry**

---

[18] Lauri had already been posthumously enshrined in the American National Freshwater Fishing Hall of Fame in 1985 (see Chapter 6).

*Fitting hooks to a special order of
Rapala lures at the factory in Estonia.*
(John Mitchell)

*Every lure is tank-tested
before it leaves the factory.*
(John Mitchell)

programme. It was immediately apparent to Juhani that the small Rapala company in Estonia, Rapala Eesti, held the key to the company's future success. Having comparatively recently gained its independence from Russia, Estonia's labour costs were very low in comparison to those in Finland, as was the cost of premises. However, the most important factor that Juhani took into account was the high quality of labour available. The decision was taken to develop Rapala Eesti as the premier manufacturing plant in Europe.

It was not until late in 1998 that market conditions were deemed suitable for a placing of Rapala shares on the Helsinki Stock Exchange. Approximately 17 million shares were placed, which left Rapala Normark NV controlling about 45 per cent of the total share capital. The cash from the sale of the shares was used to pay off a significant proportion of the company debt, and thus provide resources for further expansion. The shares started trading on the Helsinki Stock Exchange on 4 December 1998. Rapala Normark Corporation was now a publicly owned company.

Product development remained a priority throughout 1998. Risto Raps in both 5cm (2in.) and 8cm (3.25in.) models and Floating Magnums in 7cm (2.8in.) and 9cm (3.6in.) were launched. These smaller Floating Magnums did not have the worldwide appeal of the larger lures. The 7cm (2.8in.) model was discontinued in 2003, whilst the 9cm (3.6in.) model continued until 2004.

Rapala's first surface lure, the Skitter Pop, was launched in 7cm (2.8in.) and 9cm (3.6in.) models. The Skitter Pop was a balsawood popping lure featuring an almost circular cupped lip. As the lure was pulled across the surface of the water, the cupped lip would push water forward, creating a pronounced splash in front, and a wake behind the lure. It was designed primarily for the American bass-fishing markets, but it also found favour with summer pike anglers in Europe and sea-bass fishermen along the European coast.

Following their success with the special silver-plating process, Rapala now introduced stainless-steel plating using the same techniques. The stainless steel was more resistant to saltwater attack than the silver, and did not tarnish. The painting techniques used with the silver worked equally well with the stainless steel. Three stainless-steel colours were introduced to the Magnum range of lures. They were Blue Stainless Steel (BSS), Green Stainless Steel (GSS), and Stainless Steel (SS).

1999 saw the largest introduction of new lures and colours in the history of the Rapala company. The Down Deep Husky Jerk was introduced in 12cm (4.9in.) size. This lure could dive to 19ft. (5.7m) and was to bring the Husky Jerk to the attention of coastal sea fishermen who required a lure that would dive deep into rocky gullies.

A new Shad Rap was introduced. The Shad Rap RS was a plastic-bodied Shad Rap that was both rattling and suspending. It was introduced in both 5cm (2in.) and 7cm (2.8in.) models. The introduction of this lure brought the successful Shad Rap shape and action to anglers who required a suspending bait that could be fished very slowly to search likely areas for predatory fish.

Lauri's son, and Jarmo Rapala's father, Esko was honoured with the introduction of the 7cm (2.8in.) Team Esko lure. The Team Esko combined the bulkier body of the Countdown lure with the floating properties and action of the Original lure. It was primarily designed for the Scandinavian and Finnish markets where its success with trout and sea trout is almost legendary.

A new squid lure was launched for sea anglers. The 9cm (3.6in.) and 11cm (4.5in.) Velvet Squid was a plastic-bodied lure covered in a sprayed velvet flock finish. This material had a slightly soft feel, and offered a good point of purchase to squid tentacles. It was fitted with the traditional multi-point squid hook.

The Risto Rap family was extended with the introduction of the Risto Rap 4cm (1.6in.) model, and a 5cm (2in.) model was added to the Skitter Pop range.

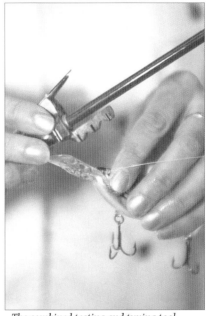

The combined testing and tuning tool used by the Rapala tank-testers.
(Rapala company archive)

Rapala's new stainless-steel technology was extended through the Magnum range of lures from 7cm (2.8in.) to 18cm (7in.). The new colours included Blue Mackerel (BM), Black Red Head (BRH), Clown (CLN) and Green Mackerel (GM). Sardine (SRD) was also added to the Magnum range.

Special saltwater colours were added to the Husky Jerk and the new Down Deep Husky Jerk lures as well as the Rattlin' Rapala range. Croaker (CR) and Pinfish (PF) were accurate imitations of common saltwater bait-fish. The introduction of these colours marked Rapala's serious move into the saltwater lure market.

A stainless steel Countdown Magnum Black Red Head (BRH) took this good barracuda.
(Rapala Media Service)

1999 saw Rapala's first major acquisition since its purchase of the Normark companies in the early 1990s. Storm Manufacturing Company was an American plastic-lure manufacturer, founded by Bill and Gary Storm in 1964. It had produced many famous models, including the Thin Fin, Hot 'n Tot, Wiggle Wart, the 'Mac' series, the ThunderStick, and the Chug Bug. Most Storm lures were sold in the USA, but Rapala's acquisition made Storm lures available to fishermen worldwide. In addition, the Rapala team rationalised the range, and improved the moulds and colour finishes in their factory at Vääksy. Today Storm lures are made in Rapala's factories at Vääksy, Finland and Schenzhen, China. Many hundreds of thousands of Storm lures are finished and packed each year in Rapala's Estonian factory at Pärnu.

Rapala Japan was formed in July 1999 to sell Rapala products to large chain stores and the wholesale trade there. Unfortunately, its establishment coincided with the country's worst recession for many years. Manabu Kimoto, the company's managing director recalls Rapala lures being sold in 'dump bins' because grey imports had wrecked the brand's price structure. However, by 2004 sales in Japan were recovering well, and the state of the economy was beginning to improve.

Changes in the Norwegian distribution arrangements were also made in 1999 when Rapala purchased 91 per cent of its distributor Elbe from the owner Einar Bjørk. Elbe is involved in all aspects of fishing in Norway including all forms of saltwater fishing, game fishing for salmon, trout, char and grayling, and pike fishing. The company distributes the Rapala brands as well as its own brands and products from Shimano, Shakespeare, Plano, Cannon/Bottomline, Cortland and Marttiini knives. It is currently the number one fishing tackle distributor in Norway. In November 1999 one of the oldest Normark companies, Normark Sport Limited in the UK, was closed. An agreement was made to sell Normark Sport's distribution business to Masterline International. John Mitchell, the managing director of Normark UK, took a seat on the board of directors at Masterline, and at the request of Jorma Kasslin took over the responsibility for aspects of the Rapala Group's press and public relations work, which ultimately resulted in the writing of this book.

Rapala Normark Corporation was rapidly gaining a reputation throughout the world as a forward-looking company that was on the acquisition trail. Jorma Kasslin commented that almost every week he would be contacted by a fishing-tackle manufacturer offering to sell the company to Rapala Normark Corporation. In most cases the company was either grossly overpriced or was in such a poor state that it was beyond saving. However, one approach was quite different to the usual pleas for financial rescue.

Painting eyes on lures in Rapala's Estonian factory.
(John Mitchell)

In 2000 Viellard Migeon et Cie (VMC), a family-owned French company, primarily involved in the manufacture of treble hooks, contacted Rapala. It was a profitable company with total annual sales of around 20 million Euros. It could trace its history back to its foundation in 1796 when it specialised in the manufacture of screws and bolts. It was not until 1910 that it started to produce fish hooks. VMC was involved in other businesses, all of which were linked to fishing. VMC has consistently led the industry in the design of treble hooks. The Needle Cone Point and the Cone Cut Point are just two of their world-famous designs. The company was amongst the first to use Vanadium, a steel alloy for hook production, and its Fastgrip triple mini-barb pattern was a world first.

Christophe Viellard, the president of the company, proposed that VMC and Rapala should work together and link themselves financially. For instance, VMC was the world's largest producer of treble hooks, but Rapala purchased very few of them. Rapala could fit VMC treble hooks to its lures, while its own distribution companies around Europe and in the USA and Canada could distribute VMC products. VMC had established distribution companies in Eastern Europe and Russia. These companies could be converted quite easily to Normark distribution companies, giving Rapala direct access to new emerging markets.

The negotiations between Rapala Normark Corporation and VMC were long, and at times difficult, but in November

2000 the purchase of Viellard Migeon et Cie, together with its subsidiary companies, was completed. Rapala financed the purchase with shares. The Viellard family received 12 per cent of the share capital of Rapala Normark Corporation; at the time each share was valued at around six Euros. This made the Viellard family the largest individual owner of Rapala shares.

As a result of the purchase of VMC, the name of the Rapala company was changed from Rapala Normark Corporation to Rapala VMC Corporation, the name by which it is known today. The vast majority of Rapala lures are now fitted with VMC treble hooks.

New lines for the millennium

In the year 2000 Rapala decided that it had to diversify in order to continue its successful expansion. A specialist company, PLI, was set up in South Carolina under the management of Bruce Brown, with a satellite office in southern China. The company's function was to identify areas within the world fishing tackle industry that the group could develop profitably.

The first area in which the company became involved was the fishing line business. In conjunction with an established monofilament manufacturer, Rapala designed two monofilaments specifically for lure fishing.

However, the major breakthrough occurred when the company investigated the fishing-tackle accessory market. It quickly established that there was a tremendous shortage of professionally designed and manufactured accessories on the market. The majority of fishermen made do with surgical forceps, electrical pliers and even domestic nail clippers to help them produce their rigs and terminal tackle.

A list of potential fishing accessory products was put together to include a series of pliers, forceps, hook removers, hook sharpeners, clippers, mechanical and digital scales, jig busters and aerators. Each item was individually designed specifically for the fisherman, including non-slip handles for a secure grip, over-sized finger holes for use with gloves, and lanyard eyelets so that items could not be dropped over the side of a boat. The Normark distribution companies throughout Europe and North America contributed their ideas and requirements to the programme.

The result of a year's work and hundreds of test samples was a comprehensive range of fishing accessories, all of which had been specifically developed for the fishing-tackle market. The Rapala accessory programme was an immediate success around the world. Since its inception it has been developed to include landing, weighing and releasing tools, such as the Rapala Lock 'n Weigh programme, landing nets that incorporate a spring balance and line counters. The programme has been divided into two distinct ranges. The Pro

Rapala VMC Corporation CEO Jorma Kasslin (left) with VMC Pêche President Christophe Viellard.
(Lars Ollberg)

Guide is the top quality range for regular or professional fishermen, whilst the Sportsman range is designed for the occasional angler who still wants the benefits of professionally designed fishing accessories.

2000 also saw Rapala break another record with the number of products they introduced to the market.

The Tail Dancer was without doubt the lure of the year. It was the first time that a banana-shaped lure had been produced from balsawood. The production required the use of special lathing techniques to form the specially shaped body. Not satisfied with this innovation, Rapala took the design one step further by building a unique rattling capsule into the balsawood body. The action of the Tail Dancer was both wider and more erratic than normal, and it was described as having a pronounced tail motion. Designed primarily for bass, zander, pike and salmon, the Tail Dancer production for 2001 was limited to 300,000 pieces of 7cm (2.8in.) and 9cm (3.6in.) lures. One American tackle dealer offered to purchase the complete 2001 production run. Needless to say, Rapala refused the offer.

The Skitter Prop 7cm (2.8in.) lure was also launched in 2000. Whilst this was a new design for Rapala, the idea of a propeller attached to the rear of a surface lure to create more disturbance was not new. However, Rapala applied their development process to the Skitter Prop and produced a balsa-bodied lure with a specially designed stainless propeller mounted on a special spindle. The propeller revolved and created surface disturbance at the slowest speeds. The body design also made the lure dive with a loud 'plop' if it was jerked into action. French sea-bass anglers enjoyed great success with lures of this type along the French Atlantic coast. Results proved that the lure not only worked in France, but also for black bass in the USA, and sea bass off the UK coast. The lure also proved its worth for pike when they remain in shallow water after spawning.

The Willtech Industrial factory complex in China.
(Willtech Industrial archive)

Other lures launched in 2000 included a 12cm (4.9in.) Saltwater Skitter Pop, a 5cm (2in.) Jointed lure, a 10cm (4in.) Down Deep Husky Jerk and a 4cm (1.6in.) Shad Rap RS.

New colours also played a major part in the product launches of 2000. The major innovation was the Rapflash Holographic range of colours. Special machines were purchased from Germany to apply these new finishes to the lures. The Original, Countdown and Shad Rap lures received three Rapflash colours; Holographic Blue Shiner (HBSH), Holographic Emerald Shiner (HESH) and Holographic Shiner (HSH). The Shad Rap RS and Rattlin' Rapala received Holographic Blue Shad (HBSD), Holographic Emerald Shad (HESD) and Holographic Shad (HSD).

The stainless steel range of colours was expanded to include Stainless Steel Blue Mullet (SSBMU), Stainless Steel Gold Mullet (SSGMU) and Stainless Steel Green Mullet (SSGRMU) for the Saltwater Husky Jerk, Saltwater Rattlin' Rapala, Saltwater Super Shad Rap and Saltwater Skitter Pop.

Among the key business decisions taken in the year 2000 were:

- Rapala's purchase of the Danish hunting-equipment distributor Sini-Guldman A/S. The company was responsible for the distribution of a number of important shotgun, rifle and hunting accessory brands. This purchase moved Steen Yde into the premier league of Danish hunting and fishing distributors. Hunting continues to play the major part in the company's activities, but the fishing division is growing rapidly.

- The change of name of Rapala's Danish distributor Steen Yde to Normark Denmark A/S.

- The appointment of Juhani Pehkonen as director of the lure division. His responsibilities now covered all operations relating to the company's lure programme, including sales, marketing, research and development. Specialist staff, and new cad-cam computer systems ensured that Rapala's research and development department was ready for the twenty-first century.

It was also in 2000 that the decision was made to investigate the possibility of purchasing a company in China, with a view to setting up a manufacturing operation to extend the group's product range in to areas where it was not currently active. It was VMC Pêche who suggested that a company called Willtech Industrial based near Schenzhen, just over the border from Hong Kong, could well be worth consideration.

Packing Storm soft baits in Willtech Industrials' new factory.
(Willtech Industrial archive)

An approach was made to William Ng, the owner and managing director of the company, and a visit was hastily arranged. In fact, a large delegation of senior Rapala managers visited Willtech. It was apparent from the very start that Willtech Industrial was not an average Chinese manufacturer. The buildings, the manufacturing equipment, the offices and indeed the management team of the company were far superior to anything that the Rapala management had seen in China before.

The fact that the company had always worked to the highest production and administrative levels was evident from the award of the ISO 9001 accreditation in 1998.

Willtech was one of the few factories in China capable of manufacturing the full range of professional fishing tackle including metal jigs, soft baits, spinners, spinner baits, spoons, rubber jigs, hard plastic lures and fly fishing accessories for both fresh and saltwater. The company offered a comprehensive range of its own products, or would manufacture products designed by its customers. William Ng told his visitors from Rapala: 'The company attaches great importance to research, development and product design. We are very responsive to both market trends and technological advances. New designs, new production methods and new materials are tested every day by our 100-strong research and development team.'

William Ng was invited to sell his company to Rapala VMC Corporation, and after some lengthy negotiations a cash and share deal was agreed and finalised in June 2001. William Ng was appointed to the Rapala VMC Corporation board of directors.

It is likely that in the future historians of the fishing tackle industry will look back and agree that Rapala's purchase of Willtech Industrial was probably the one single event that changed the course of the company's history. It was not just the matter of having a production facility in the Far East; it was the quality of the facility and its capability of development and expansion that was of such value. Product development personnel from both the Rapala and Storm divisions spent time at Willtech learning just what the company was capable of manufacturing. Senior management personnel from the Normark distribution companies in North America and Europe also visited Willtech to see if the company could manufacture items that they currently sourced from outside suppliers. There was also another brand owned by Rapala that would benefit from Willtech's knowledge and experience. That brand was Blue Fox, the American company that specialised in the manufacture of spinners, spoons and jigs, the products that Willtech specialised in producing.

The company was now in a good position to move ahead with its product development plans at Willtech. Initially the management team devised two plans. The first was to extend the Blue Fox brand with the development of spoons, spinners and jigs, products for which Blue Fox already had a good reputation. The second was to diversify the Storm brand into the soft plastic lure market. Soft plastic lures had been around for a number of years, but the quality was poor, and the baits did not last very long. Willtech Industrial was already producing soft plastic baits for some of its customers, and the quality and diversity of these baits was exceptional. It was obvious that with guidance from experienced fishermen and technology from Rapala, Willtech could quite easily lead the way in soft bait design and production, especially if the products could be branded 'Storm' a previously well-established name in the USA, which was to be the largest potential market.

One immediate result of the purchase of Willtech Industrial was the closure of the Blue Fox production and office facility in Cambridge, Minnesota. The Blue Fox range of products was rationalised severely, and the production moved to either Willtech in China or Rapala's Vääksy factory. The sales and administrative functions were brought in-house to Normark's offices at Minnetonka. In future the Blue Fox range was to be strengthened, and the brand name would be used to its full potential in the lower priced spinner, spoon and jig market. Later the Blue Fox range would be extended to include hard baits that did not conflict with either Storm or Rapala products.

The company produced its first Storm catalogue in 2000, and the impression was that the range of lures and colours had been substantially reduced. This was certainly the case, but the improvement in the moulding and painting of the Rapala-produced lures was easy to see. The lures retained by Rapala included the Chug Bug, ThunderStick, ThunderCrank and SubWart. Now, each Storm lure was packed in a bright yellow box with a transparent lid. Information including the lure's length, weight and swimming depth were printed on each box.

Normark Corporation under the guidance of Tom Mackin took responsibility for the marketing policy of Storm lures. The necessity to keep the Storm and Rapala brands distinctly separate was utmost in the minds of the marketing team as they formulated the Storm image. Storm's traditional colours of yellow and black were maintained as they contrasted well with Rapala's red. However it was necessary to promote Storm to a wider market, and to do this Normark adopted a very different approach to that of Rapala.

The traditional image of a serious, somewhat conservative, classical European lure that Rapala portrayed was totally abandoned. In its place a brash, boisterous, off the wall, and even wacky image of Storm lures and the anglers that used them was introduced. The Storm catalogue became a collector's item, not because of the products that were listed in it, but because of the unusual photographs and zany captions that were printed on every page. The Storm company's slogan says it all: 'Always Think Like a Fish, No Matter How Weird It Gets.'

2001 saw the introduction of the Rapala LC Long Cast Minnow. This balsawood lure had a special capsule inserted in its body. The capsule contained lead shot that moved towards the tail of the lure during the cast to prevent the lure tumbling and to maximise the casting distance. Once the lure hit the water, the lead shot would move forward to balance the lure and provide its special rolling action. As the lure rolled from side to side, the lead shot also produced a subtle rattle. Due to an existing patent Rapala's development team had to devise a completely new concept to achieve the casting distance, action and rattle, and its 'casting capsule' is unique in fishing-lure technology. The LC Long Cast Minnow was a shallow-diving lure typically diving to a maximum of 3ft. (0.9m). It was therefore ideal for long casting into shallow water areas.

A Dutch pike hooked on a Jointed Gold Fluorescent Red (GFR) lure.
(Jan Eggers)

The first Jointed Shad Rap lure was also launched in 2001. It was a 5cm (2in.) plastic-bodied lure with a short, jointed tail section that had a very pronounced action. One of the main advantages of the Jointed Shad Rap was the fact that it was a suspending, neutrally buoyant lure. This resulted in longer, more accurate casts, and the benefit of being able to 'suspend' the lure close to any underwater obstructions that might hold decent fish.

Another revolutionary lure was the Skitter Walk 11cm (4.5in.). Apart from the Skitter Prop, which had an entirely different function, this was the first of Rapala's lures not to have any form of diving lip. It was a surface lure designed primarily for fishermen who enjoy 'walking the dog'. The Skitter Walk's plastic body contained one large ball weight that ran to the tail of the lure during the cast, then moved from one side of the lure to the other during the retrieve. The movement of this ball weight emitted a strong cadence rattle and also resulted in the lure moving alternately to the right and left as it was jerked back towards the rod. It was claimed that the Skitter Walk was the simplest 'walk the dog' lure ever produced. It was just a matter of keeping the rod tip down, jerking the bait and winding in the slack line. It might have been simple, but it worked very well in fresh and saltwater.

The Skitter Walk also featured a new printing system developed by Rapala's research team. The body of the lure was manufactured from clear plastic, and the pattern was printed on the inside. Once the hardware was inserted, the two halves of the body were ultrasonically sealed. Bearing in mind that the Skitter Walk was initially developed as a saltwater lure, the logic of this new process can be readily understood. Saltwater predators tend to have larger, sharper teeth than their freshwater counterparts, and the body of the lure would now protect its coloured pattern.

The Tail Dancer range was also expanded yet again with a new 5cm (2in.) model that was ideal for trout, perch and zander.

A bold decision had been made at Normark Corporation in 2001 that would change the course of the company's history from a very specialist distributor to a mainstream one. That decision was to launch a range of Rapala-branded fishing rods. Never had the Rapala name been linked with rods before; it was a matter of gambling with the reputation of one of the fishing world's most respected names.

Normark Corporation did their research thoroughly. They were not satisfied with launching one range of rods – they planned to launch five at the same time. The staff at Normark, their product development division and its office in China worked continuously on the rod project. The feeling was that the company only had one chance at this. If they got it right it would be a great success, and would move the company forward. If they got it wrong it would cost hundreds of thousands of dollars plus Rapala's reputation.

Eventually the rod programme was announced. The Signature series lead the way, followed by the Pro Staff series, the Long Cast series, the Sportsman's Classic series and the Sportsman's series. The company that sold lures and knives suddenly became a major rod distributor throughout America with a total of 121 rods in four different price ranges. Most importantly, they were branded Rapala.

It is true to say that there are few if any tackle companies that could have put together a programme of this size in such a short time. If it were not for Normark's staff, their product development division and the knowledge and experience of the rod manufacturers it would not have been possible at all. The 2002 launch of the Rapala rods in the USA was a success, and Normark Corporation had instantly changed the course of America's fishing-tackle history.

Such innovation was not restricted to the Rapala product lines. Between 2001 and 2003, the following achievements were made by the management team and staff:

- VMC had established a distribution company in Poland as far back as 1994. Now this company became responsible for the distribution of Rapala group products. The company changed its name to Normark Polska SP.Z.O.O in

2003, and is based in Lomianki. Normark Polska is also the headquarters for the eastern European operation. Another VMC distribution company had been established in 1997 in the Ukraine. This company was also converted to a Rapala distribution company and started its operations in 2001. VMC Waterqueen Ukrainia is based in Kiev. VMC's Russian distribution company was founded in 1998 and began Rapala distribution in 2000–01. Now renamed Normark Russia, the company is based in Moscow.

- Back in 1995 a small Estonian fishing-tackle manufacturer was purchased to manufacture products for Normark Finland. This operation continued for a short time, but the company was converted into a distribution company, and eventually became Normark Eesti A/S, based in Härku, Estonia.

- Rapala VMC Do Brasil Ltda, based in Sao Paulo, was established to distribute the complete range of Rapala group products in Brazil.

- Fishco AG of Switzerland (later renamed Rapala-Fishco AG) was purchased to handle the distribution of Rapala and other related products throughout Switzerland.

- The factory at Willtech in China had a completely new building and 8,000m² (26,000ft.²) of factory space added, together with other buildings. Further site development was also approved in order to cope with increased demand.

- An efficiency programme was instigated in stock and credit control during 2002 to reduce the company's burden of debt following the purchase of Willtech.

2002 saw the introduction of a Rapala lure that was to meet with immediate success. The Rapala 'Dives To' series was a new name and a new concept in lure design. The rattling, balsawood lure was designed to cast well, and to dive to a specific depth, and stay there for as long as possible. As far as the fisherman was concerned, the longer his lure remained in the strike zone the better his results would be, so the lure dived very steeply to reach its optimum depth fast, and its large polycarbonate lip maintained its depth until the final few yards of the retrieve. The idea for the lure was that of David Fritts who had recently joined the Rapala operation in the USA as one of its professional fishermen. For the first time, Rapala moved away from including the length of a lure in its official description. In the case of the 'Dives To' it was more important to inform the

Examples of the 'Dives To' lure.
(Rapala company archive)

The LC Long Cast Minnow.
(Rapala company archive)

buyer of the lure's diving depth. Therefore the two 'Dives To' lures launched in 2002 were the DT-10, which dived to 10ft. (2.94m) and the DT-16, which dived to 16ft. (4.71m).

A 4cm (1.6in.) model joined the Jointed Shad Rap; the Skitter Walk range was extended with the addition of an 8cm (3.25in.) model; and the LC Long Cast Minnow saw 8cm (3.25in.) and 12cm (4.9in.) additions.

The Husky Jerk and Down Deep Husky Jerk benefited from research and development into ways of using the transparent properties of their plastic bodies to enhance new colour schemes. The 'Glass' series of colours was introduced throughout the range.

Rapala also extended its range of fishing knives to include less expensive options under the 'Sportsman' and 'Sportsman Classic' brands and top quality filleting knives from Marttiini under the 'Signature' brand.

Since the purchase of VMC Pêche in 2000, the hooks used on the vast majority of Rapala lures had been standardised in the VMC range. Having completed this programme it was now possible for the company to make available replacement hook sets for anglers to replace damaged or worn hooks. A complete replacement hook programme was established. In typical Rapala style the sets of six hooks were displayed in Rapala lure boxes.

Both freshwater and saltwater replacement hook sets were produced. The introduction of replacement hook sets also provided VMC with an additional market as anglers around the world purchased the sets to replace hooks on their favourite lures, whether they were manufactured by Rapala or not!

2003 saw the introduction of two new ranges of Rapala lures. The Glass Shad Rap was introduced in 4cm (1.6in.), 5cm (2in.) and 7cm (2.8in.) sizes. It was a deep-diving crank bait with a clear plastic body. The 'Glass Technology' previously applied to the Husky Jerk was now applied to this new range in five colours, which enhanced both the translucent and reflective properties of the clear plastic body.

The second introduction in 2003 was without doubt one of the most long-awaited and necessary introductions to the Rapala range. For three years or more, Rapala had received reports of pike fishermen in the UK and Europe adapting the Super Shad Rap to become a suspending or a countdown lure. The anglers carefully drilled the balsa body and inserted a brass rod of sufficient weight to sink the lure. The additional weight enabled longer and more accurate casts, and the lure could be fished at greater depths.

Rapala obtained samples of 'adapted' Super Shad Raps. They tested and adapted the new design in order to maintain the slow rolling action of the lure, and adjusted the position of the weight to gain the perfect balance they required. The result was the 71g (2.5oz) Countdown Super Shad Rap that European pike anglers had been requesting for years. The new lure was treated to four new colour schemes and was hailed as an immediate success.

At the other end of the size scale, Rapala's smallest lure, the Countdown 01 was launched. This 2.5cm (1in.) lure was, in the words of the Rapala design staff, 'designed to catch fish that Rapala lures have never caught before.' These fish were to include grayling, trout, perch, chub and whitefish amongst many others around the world. It weighed just 2.7g (0.10 oz).

The 'Dives To' 6 was introduced to bring the successful 'Dives To' concept into less deep water. This lure, just like its predecessors, was designed to dive to around 6ft. (1.8m) as quickly as possible, and to stay there until the last few turns of the reel on the retrieve.

The Jointed Shad Rap range was enhanced by the addition of a 7cm (2.8in.) model that was welcomed both by salmon and pike anglers. A larger size of this model was dearly needed to expand its sphere of influence into the realms of the larger predator. The lure worked well at all speeds, but most importantly, it maintained its action at the very slow speeds that are often required to take big predators. Its deep-diving and suspending qualities were an added bonus.

The very successful Tail Dancer range was extended with a special lure. The new Tail Dancer 11cm (4.5in.) was in fact a Deep Tail Dancer. The lure had gained the reputation for attracting big fish from deep water, so the Rapala design staff developed a Tail Dancer that would dive even deeper. In fact it would dive to 30ft. (9m) when trolled. The famous Tail Dancer action was still there, and the subtle rattle would be of even greater importance in the murky depths so far down.

Continuing their programme of expanding the lure fishing market by designing and producing top quality accessories, Rapala introduced their range of terminal tackle. Normark's product development division, Normark Innovations in the USA, was responsible for putting the programme together. They sourced a new snap-link, christened the Rap Snap, which could be opened at either end and locked closed. The Rap Snap had a wide, smooth loop at each end to provide the lure with unrestricted movement (the lack of which is a fault of many snap links). The Rap Snaps were sold individually, or they could be purchased already attached to perfectly matching crane or ball-bearing swivels.

In addition to the swivels and snaps, Normark Innovations also designed three ranges of wire leaders, all fitted with matching swivels and snaps. The range of leaders was made up of seven-strand, uncoated wire for freshwater use, seven-strand stainless microcable for both fresh and saltwater and 19-strand flexible stainless microcable for delicate presentation in salt and freshwater. Each range was offered in a series of three breaking strains with a choice of four lengths in each braking strain.

Landing nets were the next item to receive Rapala's attention. The company was aware that many of its customers were 'mobile anglers' who walked a considerable distance each day casting for fish. They required a net that was easy to carry, did not get caught up in bank-side vegetation, and had an easily extendable handle. Normark Innovations in the USA and China completed the design work and sourced a suitable manufacturer. The nets featured folding heads, belt loops, and one model had a spring balance incorporated in the handle.

Another fish-landing device designed by Normark Innovations was the Lock 'n Weigh, a tool that helped anglers either unhook fish in the water or lift them into a boat without resorting to a net. The Lock'n Weigh incorporated an opening cam that could be closed around a fish's lower lip, enabling the fish to be lifted from the water. The spring balance incorporated in the handle let the angler read off the weight of the fish and return it to the water without ever touching it. The original Lock'n Weigh was introduced in 2002, but for the 2004 season the company extended the range to include long-handled models, a wide gape model and a less expensive model not incorporating a spring balance that was called the Lock'n Grip.

The advent of the advanced fishing lines featuring fibres such as Dyneema had made a real impact on angling around the world. The USA and Europe were the markets most affected by the introduction of many new brands of 'advanced super lines', some of which made claims that were well beyond the realms of fiction and bordered on the realms of fantasy. Eventually the market began to settle down, and in the USA especially the lure fishermen began to return to their trusted nylon monofilament. In Europe, however, where coarse fishing for pike is often conducted with live or dead bait, and the art of carp fishing is treated with a reverence usually reserved for religious purposes, the new super lines continued their development.

The Storm Suspending WildEye Swim Bait.
(Rapala company archive)

It was in early 2003 that an American company with previous experience in the manufacture of advanced braided lines contacted Rapala. The company was working with the Performance Polymers Division of Honeywell, the manufacturers of Spectra, a gel-spun PE fibre similar to Dyneema in Europe. The company had been producing small-diameter, high-tech braids since 1994 and had manufactured some of the most famous advanced fishing lines in the USA.

It was explained that the company was ready to move the high-tech braided lines forward into the next generation of product. Research in association with Honeywell had resulted in the design of a process that would utilise nano-composite technology to impregnate and coat Spectra fibres. As a result of this new technology the company could virtually convert Spectra fibres into a composite material, and the material they had chosen was titanium.

The results of their tests revealed that Spectra Titanium Braid held many advantages over the established 'first generation' super lines. Spectra Titanium had 'body', it had a resistance similar to low-diameter nylon, and this reduced the chances of the line wrapping around the tip guide during the cast. It had excellent knot-holding characteristics and knot strength. Typically super lines were difficult to knot effectively. Spectra Titanium also had excellent abrasion resistance due to the tough resin matrix reinforced with titanium. So, in the summer of 2003 Rapala announced the launch of Rapala Titanium Braid, and for the first time entered the world of the super lines.

However, the most exciting introduction was yet to come. For almost two years Normark Corporation and its product development company Normark Innovations had been working on a secret project. It was a common sense move, and no doubt the American fishing-tackle industry was expecting it, but no-one knew when it was due to be launched. Normark selected a time well away from the fishing-tackle trade fairs to launch their range of Rapala spinning reels.

The Rapala Spinning Reels launched in 2003.
(Rapala company archive)

The range was not large, but it was effective, comprising four ranges of reels with differing price points and three reels in each range. There were enough models in the range for a fisherman to find the right-sized reel with the required specifications at a reasonable price. As we have come to expect from Normark Corporation, the presentation of the reels was excellent. The graphics were good, but conservative, just like Rapala's image.

The Rapala-owned Storm brand had not been sitting idle in the meantime. A new range of 11 Storm soft plastic baits (including jigs, shads, minnows, tubes and worms, each available in two or three sizes and in a choice of up to eight different colours) was released in May 2002. The lures were supplied in special re-sealable packs that kept the baits clean and fresh, and where necessary with the correct instructions and equipment to make a rig.

In June 2002 an additional range of 14 new Storm soft baits was announced (available for sale in 2003) including new minnows and shads as well as suspending soft baits, another jig, a squid jig and a selection of specially

Storm's WildEye Soft Shad, the company's first hybrid lure.
(Rapala Media Service)

designed Storm jig heads. Each bait was available in up to four sizes and 16 colours. The launch of these new soft baits was eagerly awaited, and the products lived up to every expectation. Top of the list was a revolutionary hybrid hard bait/soft bait called the WildEye Soft Shad. This new bait benefited from a hard bait's shape, wobble and diving ability whilst enjoying the texture and 'sexy tail wiggle' of a soft bait. The development team at Vääksy had devised a way of coating a hard plastic lure body with soft plastic, and at the same time extending the soft plastic to form a dorsal fin and a wiggling tail. The staff at Willtech were entrusted with this unique lure's production. The holographic colours of the new bait were encased inside the body, protected from the teeth of fish by the soft plastic coating. The 7cm (2.8in.) WildEye Soft Shad was Storm's first hybrid bait.

The first Storm accessories were also launched for the 2003 season in the form of a range of fishing knives.

The Storm range of hard baits was extended with two new lures, each totally different from the others. The Hopper Popper was a 1.5in. (4cm) surface lure that weighed just 2g (¹⁄₁₆ oz). It was shaped like a cricket or grasshopper, and was so light that it could be cast on a fly rod. The Hopper Popper was designed to take surface-feeding fish like trout and small bass. It also made a good lure for European sea trout.

The Storm Thunder Dog was also a surface lure, but there the similarity ended. The Thunder Dog was an 11cm (4.5in.) lure with a transparent plastic body that was designed primarily as a 'walk the dog' lure. Two ball weights inside the body assisted long, accurate casts, and the lure was retrieved with regular jerks of the rod tip that made it glide from left to right whilst emitting a loud 'click'.

Three more new lures were also introduced at the same time. The Deep Thunder 11cm (4.5in.) and the Shallow Thunder 11cm (4.5in.) complemented the 15cm (5.3in.) models introduced the previous year. The Sub Wart 7cm (2.8in.) extended the Sub Wart range into larger sized lures for the first time.

The 7cm (2.8in.) ThunderCraw was an excellent crawfish imitation to the extent that it was balanced so that it would have a natural 'falling position' when fished sink-and-draw. It swam 'backwards', just like a real crawfish, and had a wide action and a loud rattle. Special translucent crawfish colours were designed to give this lure the most realistic colour schemes.

Addtionally, the Thunder Dog 9cm (3.6in.) was introduced in 2003 to complement the 11cm (4.5in.) version introduced the previous year, and the Storm Thunder series was enhanced by the introduction of the 11cm (4.5in.) Storm Mid Thunder, which could dive to over 12ft. (4m).

Another new concept was introduced in the form of the Storm Naturistic range of baits. Willtech designers had managed to produce very accurate soft bait imitations of the major bait-fish in both fresh and saltwater. The baits were not only accurate in shape, their colouring also provided an accurate match for the real thing. The bait-fish chosen for the Naturistic range were the perch, pike, roach, trout and herring. Each bait was manufactured with an internal lead head covered in soft plastic. The belly treble hook was fitted to a split ring, and could be removed if the fisherman wanted to retrieve his lure along the river or lake bed, leaving the large single top hook protruding from the back of the bait.

In the USA Normark launched the first Storm-branded rods. It was not a large range, but the company worked hard on the design and quality of the rods and priced them competitively in order to forge a place in the market for the brand. In keeping with Storm's reputation for 'off the wall' marketing, the rods were launched by Bradshaw a WWE™ superstar wrestler standing 6ft. 6in. (1.98m) and weighing in at 290 lb. (132kg). By all accounts, his favourite finishing move was 'The Clothesline From Hell™'. Bradshaw was a favourite of the American housewives who all associated their clotheslines with hell, but for a totally different reason.

Five new WildEye baits including a revolutionary spinner bait were introduced featuring brand new colour schemes and tantalising actions.

Some 14 Blue Fox lures, comprising spoons and jigs for both fresh and saltwater use, were launched at the start of the 2003 season. In 2003, the Blue Fox range saw another expansion to its selection of jigs, many of which now sported holographic colours, and to its selection of spoons that were now fitted with top-of-the-range VMC treble and double hooks. For the first time Blue Fox became a world-wide brand with a selection of lures to suit anglers on every continent of the world.

2004 saw Rapala make two purchases that, whilst completely separate, confirmed the company's intent to move into the one lure-fishing market where they had never been represented – big-game sea fishing for fish such as marlin, tuna, albacore, wahoo and sailfish.

The first purchase was that of Guigo Marine. Constant Guigo, an avid big-game fishing enthusiast who was the first person to fish for bluefin tuna with the Rapala Magnum, had formed this small French family company in 1977. Constant won the Marlin World Cup, three European Championships and over 20 big-game tournaments worldwide.[19]

In 2000 Constant's son Philippe joined him in the business after graduating from Marseille Business School with an MBA in sales management, and took over the running of the business from his father. The company is based in Antibes in the south of France a few miles along the coast from Cannes. Guigo Marine specialises in the sale of specialist big-game fishing products, from rods and reels down to the boat equipment to land the fish. A number of products are manufactured exclusively for the company. They also arrange big-game fishing trips and charters around the world. Philippe Guigo was charged with developing Rapala's product range for the big-game market.

However, in May 2004 Rapala made another purchase that moved the company's big-game fishing plans forward with a giant leap. Rapala purchased

---

[19] He is the inventor of Rapala's CG colour, which is named after him.

the business of Williamson Lures of South Africa. Williamson was one of the few established manufacturers of big-game lures and fishing equipment that was recognised around the world. There are plenty of national and even local manufacturers that do a good job for the sport along their immediate coastline, but the research and development required to establish a worldwide reputation takes years of work. It was this knowledge and experience that Rapala purchased. The company premises in South Africa were closed, and the manufacturing machinery and stock was shipped to Willtech Industrial in China.

The plan was to use Willtech's state of the art machinery and Williamson's designs, moulds and patterns to produce a top-quality range of big-game lures and fishing accessories for the world market. Rapala already had the right man, Philippe Guigo, in position to head this new business initiative. Andrew Jones, the former managing director of Williamson Lures, also signed a two-year consultancy agreement, and relocated to Hong Kong in order to oversee the installation of the machinery, and to help train Willtech staff in the art of making blue-water lures. Rapala now had two men who would work together to develop the Williamson brand. Philippe Guigo was the expert angler who knew what the fishermen wanted, and Andrew Jones was the manufacturing expert who would ensure that the lures met all the necessary specifications. Rapala's first Williamson Lure catalogue was published in September 2004, ready for the 2005 season.

More plans were in the pipeline for Willtech Industrial, and yet another factory extension (Phase Four) was completed in 2004. The new extension was built to house another new project, kept secret during the many months of negotiation. Rapala and their premier supplier of knives, Marttiinin Puukkotehdas Oy of Finland were to set up a knife manufacturing company in China to combat the influx of low-priced knives from the Far East. Rapala was to own 51 per cent of the company, and would supply the labour and the factory premises whilst Marttiini would provide their years of experience and staff to train the Chinese workforce. On one point, the two companies were in total agreement: the Fish 'n Fillet filleting knife, initially designed by Ron Weber back in 1965, would continue to be manufactured in Finland. Now, after almost 40 years of continual association, Rapala and Marttiini would forge the closest of links that would ensure their long association would continue.

2004 saw the introduction of a new lure concept in the form of the X-Rap. This plastic-bodied lure, which marked a significant development in the evolution of the classic Rapala lure, was best described as a 'slash bait'. Whilst it had the classic Rapala 'wounded minnow' action, a slash of the rod tip would bring to life its hard cutting darting action. The X-Rap boasted an integrated weight transfer system for long, accurate casting, a built-in rattle and the ability to suspend. The plastic body displayed scale and lateral line details whilst internal holographic foil combined with clever body colour printing produced an amazing range of colours. The X-Rap was made available in 10cm (4in.) models in both fresh and saltwater versions. The freshwater version was fitted with a 'flash foil teaser tail'. Twelve freshwater and a further 12 saltwater colours made up the initial range.

Another new lure introduced in 2004 was the Glass Fat Rap. The Fat Rap had always been a popular lure, and now Rapala's 'glass technology' was put to work to bring the Fat Rap up-to-date. A complete new range of translucent colours and a loud rhythmic rattle were important new features in this lure, which was fitted with a large, square lip designed to bounce off obstructions that it would meet during its underwater travels. The Glass Fat Rap was introduced in 5cm (2in.) and 7cm (2.8in.) models in a range of eight new colours.

The third introduction was for the American market only. Their jigging market was growing as more fishermen were prepared to fish through the winter, and an increasing number of anglers used jigging techniques in the summer months. The Jigging Shad Rap was a 5cm (2in.) jigging lure with a body shape of a small shad. Fitted with up-point hooks at both ends, and a central belly treble, the Jigging Shad Rap swam in a circle as it was jigged up and down. A range of 11 new colours was introduced.

The 'Dives To' series was expanded again to include the DT-04, a lure designed to dive to about four feet.

In the USA the Rapala range of reels was extended by the introduction of a new two-ball-bearing range of three reels. The rod range was strengthened with a range of seven Xtreme Ultra Light rods, and the range of rod and reel combos was extended.

The Rapala accessories saw additions to the Lock 'n Weigh series with a Lock 'n Grip incorporating the first digital scale, and Pro Guide rod racks both for the home and for travelling.

In September 2004 the head offices of Rapala were moved from the factory at Vääksy to the outskirts of Helsinki. The international nature of Rapala's business and the requirement for a permanent meeting facility within easy reach of Helsinki's airport at Vantaa made the move necessary. It was time to say goodbye to a number of long serving members of Rapala's staff, and to welcome a younger generation who would take up the responsibility of moving the company forward into the 21st century.

At the 2004 sales meeting of Normark Corporation, held in May of that year, two special guests were enshrined in the newly formed Normark Hall of Fame: Ron Weber and Ray Ostrom. It was the first time that the founders of the Normark dynasty had met for many, many years, and it was good to see them, both now in their mid seventies, sitting together at the celebration dinner. Both Ron and Ray made speeches of thanks. Ron was typically considered and serious, whilst Ray was his old flamboyant and humorous self. In their own inimitable styles, both men happily reflected upon the chain of events that had led a fishing-tackle dealer and a tackle salesman from the USA, and a poor Finnish woodsman called Lauri Rapala to form a lifelong friendship that would spawn one of the major fishing-tackle companies of the world. Even after all these years things don't change. One cannot change the course of history unless one is a maker of history.

Appendix 1: **IGFA records held by Rapala lures**

(All International Game Fish Association records past and present, as recorded, where Rapala lures stipulated, to April 2004)

Type Category	Lure or bait	Species	Line class	Weight	Location	Capture date	Angler
All Tackle	Rapala Fat Rap	Barb, hampala	All-Tackle	14 lb 5 oz	Temenggor Lake, State of Perak, Malaysia	22-Sep-02	Teh Ah Teck
All Tackle	Rapala	Barracuda, blackfin	All-Tackle	15 lb 12 oz	Puerto Quetzal, Guatemala	10-Jun-95	Estuardo Vila S.
All Tackle	Rapala Floating	Barracuda, Guinean	All-Tackle	101 lb 3 oz	Olende, Gabon	27-Dec-02	Cyril Fabre
All Tackle	Rapala Minnow	Bass, shadow	All-Tackle	1 lb 13 oz	Spring River, Arkansas, USA	5-Jul-99	James E. Baker
All Tackle	Rapala	Binga	All-Tackle	1 lb 2 oz	Maleri Island, Lake Malawi	30-Nov-96	Garry Seymer Whitcher
All Tackle	Rapala CD 18	Bludger	All-Tackle	21 lb 6 oz	Bartholmeu Dias, Mozambique	17-Jun-97	Joh Haasbroek
All Tackle	Rapala mullet	Blue, big	All-Tackle	2 lb 5 oz	Lake Malawi, Malawi	4-Nov-00	Deon R. Haigh
All Tackle	Rapala	Burbot	All-Tackle	18 lb 11 oz	Angenmanalren, Sweden	22-Oct-96	Margit Agren
All Tackle	Rapala Magnum	Coralgrouper, highfin	All-Tackle	2 lb 10 oz	Buso Point, Huon Gulf, Papua New Guinea	1-May-94	Justin Mallett
All Tackle	J5 Rapala	Eel, marbled	All-Tackle	36 lb 1 oz	Hazelmere Dam, Durban, South Africa	10-Jun-84	Ferdie Van Nooten
All Tackle	Rapala 22	Grouper, Malabar	All-Tackle	83 lb 12 oz	Bourake, New Caledonia	27-Jan-02	Patrick Sebile
All Tackle	Rapala	Grunt, Pacific roncador	All-Tackle	3 lb 8 oz	Rio Grande de Terraba, Costa Rica	28-Jan-90	Craig Whitehead, MD
All Tackle	Rapala Rattlin' Fat Rap	Happy, pink	All-Tackle	5 lb 6 oz	Upper Zambezi, Zambia, Africa	14-Aug-98	Graham J. Glasspool
All Tackle	Rapala Husky	Jacunda	All-Tackle	1 lb 8 oz	Matapuri River, Brazil	13-Oct-99	Jack W. Wadkins
All Tackle	Rapala Rattlin'	Largemouth, humpback	All-Tackle	8 lb 7 oz	Upper Zambezi River, Zambia	15-Aug-98	Richie Peters
All Tackle	Rapala	Leatherjack, longjaw	All-Tackle	3 lb 8 oz	Rio Coto, Puntarenas, Costa Rica	6-Feb-90	Craig Whitehead, MD
All Tackle	Rapala Magnum sinking	Lookdown	All-Tackle	4 lb 10 oz	Angra Dor Reis Bay, Rio de Janeiro, Brazil	11-Nov-93	Adolpho A. Mayer Neto
All Tackle	Rapala	Mackerel, African Spanish	All-Tackle	13 lb 3 oz	Grand Bereby, Ivory Coast	27-Dec-98	Dorchies Jacques West
All Tackle	Rapala	Mcheni/lake tiger	All-Tackle	1 lb 6 oz	Maleri Islands, Lake Malawi, Malawi	31-May-97	Brendon Garry Whitcher
All Tackle	Rapala Shad Rap	Nembwe	All-Tackle	7 lb 11 oz	Tiger Camp, Zambezi River, Zambia	27-Sep-98	W. F. Reitsma
All Tackle	Rapala Fire Tiger	Piabanha	All-Tackle	4 lb 0 oz	Paraiba do Sul River, Brazil	3-Sep-02	Kdu Magalhaes
All Tackle	Rapala	Sabalo	All-Tackle	9 lb 9 oz	Rio Tambopata, Peru	10-Oct-93	James B. Wise, MD
All Tackle	Rapala Shad Rap 7	Snook, fat	All-Tackle	9 lb 5 oz	Barra Una, Sao Paulo, Brazil	14-Mar-99	Vander Afonso
All Tackle	Rapala Magnum	Threadfin, giant African	All-Tackle	109 lb 5 oz	Barra do Kwanza, Angola	17-Jan-99	Marco Roberto da Silva Couto
All Tackle	Rapala Rattlin' Rap	Tilapia, redbreast	All-Tackle	3 lb 9 oz	Zambezi River, Namibia	14-Nov-94	Bill Staveley
All Tackle	Rapala RFR5	Tilapia, threespot	All-Tackle	10 lb 6 oz	Upper Zambezi, Zambia	3-Nov-98	Ben Van Wyk
Junior	Rapala Magnum	Albacore	M-Smallfry	62 lb 6 oz	Hout Bay, South Africa	30-Mar-97	Tom De Kock
Junior	Rapala	Bluefish	M-Smallfry	15 lb 2 oz	Shrewsbury Rocks, New Jersey, USA	12-Aug-97	Dylan Robert Chayes
Junior	Rapala lure	Jack, Pacific crevalle	F-Junior	17lb 0 oz	Punta Pina, Panama	28-Jan-04	Lauren Miller
Junior	Rapala SSR14	Perch, Nile	F-Smallfry	41 lb 14 oz	Rubondo Island, Lake Victoria, Tanzania	23-Jun-99	Katie Ommanney
Junior	Rapala	Roosterfish	M-Smallfry	50 lb 0 oz	Pinas Bay, Panama	1-Mar-02	Benjamin Badofsky
Junior	Rapala CD-9	Seabass, Japanese (suzuki)	F-Junior	2 lb 12 oz	Koshien-hama, Hyogo, Japan	27-May-01	Ayaka Yamamura
Junior	Rapala	Trout, brook	M-Smallfry	3 lb 7 oz	Paulins Kill River, New Jersey, USA	31-May-97	Dylan Robert Chayes
Junior	Rapala Floating	Trout, brown	F-Junior	10 lb 10 oz	Canandaigua Lake, New York, USA	6-May-01	Shana Segbers
Junior	Rapala #7	Trout, cutthroat	F-Junior	1 lb 3 oz	Independence Lake, California, USA	26-Jun-02	Jesse Wagner
Junior	Rapala Deep Runner	Trout, rainbow	04 kg (8 lb)	27 lb 6 oz	Lake Diefenbaker, Saskatchewan, Canada	10-Jun-01	Cody Forsberg
State FW	Rapala	Bass, largemouth	02 kg (4 lb)	1 lb 4 oz	Atchison State Park, Kansas, USA	12-Oct-02	David Pesi
State FW	Rapala	Bass, largemouth	02 kg (4 lb)	2 lb 8 oz	Everett Lake, New Hampshire, USA	18-May-03	David Pesi

Type category	Lure or bait	Species	Line class	Weight	Location	Capture date	Angler
State FW	Rapala Rattlin' Fat Rap	Bass, smallmouth	06 kg (12 lb)	3 lb 1 oz	Susquehanna River, New York, USA	13-Aug-00	Jeffrey S. Weibly
State FW	Rapala Rattlin' Fat Rap	Bass, smallmouth	02 kg (4 lb)	3 lb 14 oz	Susquehanna River, New York, USA	19-Aug-00	Jeffrey S. Weibly
State FW	Rapala	Pike, northern	02 kg (4 lb)	12 lb 0 oz	Lake Superior, Minnesota, USA	24-Sep-99	Justin Zachery Powers
State FW	Rapala	Trout, brown	06 kg (12 lb)	6 lb 11 oz	Beaver Brook, New Jersey, USA	4-May-01	Frank DeBlasio
State FW	Rapala	Trout, lake	10 kg (20 lb)	20 lb 0 oz	Lake Superior, Michigan, USA	31-May-00	Luke A. Stout
State FW	Rapala Minnow	Trout, rainbow	02 kg (4 lb)	2 lb 8 oz	Wachusett Reservoir, Massachusetts, USA	7-Apr-03	Christopher Montuori
State FW	Rapala	Walleye	02 kg (4 lb)	9 lb 0 oz	Boulder Lake, Minnesota, USA	6-Sep-99	Justin Zachery Powers
State FW-LC	Rapala Husky Jerk	Pike, northern	10 kg (20 lb) Tie	6 lb 0 oz	Cayuga Lake, New York, USA	14-Feb-04	Jeffrey S. Weibly
State FW-LC; Junior	Rapala Mini Fat Rap	Crappie, black/white	06 kg (12 lb)	2 lb 0oz	Painer, Virginia, USA	4-Apr-04	Trevor T. Hill
World Rec	Rapala CD18 Magnum	Albacore	W-08 kg (16 lb)	59 lb 15 oz	Hout Bay, Republic of South Africa	21-Aug-88	Maureen K. Colyn
World Rec	Rapala CD 14 Magnum	Albacore	M-04 kg (8 lb)	60 lb 11 oz	Hout Bay, Cape Town, Republic of South Africa	30-Apr-92	Hubert Meyer
World Rec	Rapala	Barracuda, great	M-08 kg (16 lb)	65 lb 11 oz	Port Michel, Gabon	22-Jan-84	Anestis Arnopoulos
World Rec	Rapala Mackerel Magnum	Barracuda, great	M-10 kg (20 lb)	65 lb 0 oz	Bonee Sifflante, Cameroon	5-Oct-86	Pierre Boursier
World Rec	Rapala Concorde	Barracuda, great	M-15 kg (30 lb)	79 lb 5 oz	Libreville, Gabon	25-Aug-91	Robert Courdesses
World Rec	Rapala Magnum 26	Barracuda, great	W-15 kg (30 lb)	60 lb 10 oz	Bom Bom Island, West Africa	24-May-93	Ursula Marais
World Rec	Rapala Mag CD18	Barracuda, Guinean	M-15 kg (30 lb)	48 lb 8 oz	Macha Branca, Luanda, Angola	8-Mar-04	Cam Nicolson
World Rec	Rapala Magnum	Barracuda, Guinean	M-24 kg (50 lb)	37 lb 7 oz	Macha Branca, Luanda, Angola	8-Mar-04	Hakan Ekberg
World Rec	Rapala	Barracuda, Guinean	M-37 kg (80 lb)	68 lb 5 oz	Rubane, Guinee-Bissau	29-Mar-04	Gerard Duquesnois
World Rec	Shad Rap Rapala	Bass, striped (landlocked)	04 kg (8 lb)	53 lb 0 oz	Bull Shoals, Arkansas, USA	1-May-87	William G. Sligar
World Rec	Rapala Countdown	Bass, yellow	04 kg (8 lb)	1 lb 2 oz	Canyon Lake, Arizona, USA	7-Aug-88	John H. Melisko
World Rec	Rapala	Bonito, Atlantic	M-15 kg (30 lb)	17 lb 15 oz	Isla Graciosa, Canary Islands, Spain	2-Jan-93	Pierangelo Dellabona
World Rec	Rapala Silver	Bonito, Atlantic	W-15 kg (30 lb)	14 lb 7 oz	Faial, Azores, Portugal	21-Jul-97	Kori Ann Valenta
World Rec	Rapala Mackerel #13	Bonito, Pacific	W-10 kg (20 lb)	11 lb 9 oz	San Diego, California, USA	16-Jul-83	Christine Ann Clark
World Rec	Rapala	Bonito, Pacific	M-03 kg (6 lb)	12 lb 9 oz	Balboa, California, USA	14-May-97	James Duncan
World Rec	Rapala 14 Magnum	Bonito, Pacific	M-10 kg (20 lb)	12 lb 14 oz	Cuajiniquil, Costa Rica	31-Aug-01	Christian Hampl
World Rec	Rapala Original 7mn	Carp, grass	02 kg (4 lb)	53 lb 1 oz	William R. Logan Wildlife Area, Missouri, USA	27-Jul-00	Marvin Earl O'Neal
World Rec	Rapala Countdown	Carp, grass	06 kg (12 lb)	58 lb 14 oz	Lake Ouachita, Arkansas, USA	6-Apr-02	Jon Dixon
World Rec	Rapala	Dorado	01 kg (2 lb)	9 lb 7 oz	Vallemi, Paraguay River, Paraguay	4-Dec-84	Jorge E. Xifra
World Rec	Rapala Shad Rap	Drum, freshwater	08 kg (16 lb)	31 lb 6 oz	Nickajack Reservoir, Tennessee, USA	12-Mar-88	Joseph E. Willard, Jr.
World Rec	Rapala 18cm Magnum	Huchen	15 kg (30 lb)	70 lb 12 oz	Carinthia, Austria	1-Jan-80	Martin F.P. Ester
World Rec	Rapala Magnum	Jack, crevalle	M-15 kg (30 lb)	57 lb 5 oz	Barra do Kwanza, Angola	10-Oct-92	Cam Nicolson
World Rec	Rapala	Jack, Pacific crevalle	W-03 kg (6 lb)	11 lb 2 oz	Zihuatanejo, Mexico	3-Apr-95	Irene McDonald Johnson
World Rec	Rapala	Jack, Pacific crevalle	W-04 kg (8 lb)	15 lb 0 oz	Playa Zancudo, Bahia Dulce, Costa Rica	5-Dec-98	Irene McDonald Johnson
World Rec	Rapala	Ladyfish	M-15 kg (30 lb)	2 lb 12 oz	Homestead, Florida, USA	15-Jul-02	David Pesi
World Rec	Rapala Magnum	Mackerel, narrowbarred	M-04 kg (8 lb)	72 lb 12 oz	Lee Point, Darwin, N.T., Australia	24-Aug-85	Henry J. Fehres

Type category	Lure or bait	Species	Line class	Weight	Location	Capture date	Angler
World Rec	Rapala CD18	Mackerel, narrowbarred	W-08 kg (16 lb)	66 lb 9 oz	Port Hedland, W.A., Australia	16-Aug-98	Joy Burrage
World Rec	Rapala Magnum 14	Mackerel, Pacific sierra	M-10 kg (20 lb)	14 lb 14 oz	Cuajiniquil, Costa Rica	3-Sep-00	Antonio Morell Corradi
World Rec	Rapala CD	Mackerel, Pacific sierra	M-04 kg (8 lb)	10 lb 0 oz	Playa Zancudo, Costa Rica	13-Dec-00	Craig Whitehead, MD
World Rec	Rapala 18 Magnum	Mackerel, Pacific sierra	M-08 kg (16 lb)	16 lb 2 oz	Cuajiniquil, Costa Rica	13-Aug-01	Christian Hampl
World Rec	Rapala 14	Mackerel, Pacific sierra	M-02 kg (4 lb)	10 lb 7 oz	Cuajiniquil, Costa Rica	26-Aug-01	Christian Hampl
World Rec	Rapala Floating	Mackerel, Pacific sierra	M-03 kg (6 lb)	11 lb 12 oz	Cuajiniquil, Costa Rica	9-Sep-01	Christian Hampl
World Rec	Rapala lure	Mackerel, Pacific sierra	W-08 kg (16 lb)	5 lb 12 oz	Golfito, Costa Rica	4-Apr-03	Irene McDonald Johnson
World Rec	Rapala	Muskellunge	15 kg (30 lb)	56 lb 7 oz	Manitou Lake, Ontario, Canada	30-Aug-84	Gene Borucki
World Rec	4" Rapala	Muskellunge	06 kg (12 lb)	65 lb 0 oz	Blackstone Harbor, Ontario, Canada	16-Oct-88	Kenneth J. O'Brien
World Rec	Floating Rapala	Muskellunge, tiger	02 kg (4 lb)	23 lb 9 oz	Lake Rolard, Twin Lakes, Michigan, USA	8-Aug-87	Bryan Guzek
World Rec	Shad Rap Rapala	Muskellunge, tiger	06 kg (12 lb)	26 lb 2 oz	Lake Summerset, Davis, Illinois, USA	4-Aug-89	David Pan
World Rec	Rapala Magnum	Nembwe	03 kg (6 lb)	5 lb 2 oz	Upper Zambezi River, Mongu, Zambia	9-Sep-02	Donald John Bousfield
World Rec	Rapala	Payara	08 kg (16 lb)	32 lb 8 oz	Uraima Falls, Venezuela	13-Apr-96	Lance Glaser
World Rec	Rapala	Payara	06 kg (12 lb)	32 lb 0 oz	Uraima Falls, Venezuela	14-Apr-96	Lance Glaser
World Rec	Rapala Magnum	Payara	02 kg (4 lb)	18 lb 0 oz	Uraima Falls, Venezuela	9-Feb-98	Shoichiro Kawai
World Rec	Rapala CD18	Payara	10 kg (20 lb)	33 lb 8 oz	Uraima Falls, Venezuela	5-Mar-99	Bill Keeley
World Rec	Rapala Magnum 26	Payara	03 kg (6 lb)	18 lb 8 oz	Uraima Falls, Venezuela	7-Feb-03	Carlos Barrantes Araya
World Rec	Rapala Shad Rap	Peacock, blackstriped	01 kg (2 lb)	1 lb 4 oz	Rio Cinaruco, Venezuela	18-Jan-99	Eric R. Ostmark
World Rec	Rapala Mag 18	Peacock, speckled	10 kg (20 lb)	24 lb 0 oz	Mataveni River, Orinoco, Colombia	15-Jan-82	J. Hatcher James, III
World Rec	Rapala Magnum	Peacock, speckled	03 kg (6 lb)	20 lb 10 oz	Rio Sipapo, Amazonas, Venezuela	6-Jan-95	Carlos A. Aristeguieta L.
World Rec	Rapala Magnum	Perch, Nile	60 kg (130 lb)	124 lb 8 oz	Lake Victoria, Kenya	31-Mar-94	Derek Brink
World Rec	Rapala Super Shad Rap	Perch, Nile	24 kg (50 lb)	210 lb 0 oz	Lake Nasser, Egypt	24-Jun-98	Darren Robert Lord
World Rec	3" Rapala	Perch, yellow	06 kg (12 lb)	1 lb 15 oz	Barbers Pond, W. Kingston, Rhode Island, USA	26-Sep-86	Holly Kristen Ferris
World Rec	Rapala	Pollack, European	M-15 kg (30 lb)	26 lb 0 oz	Ile de Ouessant, France	30-Aug-81	Loik Le Chat
World Rec	Rapala	Queenfish, talang	W-08 kg (16 lb)	18 lb 8 oz	Coburg Peninsula, N.T., Australia	6-Jul-92	Carla Beck
World Rec	Rapala	Skipjack, black	W-06 kg (12 lb)	17 lb 0 oz	La Paz, Baja California, Mexico	27-May-88	Agnes H. (Pug) Jones
World Rec	Rapala	Skipjack, black	W-08 kg (16 lb)	17 lb 0 oz	La Paz, Baja California, Mexico	27-May-88	Agnes H. (Pug) Jones
World Rec	Rapala	Skipjack, black	W-15 kg (30 lb)	15 lb 0 oz	La Paz, Baja California, Mexico	27-May-88	Agnes H. (Pug) Jones
World Rec	Rapala	Skipjack, black	W-04 kg (8 lb)	5 lb 8 oz	Zihuatanejo, Mexico	6-Apr-96	Irene McDonald Johnson
World Rec	Rapala	Snakehead	10 kg (20 lb)	9 lb 4 oz	Krassio Dam, Suphanburi, Thailand	17-Dec-02	Jean-Francois Helias
World Rec	Rapala	Snakehead	08 kg (16 lb)	13 lb 3 oz	Krassio Dam, Suphanburi, Thailand	18-Dec-02	Jean-Francois Helias
World Rec	Rapala Floating	Snakehead	08 kg (16 lb) Tie	13 lb 3 oz	Dan Tchang, Suphanburi, Thailand	1-Jan-03	Jean-Francois Helias
World Rec	Rapala Floating	Snakehead	06 kg (12 lb)	9 lb 14 oz	Dan Tchang, Suphanburi, Thailand	2-Jan-03	Jean-Francois Helias
World Rec	Rapala Floating	Snakehead	04 kg (8 lb)	4lb 15 oz	Khao Laem Reservoir, Thailand	2-Apr-04	Jean-Francois Helias
World Rec	Rapala CD-14 Mag	Snapper, cubera	W-24 kg (50 lb)	78 lb 0 oz	Cannon Key, Brus Laguna, Honduras	19-Jan-95	Ruth Kryger
World Rec	Rapala CD11 GM	Snook, Atlantic	W-04 kg (8 lb)	27 lb 8 oz	Barra del Colorado, Costa Rica	2-Oct-89	Donna L. Davenport
World Rec	Shad Rapala	Sunfish, redbreast	06 kg (12 lb)	1 lb 2 oz	Suwannee River, Chiefland, Florida, USA	23-Jul-86	Bernard L. Schultz
World Rec	Rapala	Tarpon	M-15 kg (30 lb) Tie	283 lb 4 oz	Sherbro Island, Sierra Leone	16-Apr-91	Yvon Victor Sebag
World Rec	Rapala Shad Rap	Threadfin, king	W-08 kg (16 lb)	19 lb 6 oz	Bathurst Island, N.T., Australia	16-Jun-86	Lorrie Fay

Type category	Lure or bait	Species	Line class	Weight	Location	Capture date	Angler
World Rec	Rapala Shad Rap	Threadfin, king	M-08 kg (16 lb)	22 lb 0 oz	Port Hurd, Bathurst Island, N.T., Australia	24-Nov-90	Wayne Andrew Ross
World Rec	Rapala Floater	Threadfin, king	W-06 kg (12 lb)	21 lb 2 oz	Port Hurd, Bathurst Island, N.T., Australia	4-Aug-91	Dottie Wing
World Rec	Rapala CD18	Trevally, bigeye	W-15 kg (30 lb)	15 lb 0 oz	Isla Coiba, Panama	18-Jan-84	Sally S. Timms
World Rec	Rapala CD14 Mag	Trevally, bigeye	W-24 kg (50 lb)	15 lb 3 oz	Magojima, Ogasawara, Tokyo, Japan	9-Aug-98	Mutsumi Shoji
World Rec	Rapala	Trevally, bluefin	M-01 kg (2 lb)	6 lb 6 oz	Isla San Benedicto, Revillagigedo Islands, Mexico	19-May-87	Butch Green
World Rec	Rapala B. Mag 9	Trevally, bluefin	M-02 kg (4 lb)	13 lb 0 oz	Gangehi, Ari Atoll, Republic of Maldives	10-Jul-89	Roberto Ferrario
World Rec	Rapala Red Head CD7	Trevally, giant	W-02 kg (4 lb)	10 lb 14 oz	Singaua, Huon Gulf, Papua New Guinea	24-Sep-89	Rebecca Jane Mallett
World Rec	Rapala	Trout, brown	24 kg (50 lb)	14 lb 4 oz	Lake Ontario, New York, USA	29-Apr-86	Paul Loquasto
World Rec	Rapala Shad Rap	Trout, bull	04 kg (8 lb)	12 lb 4 oz	Flathead River, Montana, USA	4-Jul-87	William J. Harris, DDS
World Rec	Rapala Fat Rap	Trout, bull	06 kg (12 lb)	23 lb 2 oz	Lake Billy Chinook, Culver, Oregon, USA	25-Mar-89	Don Yow
World Rec	Rapala	Trout, lake	03 kg (6 lb)	36 lb 9 oz	Lake Grandby, Colorado, USA	17-Nov-01	Robert Mason
World Rec	CD18 Rapala Magnum	Tuna, bigeye (Atlantic)	M-08 kg (16 lb)	140 lb 1 oz	Cape Point, South Africa	20-Oct-95	D.E.L. Carter
World Rec	Rapala	Tuna, yellowfin	M-24 kg (50 lb)	385 lb 12 oz	Lome, West Africa	20-Apr-03	Philippe Marn
World Rec	Rapala	Tunny, little	M-06 kg (12 lb)	28 lb 3 oz	Annaba, Cap de Garde, Algeria	25-Dec-88	Raymond Madau
World Rec	Rapala	Walleye	01 kg (2 lb)	10 lb 6 oz	Branched Oak Lake, Lincoln, Nebraska, USA	18-Apr-84	Thomas G. Bitting
World Rec	Rapala CD11	Bass, European	M-15 kg (30 lb)	20 lb 14 oz	Cap d'Agde, France	8-Sep-99	Robert Mari
World Rec	Rapala CD18	Jack, crevalle	M-24 kg (50 lb)	58 lb 6 oz	Barra do Kwanza, Angola	10-Dec-00	Nuno Abohbot P. da Silva
World Rec	Rapala Fire Tiger	Perch, Nile	15 kg (30 lb)	230 lb 0 oz	Lake Nasser, Egypt	20-Dec-00	William Toth
World Rec	Rapala Magnum	Snook, Pacific	M-15 kg (30 lb)	57 lb 12 oz	Rio Naranjo, Quepos, Costa Rica	23-Aug-91	George Beck
World Rec	J9 Rapala	Splake	04 kg (8 lb)	20 lb 11 oz	Georgian Bay, Ontario, Canada	17-May-87	Paul S. Thompson
World Rec	Rapala 11cm	Tunny, little	M-15 kg (30 lb)	35 lb 2 oz	Cap de Garde, Algeria	14-Dec-88	Jean Yves Chatard
World Rec; Junior	Rapala Mag CD18	Barracuda, Guinean	M-08 kg (16 lb)	52 lb 14 oz	Macha Branca, Luanda, Angola	8-Mar-04	Alex Nicholson
World Rec; Junior	Rapala Magnum	Queenfish, talang	W-10 kg (20 lb)	19 lb 6 oz	Groote Eylandt, Australia	13-Jun-98	Cheree Collins
World Rec; State FW	Shad Rapala	Crappie, black	06 kg (12 lb)	4 lb 4 oz	Paint Creek, Coosa River, Alabama, USA	18-Mar-84	Sherril S. Harris
Retired	Rapala	Albacore	F-Smallfry	20 lb 4 oz	San Diego, California, USA	21-Jul-99	Rachel Ann Heim
Retired	Rapala CD18	Barracuda, great	F-Junior	17 lb 6 oz	Shimoni, Kenya	17-Aug-98	Lyndsay Hemphill
Retired	Rapala Magnum	Bass, European	M-15 kg (30 lb)	13 lb 5 oz	Oessant, France	14-Sep-86	Pierre Serralta
Retired	Rapala	Bass, shoal	01 kg (2 lb)	1 lb 3 oz	Big Lazar Creek, Talbot County, Georgia, USA	25-Aug-84	Winston H. Baker
Retired	Rapala Rattlin' Rapala	Bass, smallmouth	M-Smallfry	2 lb 12 oz	Rainy Lake, Ontario, Canada	8-Aug-98	Hunter Morris
Retired	Rapala	Bass, smallmouth	F-Smallfry	2 lb 6 oz	Green Lake, Quebec, Canada	28-Jul-98	Cameron McLain Nutting
Retired	Rapala	Bass, white	01 kg (2 lb)	3 lb 6 oz	Devils Lake, North Dakota, USA	30-Dec-86	Richard E. LaBouy
Retired	Rapala Floating	Bass, whiterock	01 kg (2 lb)	10 lb 6 oz	Little Red River, Heber Springs, Arkansas, USA	9-May-88	Gary Lee Evans
Retired	Rapala CD9S	Bass, whiterock	06 kg (12 lb)	16 lb 2 oz	Little Three Mile Creek, Ohio, USA	23-Jan-85	Ralph E. Campbell
Retired	Rapala	Blue, big	All-Tackle	1 lb 3 oz	Maleri Islands, Lake Malawi, Malawi	7-May-97	Brendon Garry Whitcher
Retired	Rapala Shad Rap	Characoid, pike	All-Tackle	2 lb 0 oz	Orinoco River, Venezuela	15-Jan-99	Jose Cristobal Nieto
Retired	Rapala Shad Rap	Crappie, black	04 kg (8 lb)	2 lb 6 oz	Lake San Antonio, California, USA	28-Mar-01	Doreen J. Lewallen

Type Category	Lure or bait	Species	Line class	Weight	Location	Capture date	Angler
Retired	Rapala	Crappie, black	M-Junior	2 lb 0 oz	San Antonio Lake, California, USA	12-Apr-99	Cory Miyamoto
Retired	Rapala	Croaker, S. A. silver	All-Tackle	5 lb 11 oz	Xingu River, Estado Mato Grosso, Brazil	6-May-96	Sergio Roberto Rothier
Retired	Rapala	Dentex	M-10 kg (20 lb)	16 lb 6 oz	Isle of Lanzarote, Canary Islands, Spain	8-Mar-98	Sergio Bacchetti
Retired	Rapala Fat Rap	Drum, freshwater	F-Smallfry	3 lb 6 oz	Red Rock Dam, Pella, Iowa, USA	18-Jul-98	Miranda Lopez
Retired	Rapala 22	Grouper, broomtail	All-Tackle	89 lb 0 oz	El Muerto Island, Ecuador	20-Jun-97	Jorge Jurado
Retired	Rapala CD9	Jack, Pacific crevalle	W-04 kg (8 lb)	14 lb 5 oz	Zihuatanejo, Mexico	4-Apr-94	Irene McDonald Johnson
Retired	Rapala CD9	Jack, Pacific crevalle	W-10 kg (20 lb)	18 lb 6 oz	Zihuatanejo, Mexico	12-Jun-90	Irene McDonald Johnson
Retired	Rapala	Jack, Pacific crevalle	W-10 kg (20 lb)	14 lb 0 oz	Zihuatanejo, Mexico	1-Nov-84	Virginia T. Pena
Retired	Rapala	Jack, Pacific crevalle	M-24 kg (50 lb)	11 lb 12 oz	Zihuatanejo, Mexico	10-Oct-84	Tony A. Pena
Retired	Rapala	Jack, Pacific crevalle	M-24 kg (50 lb)	8 lb 14 oz	Zihuatanejo, Mexico	10-Aug-84	Tony A. Pena
Retired	Rapala	Jack, Pacific crevalle	W-15 kg (30 lb)	16 lb 4 oz	Zihuatanejo, Mexico	1-Aug-84	Virginia T. Pena
Retired	Rapala Shad Rap	Largemouth, humpback	All-Tackle	7 lb 4 oz	Tiger Camp, Zambezi River, Zambezi	23-Aug-96	Colin Snyman
Retired	Rapala	Leerfish (Garrick)	All-Tackle	54 lb 10 oz	Nice, France	20-Feb-97	Dominique Loiseau
Retired	Rapala	Mackerel, narrowbarred	M-02 kg (4 lb)	23 lb 0 oz	Port Hedland, Australia	29-Jun-86	Len Laughton
Retired	Rapala 14 B	Mackerel, narrowbarred	M-06 kg (12 lb)	73 lb 3 oz	Cape Cuvier, W.A., Australia	27-Aug-82	Shane Quinlan
Retired	Rapala Sinking	Mackerel, Pacific sierra	M-Junior	4 lb 2 oz	Isla Meanquera, El Salvador	17-Apr-04	Javier Saca Bahaia
Retired	Rapala CD	Mackerel, Pacific sierra	M-02 kg (4 lb)	5 lb 0 oz	Playa Zancudo, Costa Rica	16-Dec-00	Craig Whitehead, MD
Retired	Rapala CD	Mackerel, Pacific sierra	M-03 kg (6 lb)	8 lb 0 oz	Playa Zancudo, Costa Rica	13-Dec-00	Craig Whitehead, MD
Retired	Rapala CD Magnum	Mackerel, Pacific sierra	W-04 kg (8 lb)	3 lb 1 oz	Zihuatanejo, Mexico	26-Oct-00	Irene McDonald Johnson
Retired	Rapala	Mackerel, Pacific sierra	W-04 kg (8 lb)	2 lb 6 oz	Cabo San Lucas, Baja California Sur, Mexico	1-Oct-00	Cheryl Duncan
Retired	Rapala	Mackerel, Pacific sierra	M-02 kg (4 lb)	4 lb 11 oz	Cabo San Lucas, Baja California Sur, Mexico	15-Jan-00	Stein Cozad
Retired	Rapala	Mackerel, Pacific sierra	M-03 kg (6 lb)	4 lb 8 oz	Cabo San Lucas, Baja California Sur, Mexico	14-Jan-00	James Duncan
Retired	Rapala	Mackerel, Pacific sierra	M-04 kg (8 lb)	4 lb 8 oz	Cabo San Lucas, Baja California Sur, Mexico	14-Jan-00	James Duncan
Retired	Rapala	Mackerel, Pacific sierra	M-06 kg (12 lb)	5 lb 1 oz	Cabo San Lucas, Baja California Sur, Mexico	14-Jan-00	Stein Cozad
Retired	Rapala CD Magnum	Mackerel, Pacific sierra	M-04 kg (8 lb)	3 lb 0 oz	Playa Zancudo, Costa Rica	7-Aug-99	Craig Whitehead, MD
Retired	Rapala 5.5in	Mackerel, Pacific sierra	M-08 kg (16 lb)	9 lb 0 oz	Playa Zancudo, Costa Rica	7-Jul-99	Craig Whitehead, MD
Retired	Rapala 5.5in	Mackerel, Pacific sierra	M-10 kg (20 lb)	7 lb 0 oz	Playa Zancudo, Costa Rica	7-Jul-99	Craig Whitehead, MD
Retired	Rapala CD 4in	Mackerel, Pacific sierra	M-02 kg (4 lb)	2 lb 8 oz	Playa Zancudo, Costa Rica	25-Jun-99	Craig Whitehead, MD
Retired	Rapala 4in	Mackerel, Pacific sierra	M-03 kg (6 lb)	2 lb 8 oz	Playa Zancudo, Costa Rica	23-Jun-99	Craig Whitehead, MD
Retired	Rapala CD 4in	Mackerel, Pacific sierra	M-04 kg (8 lb)	2 lb 8 oz	Playa Zancudo, Costa Rica	23-Jun-99	Craig Whitehead, MD
Retired	Rapala CD 4in	Mackerel, Pacific sierra	M-08 kg (16 lb)	4 lb 0 oz	Playa Zancudo, Costa Rica	18-Jun-99	Craig Whitehead, MD
Retired	Rapala CD	Mackerel, Pacific sierra	M-10 kg (20 lb)	5 lb 0 oz	Playa Zancudo, Costa Rica	18-Jun-99	Craig Whitehead, MD
Retired	Rapala	Mackerel, West African Spanish	All-Tackle	11 lb 0 oz	Ada, Ghana, West Africa	20-Apr-95	E. Leon Buckles
Retired	Rapala	Muskellunge	02 kg (4 lb) WI	9 lb 8 oz	Pokegama Bay, Lake Superior, Wisconsin, USA	27-Nov-90	Justin Zachery Powers
Retired	Rapala	Muskellunge	01 kg (2 lb)	5 lb 13 oz	Pincher Lake, Ontario, Canada	14-Aug-84	Jim Gamlin
Retired	Rapala	Otolithe	All-Tackle	25 lb 0 oz	Bijagos, Guinee-Bissau	19-Apr-95	Ernest Lopez
Retired	Rapala	Payara	03 kg (6 lb)	10 lb 4 oz	Orinoco River, Puerto Ayacucho, Venezuela	13-Jan-98	Eric R. Ostmark

Type category	Lure or bait	Species	Line class	Weight	Location	Capture date	Angler
Retired	Rapala Rattlin' Rapala	Payara	01 kg (2 lb)	3 lb 4 oz	Orinoco River, Puerto Ayacucho, Venezuela	20-Jan-97	Eric Ostmark
Retired	Rapala CD18 Mag	Payara	02 kg (4 lb)	6 lb 9 oz	Rio Paragua, Venezuela	15-Mar-96	James B. Wise, MD
Retired	Rapala Shad Rap	Peacock, butterfly	06 kg (12 lb)	7 lb 7 oz	Miami, Florida, USA	24-May-99	Robert Gimenez
Retired	Rapala Magnum	Peacock, butterfly	02 kg (4 lb)	5 lb 13 oz	Rio Sipapo, Amazonas, Venezuela	20-Nov-96	Carlos Aristeguieta L.
Retired	Rapala	Pellona, Amazon	08 kg (16 lb)	1 lb 12 oz	Rio Caura, Venezuela	21-Jan-00	E. R. Ostmark
Retired	Rapala Shad Rap	Perch, Nile	M-Smallfry	112 lb 6 oz	Entebbe, Uganda, East Africa	27-Aug-99	Anthony Outram
Retired	Rapala	Perch, Nile	02 kg (4 lb)	24 lb 4 oz	South Island, Lake Turkana, Kenya	15-May-97	Gai Cullien
Retired	Rapala	Pike, northern	03 kg (6 lb)	33 lb 4 oz	Smith Bay, Ontario, Canada	7-Jul-96	Marion M. Heffren
Retired	Rapala	Pike, northern	24 kg (50 lb)	25 lb 3 oz	Norrtalje Archipelago, Sweden	29-May-85	Dan Jonasson
Retired	Rapala	Salmon, chum	02 kg (4 lb)	11 lb 2 oz	Noatak River, Alaska, USA	15-Aug-84	David Lloyd
Retired	Rapala Rattlin' Rapala	Seabass, Japanese (suzuki)	M-Junior	5 lb 9 oz	Keihin Unga, Yokohama, Japan	11-Mar-00	Hayato Wakabayashi
Retired	Rapala CD9	Seabass, Japanese (suzuki)	M-Junior	4 lb 1 oz	Keihin Unga, Yokohama, Kanagawara, Japan	31-Mar-98	Hayato Wakabayashi
Retired	Rapala CD9	Seabass, Japanese (suzuki)	W-03 kg (6 lb)	5 lb 9 oz	Tsubasa-bashi, Tsurumi, Yokohama, Kanagawa, Japan	24-Feb-96	Yuko Mizukami
Retired	Rapala	Snapper, cubera	M-Junior	30 lb 13 oz	Gardens of the Queen, Cuba	27-Mar-97	William Gay
Retired	Rapala CD14	Snapper, cubera	M-10 kg (20 lb)	66 lb 0 oz	Tortuga Lodge, Tortuguero, Costa Rica	5-Mar-85	Eduardo Brown Silva
Retired	Rapala	Splake	04 kg (8 lb)	1 lb 10 oz	Smokey Lake, Phelps, Wisconsin, USA	11-Feb-85	Kenneth J. McDaniel
Retired	Rapala	Splake	Tie 15 kg (30 lb)	1 lb 4 oz	Smokey Lake, Phelps, Wisconsin, USA	11-Feb-85	Robert Page
Retired	Rapala	Sunfish, redbreast	02 kg (4 lb)	1 lb 4 oz	Suwannee River, Florida, USA	11-Apr-84	Winston H. Baker
Retired	Rapala	Sunfish, redbreast	06 kg (12 lb)	1 lb 0 oz	Suwannee River, Florida, USA	11-Apr-84	Winston H. Baker
Retired	Rapala	Sunfish, redbreast	02 kg (4 lb)	1 lb 0 oz	Suwannee River, Florida, USA	11-Feb-84	Winston H. Baker
Retired	Rapala Fat Rap	Tilapia, threespot	All-Tackle	10 lb 2 oz	Tiger Camp, Zambezi River, Zambia	18-Oct-98	Greg Marshbank
Retired	Rapala Fat Rap	Tilapia, threespot	All-Tackle	9 lb 7 oz	Tiger Camp, Zambezi River, Zambia	11-Feb-97	Michael Harris
Retired	Rapala Rattlin' Fat Rap	Tilapia, threespot	All-Tackle	9 lb 4 oz	Tiger Camp, Zambezi River, Zambia	16-Nov-94	Colin Armstrong
Retired	Rapala CD22	Trahira, giant	All-Tackle	23 lb 0 oz	Uraima Falls, Venezuela	3-Jan-01	Debbie Raker
Retired	Rapala CD22	Trevally, giant	M-Smallfry	38 lb 9 oz	Rai Coast, Madang, Papua New Guinea	4-Oct-01	Lincoln A. Smith
Retired	Rapala	Trevally, giant	M-02 kg (4 lb)	2 lb 10 oz	Woody Wallis Rock, N. Qld., Australia	16-Jun-84	Tony A. Pena
Retired	Rapala Floating	Trout, brown	M-Smallfry	7 lb 14 oz	Lake Michigan, Michigan, USA	4-Apr-01	John Jackoviak
Retired	Rapala Floating	Trout, brown	F-Junior	10 lb 8 oz	Lake Michigan, Michigan, USA	27-Mar-01	Juliana Jackoviak
Retired	Rapala Floating	Trout, brown	M-Smallfry	7 lb 8 oz	Lake Michigan, Michigan, USA	20-Mar-01	John Jackoviak
Retired	Rapala	Trout, brown	F-Smallfry	2 lb 8 oz	Lake Michigan, Michigan, USA	28-Apr-98	Juliana Jackoviak
Retired	Rapala	Trout, brown	M-Smallfry	5 lb 4 oz	Paulins Kill River, New Jersey, USA	24-May-97	Dylan Robert Chayes
Retired	Rapala	Trout, brown	24 kg (50 lb)	11 lb 2 oz	Mjosa, Brumunddal, Norway	12-Mar-84	Morten Aarsten
Retired	Rapala	Trout, bull	02 kg (4 lb)	6 lb 8 oz	Duncan River, B.C., Canada	9-Feb-84	Michael B. Haw
Retired	Rapala	Trout, rainbow	F-Junior	7 lb 8 oz	Palmdale, California, USA	2-Apr-01	Nicole Smith
Retired	Rapala CD18	Tuna, bigeye (Atlantic)	M-08 kg (16 lb)	63 lb 14 oz	St. Helena Island, United Kingdom	24-Jun-85	Baba Joubert
Retired	Rapala Magnum	Tuna, yellowfin	M-Smallfry	115 lb 15 oz	Hout Bay, South Africa	23-Mar-97	Tom De Kock
Retired	Rapala	Wahoo	M-04 kg (8 lb)	49 lb 13 oz	Ponta da Barra, Mozambique	29-Sep-97	Hennie Geldennuys
Retired	Rapala	Yellowtail, California	F-Smallfry	13 lb 0 oz	San Diego, California, USA	22-May-97	Danielle Barnett

Appendix 2: **Depth charts – casting and trolling**

Original | Countdown | 'Dives To' | X-Rap

Depth	Original 3cm	5cm	7cm	9cm	11cm	13cm	18cm	Countdown 1cm	3cm	5cm	7cm	9cm	11cm	'Dives To' 4cm	6cm	10cm	16cm	X-Rap 10cm
Top water																		
0.3m / 1ft.																		
0.6m / 2ft.																		
0.9m / 3ft.																		
1.2m / 4ft.																		
1.5m / 5ft.																		
1.8m / 6ft.																		
2.1m / 7ft.																		
2.4m / 8ft.																		
2.7m / 9ft.																		
3.0m / 10ft.																		
3.3m / 11ft.																		
3.6m / 12ft.																		
3.9m / 13ft.																		
4.2m / 14ft.																		
4.5m / 15ft.																		
4.8m / 16ft.																		
5.1m / 17ft.																		
5.4m / 18ft.																		
5.7m / 19ft.																		
6.0m / 20ft.																		

Glass Fat Rap | Team Esko | Husky Jerk | Deep Down Husky Jerk | Jointed | Mini Fat Rap | Fat Rap

Depth	Glass Fat Rap 5cm	7cm	Team Esko 7cm	Husky Jerk 6cm	8cm	10cm	12cm	14cm	Deep Down Husky Jerk 10cm	12cm	Jointed 5cm	7cm	9cm	11cm	13cm	Mini Fat Rap 3cm	Fat Rap 5cm	7cm
Top water																		
0.3m / 1ft.																		
0.6m / 2ft.																		
0.9m / 3ft.																		
1.2m / 4ft.																		
1.5m / 5ft.																		
1.8m / 6ft.																		
2.1m / 7ft.																		
2.4m / 8ft.																		
2.7m / 9ft.																		
3.0m / 10ft.																		
3.3m / 11ft.																		
3.6m / 12ft.																		
3.9m / 13ft.																		
4.2m / 14ft.																		
4.5m / 15ft.																		
4.8m / 16ft.																		
5.1m / 17ft.																		
5.4m / 18ft.																		
5.7 m / 19 ft																		
6.0 m / 20 ft																		

	Shallow Shad Rap			Deep Shad Rap			Glass Shad Rap			Shad Rap RS			Jointed Shad Rap			Super Shad Rap	CD Super Shad Rap
	5cm	7cm	9cm	5cm	7cm	9cm	4cm	5cm	7cm	4cm	5cm	7cm	4cm	5cm	7cm	14cm	14cm
Top water																	
0.3m / 1ft.																	
0.6m / 2ft.																	
0.9m / 3ft.																	
1.2m / 4ft.																	
1.5m / 5ft.																	
1.8m / 6ft.																	
2.1m / 7ft.																	
2.4m / 8ft.																	
2.7m / 9ft.																	
3.0m / 10ft.																	
3.3m / 11ft.																	
3.6m / 12ft.																	
3.9m / 13ft.																	
4.2m / 14ft.																	
4.5m / 15ft.																	
4.8m / 16ft.																	
5.1m / 17ft.																	

	Tail Dancer				Long Cast Minnow			Sliver		Magnum Floating				Countdown Magnum						
	5cm	7cm	9cm	11cm	8cm	10cm	12cm	13cm	20cm	9cm	11cm	14cm	18cm	7cm	9cm	11cm	14cm	18cm	22cm	26cm
Top water																				
0.3m / 1ft.																				
0.6m / 2ft.																				
0.9m / 3ft.																				
1.2m / 4ft.																				
1.5m / 5ft.																				
1.8m / 6ft.																				
2.1m / 7ft.																				
2.4m / 8ft.																				
2.7m / 9ft.																				
3.0m / 10ft.																				
3.3m / 11ft.																				
3.6m / 12ft.																				
3.9m / 13ft.																				
4.2m / 14ft.																				
4.5m / 15ft.																				
4.8m / 16ft.																				
5.1m / 17ft.																				
5.4m / 18ft.																				
5.7m / 19ft.																				
6.0m / 20ft.																				
6.3m / 21ft.																				
6.6m / 22ft.																				
6.9m / 23ft.																				
7.2m / 24ft.																				
7.5m / 25ft.																				
7.8m / 26ft.																				
8.1m / 27ft.																				
8.4m / 28ft.																				
8.7m / 29ft.																				
9.0m / 30ft.																				

Appendix 3: **Matching snaps, lines, and hooks**

Lure family	Lure	Knot	Snap size	Leader size	Line diameter (mm)	Replacement hook Set
Countdown	CD-01	loop knot	0	-	0.14–0.25	RRHK 12
Countdown	CD-3	loop knot	0	-	0.14–0.25	RRHK 12
Countdown	CD-5	loop knot	0	-	0.16–0.28	RRHK 10
Countdown	CD-7	loop knot	0–1	1	0.18–0.30	RHK 7
Countdown	CD-9	loop knot	1–2	1	0.25–0.35	RHK 5
Countdown	CD-11	loop knot	1–2	1–2	0.28–0.40	RHK 3
Countdown Magnum	CDMAG-7	uni knot	1–2	2	0.30–0.40	RSHK 3
Countdown Magnum	CDMAG-9	uni knot	2–3	2–3	0.30–0.45	RSHK 2
Countdown Magnum	CDMAG-11	uni knot	2–3	2–3	0.33–0.50	RSHK 1
Countdown Magnum	CDMAG-14	uni knot	2–3	2–3	0.35–0.60	RSHK 2/0
Countdown Magnum	CDMAG-18	uni knot	4–5	3–4	0.35–1.00	RSHK 4/0
Countdown Magnum	CDMAG-22	uni knot	4–6	3–4	0.35–1.00	
Countdown Magnum	CDMAG-26	uni knot	5–6	3–4	0.35–1.00	
Countdown Super Shad Rap	CDSR-14	loop knot	2–4	2–3	0.30–0.60	RSHK 2/0
DD Husky Jerk	DHJ-10	uni knot	1–2	1	0.25–0.35	RHK 3
DD Husky Jerk	DHJ-12	uni knot	2–3	2	0.30–0.40	RRHK 5
'Dives To'	DT-04	uni knot	0	-	0.14–0.25	RRHK 6
'Dives-To'	DT-06	uni knot	0–1	1	0.16–0.25	RRHK 5/6
'Dives-To'	DT-10	uni knot	1	1	0.18–0.30	RRHK 5
'Dives-To'	DT-16	uni knot	1–2	1	0.20–0.35	RRHK 3
Floating Magnum	FMAG-7	loop knot	1–2	2	0.28–0.35	RSHK 3
Floating Magnum	FMAG-9	loop knot	1–2	2	0.30–0.40	RSHK 2
Floating Magnum	FMAG-11	loop knot	2–3	2–3	0.30–0.42	RSHK 1
Floating Magnum	FMAG14	loop knot	2–3	2–3	0.33–0.45	RSHK 2/0
Floating Magnum	FMAG18	loop knot	2–3	2–3	0.35–0.60	RSHK 4/0
Glass Fat Rap	GFR-5	uni knot	0–1	1	0.22–0.33	RRHK 5
Glass Fat Rap	GFR-7	uni knot	1–2	1	0.25–0.35	RHK 3
Glass Shad Rap	GSR-04	uni knot	0	-	0.16–0.28	RHK 6
Glass Shad Rap	GSR-05	uni knot	0–1	-	0.18–0.30	RHK 5
Glass Shad Rap	GSR-07	uni knot	1–2	1	0.20–0.33	RHK 3
Husky Jerk	HJ-6	uni knot	0	-	0.16–0.25	RRHK 10
Husky Jerk	HJ-8	uni knot	0–1	1	0.20–0.30	RRHK 6
Husky Jerk	HJ-10	uni knot	1	1–2	0.22–0.33	RRHK 5
Husky Jerk	HJ-12	uni knot	1–2	1–2	0.25–0.35	RRHK 5
Husky Jerk	HJ-14	uni knot	2–3	2	0.30–0.40	RHK 5
Jointed	J-5	loop knot	0	-	0.16–0.25	RRHK 10
Jointed	J-7	loop knot	0–1	-	0.16–0.28	RHK 6
Jointed	J-9	loop knot	1–2	1	0.18–0.30	RHK 5
Jointed	J-11	loop knot	1–2	1–2	0.20–0.35	RHK 3
Jointed	J-13	loop knot	2–3	2	0.30–0.40	RHK 2
Jointed Shad Rap	JSR-4	uni knot	0	-	0.16–0.28	RRHK 10
Jointed Shad Rap	JSR-5	uni knot	0–1	1	0.18–0.30	RHK 7

Lure Family	Lure	Knot	Snap size	Leader size	Line diameter (mm)	Replacement hook Set
Jointed Shad Rap	JSR-7	uni knot	1–2	1	0.20–0.33	RHK 5
LC Long Cast Minnow	LC-08	uni knot	0–1	-	0.18–0.30	RRHK 6
LC Long Cast Minnow	LC-10	uni knot	1–2	1	0.20–0.30	RRHK 5
LC Long Cast Minnow	LC-12	uni knot	2–3	2	0.22–0.33	RHK 2
Mini Fat Rap	MFR-3	loop knot	0	-	0.14–0.20	RRHK 12
Original	F-3	loop knot	0	-	0.14–0.20	RRHK 12
Original	F-5	loop knot	0	-	0.14–0.25	RRHK 10
Original	F-7	loop knot	0–1	1	0.16–0.25	RHK 7
Original	F-9	loop knot	0–1	1	0.18–0.30	RHK 7
Original	F-11	loop knot	1–2	1–2	0.20–0.33	RHK 6
Original	F-13	loop knot	1–2	1–2	0.25–0.33	RHK 5
Original	F-18	loop knot	1–3	2	0.30–0.40	RHK 2
Rattlin' Rapala	RNR-5	uni knot	0–1	1	0.20–0.30	RHK 5
Rattlin' Rapala	RNR-7	uni knot	1–2	1	0.20–0.33	RHK 3
Rattlin' Rapala	RNR-8	uni knot	1–2	1–2	0.25–0.40	RHK 3
Shad Rap Deep Runner	SR-5	uni knot	0	-	0.18–0.30	RHK 6
Shad Rap Deep Runner	SR-7	uni knot	0–1	1	0.20–0.33	RHK 5
Shad Rap Deep Runner	SR-8	uni knot	1–2	1–2	0.25–0.35	RHK 3
Shad Rap Deep Runner	SR-9	uni knot	1–2	2–3	0.30–0.40	RHK 3
Shallow Shad Rap	SSR-5	loop knot	0	-	0.18–0.30	RHK 6
Shallow Shad Rap	SSR-7	loop knot	0–1	1	0.20–0.33	RHK 5
Shallow Shad Rap	SSR-8	loop knot	1–2	2	0.25–0.35	RHK 3
Shallow Shad Rap	SSR-9	loop knot	1–2	2–3	0.30–0.40	RHK 3
Skitter Pop	SP-5	uni knot	0–1	-	0.22–0.30	RRHK 5
Skitter Pop	SP-7	uni knot	1–2	-	0.25–0.33	RRHK 5
Skitter Pop	SP-9	uni knot	2–3	1	0.30–0.40	RHK 3
Skitter Pop	SSP-12	uni knot	3–4	2	0.35–0.50	RSHK 1
Skitter Prop	SPR-07	uni knot	1–2	-	0.30–0.40	RHK 3
Skitter Walk	SW-8	uni knot	1–2	1–2	0.28–0.35	RHK 3
Skitter Walk	SSW-11	uni knot	2–3	2–3	0.30–0.45	RSHK 2
Sliver	SL-13	uni knot	2–3	2	0.30–0.50	RSHK 2
Sliver	SL-20	uni knot	2–4	2–3	0.35–0.60	RSHK 2/0
Super Shad Rap	SSR-14	loop knot	2–4	2–3	0.30–0.60	RSHK 2/0
Tail Dancer	TD-5	uni knot	0–1	-	0.22–0.30	RHK 7
Tail Dancer	TD-7	uni knot	1–2	1	0.25–0.33	RHK 5
Tail Dancer	TD-9	uni knot	2–3	1–2	0.30–0.40	RHK 3
Tail Dancer	TDD-11	uni knot	2–3	2–3	0.30–0.42	RHK 3
Team Esko	TE-7	loop knot	0–1	1	0.18–0.30	RRHK 6
X-Rap	XR-10	uni knot	1–2	1–2	0.20–0.30	RHK 5
X-Rap	SXR-10	uni knot	1–2	1–2	0.20–0.30	RSHK 3

Appendix 4A: Colour availablity chart – freshwater.

KEY: **GREEN: USA ONLY** **ORANGE: REST OF WORLD** **RED: WORLDWIDE**

The number in the box represents the sizes of lure in that colour

Code	Description	F / HF Floating	CD / HCD Countdown	DT Dives To	TE Team Esko	HJ / HHJ Husky Jerk	DHJ Down Deep Husky Jerk	J Jointed	MFR / FR Mini Fat Rap Fat Rap	GFR Glass Fat Rap	SSR Shallow Shad Rap	SR Deep Shad Rap	SRRS Shad Rap RS
B	Blue / Silver	3,5,7,9, 11,13,18	3,5,7,9,11					5,7,9, 11,13			5,7,8,9	5,7,8,9	
BB	Baby Bass			4,6,10,16		6,8,10,12,14	10,12				5,7,8,9	5,7,8,9	
BCW	Brown Crawdad								1,3,5				
BF	Blue Foil				7								
BFL	Blue Flash												
BG	Bluegill			4,6,10,16							5,7,8,9	5,7,8,9	
BLM	Bleeding Minnow	3,5,7,9, 11,13,18	3,5,7,9,11										
BLT	Bleeding Tiger												
BMD	Black Muddler	3,5,7,9, 11,13,18	1,3,5,7,9,11										
BOB	Baby Bass Orange Belly												
BRT	Brown Tiger				7								
BSD	Blue Shad			4,6,10,16									
BSH	Blue Shiner										5,7,9	5,7,9	
BSM	Blue Spotted Minnow	3,5,7,9, 11,13,18	3,5,7,9,11										
BTR	Brook Trout	3,5,7,9, 11,13,18	1,3,5,7,9,11										
CHB	Chrome Blue												
CHS	Chartreuse Shiner												
CLF	Clown Flash												
CLN	Clown	3,5,7,9, 11,13,18				6,8,10,12,14	10,12					5,7,8,9	
CW	Crawdad								1,3,5		5,7,8,9	5,7,8,9	4,5,7
DCW	Dark Brown Crawdad			4,6,10,16									
ESH	Emerald Shiner												
F	Frog												
FCW	Fire Crawdad								1,3,5				
FLP	Flash Perch												
FMN	Fire Minnow	3,5,7,9, 11,13,18	1,3,5,7,9,11										
FP	Fire Perch										5,7,9	5,7,9	
FSD	Fire Shad												
FSRD	Foil Sardine												
FT	Firetiger	3,5,7,9, 11,13,18	3,5,7,9,11	4,6,10,16		6,8,10,12,14	10,12	5,7,9, 11,13	1,3,5		5,7,8,9	5,7,8,9	4,5,7
FTB	Firetiger Black Head												
G	Gold / Black	3,5,7,9, 11,13,18	3,5,7,9,11			6,8,10,12,14	10,12	5,7,9 11,13				5,7,8,9	
GB	Glow Blue												
GBCW	Glass Brown Crawdad									5,7			
GBK	Glass Black					6,8,10,12,14	10,12			5,7			
GBM	Glass Blue Minnow					6,8,10,12,14	10,12						
GBSD	Glass Blue Shad									5,7			
GC	Gold Chub												

KEY: GREEN: USA ONLY   ORANGE: REST OF WORLD   RED: WORLDWIDE
The number in the box represents the sizes of lure in that colour

GSR Glass Shad Rap	JSR Jointed Shad Rap	RNR / HRNR Rattlin' Rapala	SP Skitter Pop	SPR Skitter Prop	TD Tail Dancer	TDD Deep Tail Dancer	LC Long Cast Minnow	SW Skitter Walk	WSR Jigging Rap	W Jigging Rap	XR X-Rap	Description	Code
					5,7,9		8,10	5				Blue / Silver	B
	4,5,7	4,5,7,8						8				Baby Bass	BB
	4,5,7											Brown Crawdad	BCW
						11						Blue Foil	BF
						11						Blue Flash	BFL
		4,5,7,8						8				Bluegill	BG
												Bleeding Minnow	BLM
						11						Bleeding Tiger	BLT
												Black Muddler	BMD
		4,5,7,8										Baby Bass Orange Belly	BOB
					5,7,9	11						Brown Tiger	BRT
	4,5,7	4,5,7,8										Blue Shad	BSD
												Blue Shiner	BSH
												Blue Spotted Minnow	BSM
												Brook Trout	BTR
		4,5,7,8								2,3,5,7,9		Chrome Blue	CHB
		4,5,7,8										Chartreuse Shiner	CHS
						11						Clown Flash	CLF
										2,3,5,7,9	10	Clown	CLN
	4,5,7											Crawdad	CW
												Dark Brown Crawdad	DCW
					5,7,9							Emerald Shiner	ESH
			5,7,9	7				8				Frog	F
	4,5,7											Fire Crawdad	FCW
						11						Flash Perch	FLP
												Fire Minnow	FMN
												Fire Perch	FP
								8				Fire Shad	FSD
							8,10					Foil Sardine	FSRD
	4,5,7	4,5,7,8	5,7,9	7	5,7,9		8,10					Firetiger	FT
		4,5,7,8										Firetiger Black Head	FTB
										2,3,5,7,9	10	Gold / Black	G
								5				Glow Blue	GB
4,5,7												Glass Brown Crawdad	GBCW
4,5,7												Glass Black	GBK
												Glass Blue Minnow	GBM
4,5,7												Glass Blue Shad	GBSD
							8,10					Gold Chub	GC

KEY: GREEN: USA ONLY ORANGE: REST OF WORLD RED: WORLDWIDE
The number in the box represents the sizes of lure in that colour

Code	Description	F/HF Floating	CD/HCD Countdown	DT Dives To	TE Team Esko	HJ/HHJ Husky Jerk	DHJ Down Deep Husky Jerk	J Jointed	MFR/FR Mini Fat Rap Fat Rap	GFR Glass Fat Rap	SSR Shallow Shad Rap	SR Deep Shad Rap	SRRS Shad Rap RS
GCL	Glass Clown					6,8,10,12,14	10,12						
GCLN	Glow Clown												
GCM	Glass Copper Minnow					6,8,10,12,14	10,12						
GCS	Glass Citrus Shad										5,7		
GF	Gold Fish										5,7,9	5,7,9	
GFP	Glass Fire Perch					6,8,10,12,14	10,12						
GFR	Gold Flourescent Red	3,5,7,9 11,13,18	1,3,5,7,9,11	4,6,10,16				5,7,9 11,13					
GFT	Glow Fire Tiger												
GG	Glow Green												
GGH	Glass Ghost												
GGR	Glass Gold Red												
GL	Glow												
GMD	Glass Muddler					6,8,10,12,14	10,12						
GMN	Glass Minnow					6,8,10,12,14	10,12						
GOMD	Gold Muddler	3,5,7,9	3,5,7,9,11										
GP	Glass Perch					6,8,10,12,14	10,12				5,7		
GPCH	Glass Purple Chartreuse										5,7		
GPCL	Glass Pink Clown					6,8,10.12.14	10,12						
GPS	Glass Purple Shad										5,7		
GPP	Glass Purple Perch					6,8,10,12,14	10,12						
GPSF	Glass Purple Sunfire					6,8,10,12,14	10,12						
GPT	Green Parrot				7								
GR	Glow Red												
GRB	Gold Rainbow Foil				7								
GRH	Glass Red Head					6,8,10,12,14	10,12						
GSD	Glass Shad										5,7		
GTR	Glow Tiger												
GTR	Green Tiger			4,6,10,16									
HB	Holographic Blue												
HBM	Hot Blue Minnow												
HBSD	Holographic Blue Shad												
HC	Hot Chub												
HESD	Holographic Emerald Shad												
HFL	Hot Flash												
HH	Hot Head												
HM	Hot Mustard			4,6,10,16									
HMMD	Hot Mustard Muddler		1,3,5,7,9,11										
HP	Hot Pink												
HS	Hot Steel	3,5,7,9 11,13,18	1,3,5,7,9,11								5,7,8,9	5,7,8,9	
HSD	Holographic Shad												
HT	Hot Tiger				7			5,7,9 11,13					
HTP	Hot Tiger Perch												
LF	Lime Frog												
MD	Muddler	3,5,7,9	1,3,5,7					5,7,9 11,13					
MN	Minnow	3,5,7,9	1,3,5,7										

GSR Glass Shad Rap	JSR Jointed Shad Rap	RNR / HRNR Rattlin' Rapala	SP Skitter Pop	SPR Skitter Prop	TD Tail Dancer	TDD Deep Tail Dancer	LC Long Cast Minnow	SW Skitter Walk	WSR Jigging Rap	W Jigging Rap	XR X-Rap	Description	Code
								8,10				Glass Clown	GCL
									5			Glow Clown	GCLN
												Glass Copper Minnow	GCM
4,5,7												Glass Citrus Shad	GCS
												Gold Fish	GF
4,5,7												Glass Fire Perch	GFP
					5,7,9		8,10			2,3,5,7,9		Gold Flourescent Red	GFR
									5			Glow Fire Tiger	GFT
									5			Glow Green	GG
											10	Glass Ghost	GGH
4,5,7												Glass Gold Red	GGR
									5	2,3,5,7,9		Glow	GL
												Glass Muddler	GMD
												Glass Minnow	GMN
												Gold Muddler	GOMD
4,5,7												Glass Perch	GP
												Glass Purple Chartreuse	GPCH
												Glass Pink Clown	GPCL
4,5,7												Glass Purple Shad	GPS
												Glass Purple Perch	GPP
4,5,7												Glass Purple Sunfire	GPSF
					5,7,9	11						Green Parrot	GPT
									5			Glow Red	GR
						11						Gold Rainbow Foil	GRB
												Glass Red Head	GRH
4,5,7												Glass Shad	GSD
										2,3,5,7,9		Glow Tiger	GTR
												Green Tiger	GTR
								8				Holographic Blue	HB
							8,10					Hot Blue Minnow	HBM
		4,5,7										Holographic Blue Shad	HBSD
					5,7,9		8,10					Hot Chub	HC
		4,5,7										Holographic Emerald Shad	HESD
						11						Hot Flash	HFL
											10	Hot Head	HH
												Hot Mustard	HM
												Hot Mustard Muddler	HMMD
											10	Hot Pink	HP
								8			10	Hot Steel	HS
		4,5,7										Holographic Shad	HSD
						11						Hot Tiger	HT
	4,5,7											Hot Tiger Perch	HTP
			5,7,9	7								Lime Frog	LF
												Muddler	MD
												Minnow	MN

KEY: GREEN: USA ONLY ORANGE: REST OF WORLD RED: WORLDWIDE

The number in the box represents the sizes of lure in that colour

Code	Description	F/HF Floating	CD/HCD Countdown	DT Dives To	TE Team Esko	HJ/HHJ Husky Jerk	DHJ Down Deep Husky Jerk	J Jointed	MFR/FR Mini Fat Rap Fat Rap	GFR Glass Fat Rap	SSR Shallow Shad Rap	SR Deep Shad Rap	SRRS Shad Rap RS
NP	Nordic Perch				7								
OG	Olive Green												
OGMD	Olive Green Muddler	3,5,7,9	1,3,5,7,9,11										
P	Perch	3,5,7,9 11,13,18	3,5,7,9,11	4,6,10,16				5,7,9 11,13	1,3,5		5,7,8,9	5,7,8,9	4,5,7
PCLF	Purple Clown Flash												
PD	Purpledescent	3,5,7,9 11,13,18	1,3,5,7,9,11								5,7,8,9	5,7,8,9	
PG	Purple Gold												
PGH	Purple Ghost												
PK	Pike							9,11,13					
PRL	Pearl												
PRT	Parrot			4,6,10,16									
RC	Red Tail Chub												
RCW	Red Crawdad			4,6,10,16					1,3,5				
RDT	Red Tiger				7								
RFCW	Redfire Crawdad												
RFSH	Redfin Shiner										5,7,9	5,7,9	
RFSM	Redfin Spotted Minnow	3,5,7,9 11,13,18	3,5,7,9,11										
RT	Rainbow Trout	3,5,7,9 11,13,18	1,3,5,7,9,11					5,7,9 11,13					
RTF	Rainbow Trout												
S	Silver / Black	3,5,7,9 11,13,18	1,3,5,7,9,11	4,6,10,16		6,8,10,12,14	10,12	5,7,9 11,13	1,3,5		5,7,8,9	5,7,8,9	4,5,7
SB	Silver / Blue					6,8,10,12,14	10,12						4,5,7
SBB	Silver Baby Bass												
SD	Shad			4,6,10,16							5,7,8,9	5,7,8,9	4,5,7
SDT	Translucent Shad												
SF	Silver Foil				7								
SFC	Silver Flourescent Chartreuse	3,5,7,9 11,13,18	3,5,7,9,11					5,7,9 11,13			5,7,8,9	5,7,8,9	
SFL	Silver Flash												
SG	Silver / Gold												4,5,7
SH	Shiner	3,5,7,9 11,13,18											
SSD	Silver Shad												
SSH	Silver Shiner										5,7,9	5,7,9	
SSM	Silver Spotted Minnow		3,5,7,9,11										
STS	Silver Tennessee Shad												
TR	Brown Trout	3,5,7,9, 11,13,18	1,3,5,7,9,11					5,7,9 11,13					
TSD	Tenessee Shad					6,8,10,12,14	10,12						
V	Vampire	3,5,7,9 11,13,18	3,5,7,9,11										
W	Walleye										5,7,8,9	5,7,8,9	

KEY: **GREEN: USA ONLY** **ORANGE: REST OF WORLD** **RED: WORLDWIDE**
The number in the box represents the sizes of lure in that colour

GSR Glass Shad Rap	JSR Jointed Shad Rap	RNR / HRNR Rattlin' Rapala	SP Skitter Pop	SPR Skitter Prop	TD Tail Dancer	TDD Deep Tail Dancer	LC Long Cast Minnow	SW Skitter Walk	WSR Jigging Rap	W Jigging Rap	XR X-Rap	Description	Code
						11						Nordic Perch	NP
											10	Olive Green	OG
												Olive Green Muddler	OGMD
	4,5,7				5,7,9		8,10	5		2,3,5,7,9	10	Perch	P
						11						Purple Clown Flash	PCLF
						11						Purpledescent	PD
											10	Purple Gold	PG
											10	Purple Ghost	PGH
												Pike	PK
									5			Pearl	PRL
										2,3,5,7,9,11		Parrot	PRT
					5,7,9							Red Tail Chub	RC
	4,5,7	4,5,7,8										Red Crawdad	RCW
						11						Red Tiger	RDT
		4,5,7,8										Redfire Crawdad	RFCW
												Redfin Shiner	RFSH
												Redfin Spotted Minnow	RFSM
					5,7,9		8,10			2,3,5,7,9		Rainbow Trout	RT
						11						Rainbow Trout	RTF
		4,5,7,8	5,7,9	7	5,7,9		8,10	5		2,3,5,7,9	10	Silver / Black	S
		4,5,7,8	5,7,9	7							10	Silver / Blue	SB
	4,5,7											Silver Baby Bass	SBB
	4,5,7	4,5,7,8	5,7,9	7	5,7,9		8,10		5			Shad	SD
								8				Translucent Shad	SDT
						11						Silver Foil	SF
										2,3,5,7,9		Silver Flourescent Chartreuse	SFC
						11						Silver Flash	SFL
		4,5,7,8										Silver / Gold	SG
												Shiner	SH
	4,5,7											Silver Shad	SSD
												Silver Shiner	SSH
												Silver Spotted Minnow	SSM
		4,5,7,8										Silver Tennessee Shad	STS
							8,10					Brown Trout	TR
												Tenessee Shad	TSD
												Vampire	V
	4,5,7											Walleye	W

207

Appendix 4B: **Colour availablity chart – saltwater**

KEY: **GREEN: USA ONLY** ORANGE: REST OF WORLD **RED: WORLDWIDE**
The number in the box represents the sizes of lure in that colour

Code	Description	CDSR Countdown Super Shad Rap	SSR Super Shad Rap	LC Long Cast Minnow	SL Sliver	SSP Saltwater Skitter Pop	SSW Skitter Walk	F-MAG Floating Magnum	CD-Mag Countdown Magnum	SXR Saltwater X-Rap
AYU	Ayu									10
B	Blue / Silver								7,9,11,14,18	
BG	Bluegill		14							
BH	Blue Herring			12						
BKCH	Black Chartreuse Head						11			
BMU	Blue Mullet					9,12	11			
BN	Bone						11			
BSD	Blue Shad	14								
BSH	Blue Shiner		14					9,11,14,18	7,9,11,14,18	
BSRD	Blue Sardine								7,9,11,14,18	10
BTO	Bonito								7,9,11,14,18	
CG	Pearl Fluorescent Orange			12		9,12			7,9,11,14,18,22,26	
CLN	Clown									10
CM	Chartreuse Mackerel					9,12				
D	Dorado							11,14,18	11,14,18	
DZ	Donzella								7,9,11,14,18	
FCW	Fire Charetreuse					12				
FSRD	Foil Sardine			12						
FT	Firetiger		14	12				9,11,14,18	7,9,11,14,18,22,26	
G	Gold / Black									10
GF	Gold Fish		14					9,11,14,18		
GFP	Glass Fire Perch									
GFR	Gold Flourescent Red			12	13,20			11,14,18	11,14,18,22,26	
GGH	Glass Ghost									10
GM	Gold Green Mackerel					9,12		11,14,18	7,9,11,14,18,22,26	
GMU	Gold Mullet			12			11			
GR	Gold / Green				13,20					
GRMU	Green Mullet						11			
GSH	Gold Shiner		14							
HB	Holographic Blue						11			
HBM	Hot Blue Minnow			12						
HBNC	Holographic Bone Chartreuse						11			
HCH	Hot Chartreuse			12			11			
HH	Hot Head									10
HOG	Holographic Orange Gold						11			
HP	Hot Pink			12		12	11			

Appendix 4B: Colour availability chart – saltwater

KEY: GREEN: USA ONLY ORANGE: REST OF WORLD RED: WORLDWIDE
The number in the box represents the sizes of lure in that colour

Code	Description	CDSR Countdown Super Shad Rap	SSR Super Shad Rap	LC Long Cast Minnow	SL Sliver	SSP Saltwater Skitter Pop	SSW Skitter Walk	F-MAG Floating Magnum	CD-Mag Countdown Magnum	SXR Saltwater X-Rap
HS	Hot Steel						11			10
HT	Hot Tiger		14					9,11,14,18		
HTP	Hot Tiger Perch	14								
MB	Moss Bunker			12						
MU	Mullet		14	12		9,12		11,14,18	11,14,18	
NF	Needlefish				13,20					
NP	Nordic Perch	14								
OG	Olive Green									10
P	Perch		14	12				9,11,14,18		
PGH	Purple Ghost									10
PK	Pike							9,11,14,18	7,9,11,14,18	
PM	Purple Mackerel								11,14,18,22,26	
PSRD	Pink Sardine							9,11,14,18	7,9,11,14,18	
RD	Red Dorado								7,9,11,14,18	
RF	Red Fish						11			
RFSH	Redfin Shiner		14					9,11,14,18	7,9,11,14,18	
RH	Red Head		14	12	13,20	9,12	11	9,11,14,18	7,9,11,14,18,22,26	
RT	Rainbow Trout	14								
S	Silver / Black				13,20			11,14,18	7,9,11,14,18,22,26	10
SB	Silver / Blue									10
SBM	Silver Blue Mackerel									10
SD	Shad		14							
SGM	Silver Green Mackerel									10
SH	Shiner		14					9,11,14,18	7,9,11,14,18	
SM	Silver Blue Mackerel					9,12		9,11,14,18	7,9,11,14,18,22,26	
SMU	Silver Mullet						11			
SPM	Spotted Minnow			12						10
SRD	Sardine							11,14,18	7,9,11,14,18	
SSD	Silver Shad	14								
ST	Speckled Trout						11			
TR	Brown Trout	14								
W	Walleye		14							
YT	Yellow Tiger		14					9,11,14,18		

209

Appendix 5: Rapala VMC Corporation group structure

DISTRIBUTION

USA	Finland	Spain	Russia
Canada	Sweden	Switzerland	Ukraine
Japan	Denmark	Portugal	Lithuania
Brasil	Norway	Estonia	Latvia
Malaysia	France	Poland	Czech Republic

OWN DISTRIBUTION

GROUP BRANDS

Rapala® · STORM · VMC® · BLUE FOX®

MANUFACTURING AND R&D

SUPPLY

PRODUCT

Hardbaits
Rapala
Storm

Softbaits
Storm

Hardbaits
Rapala
Storm

Spinners
Blue Fox

Other lures
Blue Fox

SOURCE

Rapala
Finland
Ireland
Estonia

Willtech
Hong Kong
China

VMC France
Willtech
China

OWN R&D AND MANUFACTURING OR SOURCING

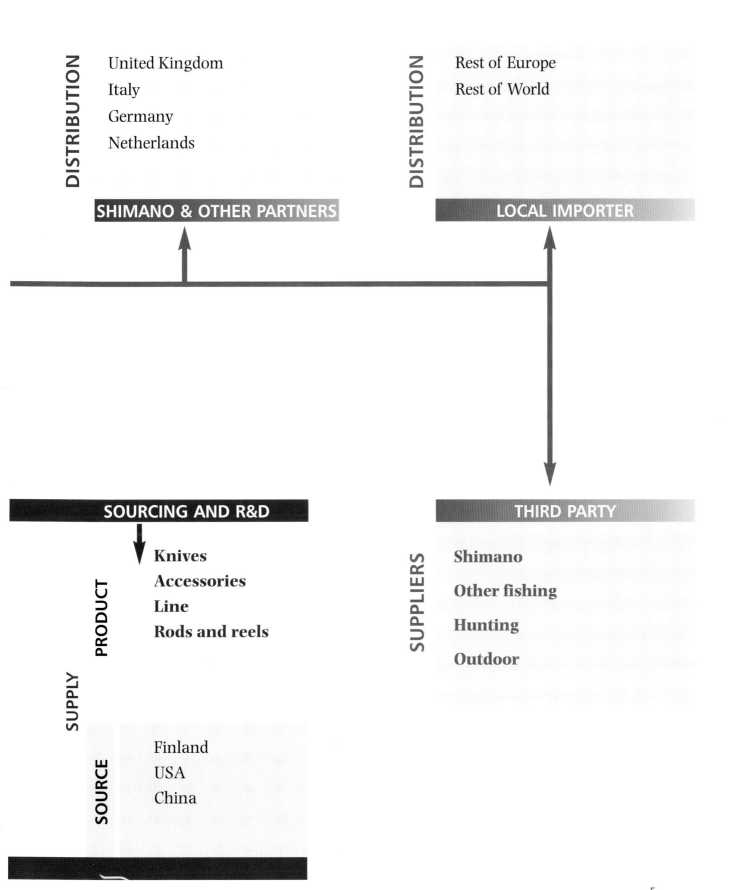

DISTRIBUTION

United Kingdom
Italy
Germany
Netherlands

DISTRIBUTION

Rest of Europe
Rest of World

SHIMANO & OTHER PARTNERS

LOCAL IMPORTER

SOURCING AND R&D

PRODUCT

Knives
Accessories
Line
Rods and reels

SUPPLY

SOURCE

Finland
USA
China

THIRD PARTY

SUPPLIERS

Shimano

Other fishing

Hunting

Outdoor

Index

Page numbers in bold refer to illustrations

'advanced super lines' 186–7
American Fishing Tackle Manufacturers Association
    121, 123, 148
Asikkala village 9, 15, **20,** 31, 32, 50, 70, 89, 124

Baronowski, Mike 74
big-game/blue water sea fishing 189–90
Blue Fox products 123, 125, 154–5, 157, 180, 189
Brown, Bruce 177
Brunou, Harald 72, 76, 96, **97–9,** 126
Brunou, Thorsten **75**

Calengor, Jerry 133
Cannon, Roger **102**, 103, 107, 126, 128, 131
Carmichael Lynch 121, 123, 128, 129, 135
Carrera, Bill 128
China, manufacturing in 178, 179, 182, 190
countdown fishing 92, 97, 185
Cronin, Ramon 92, 93
Cullerton Sr., Bill 74

Dahlberg, Larry 24
deep-diving lures
    'Dives To' 136, 137, 183–4, **183**, 185, 191, 198,
        200, 202, 204, 206
    Glass Shad Rap 162, 163, 184, 199, 200, 203,
        205, 207

Eerikintytär, Maria 8, 9, 10, **15**, 15, 18
Elmgren, Hans O. 70
Emby, Ab 79, **102**, 107
Emby, Marge 79, **102**, 107
Engel, Marty 79
Rapala, Elma (née Leppänen) 18, **18**, 19, **19**, 20, 25–6,
    28, 33, 49, 50, 51, 52, 56–7, 76, 94, 119
Estonia, manufacturing in 174, 175, 176

filleting knives 95–6, **96,** 100, 103, 121, 156, 176, 184,
    188, 190
Finland 8, 9, **10**, 11, 12, 13, 15, 29, 69
    agriculture/forestry **11–12**, **14**, 15, 19
    army 13, 31, 32, 33, 34, 36, 52, **52**, 53
    civil unrest 8, 10, 11–12, 13–14, 15
    early history 7–9
    and First World War 10, 11, 15
    fishing/hunting in 16–17, 52

independence (gain/loss) 7, 8, 9, 10, 13, 14
    neutrality 31, 33
    and Russia/Soviet Union 7–8, 9, 10, 11–12, 13,
        30–3, 34, 35
    and Second World War 30–7, **34**
fishing nets/traps 17, 25, 27, 186
fishing rods 182, 189, 191
fishing tackle accessories 177–8
Flipper Boats Oy 134, 147
floating lures 154
    Deep Tail Dancer 142, 143, 203, 205, 207
    Fat Rap 58, 59, 105, 122, **123**, 123, 130, 152, 153,
        191, 198, 202, 204, 206
    Floating Magnum 44, 45, 101, 126–7, 174, 199,
        200, 208, 209
    Glass Fat Rap 166, 167, 191, 198, 200, 202,
        204, 206
    Jointed 46, 47, 107, 119, 120, 123, 125, 130, 178,
        198, 200, 202, 204, 206
    Long Cast Minnow 138, 139, 181, **184**, 184, 199,
        201, 203, 205, 207, 208, 209
    Original 22, 23, 48, 89, 91, 92, 93, 97, 103, 105,
        119, **121**, 122, 124, 129, 157, 175, 178, 198, 201,
        202, 204, 206
    Shad Rap Deep Runner 62, 63, 130, 132, 152, 201,
        202, 204, 206
    Shallow Shad Rap 64, 65, 130, 132, 152, 199, 201,
        202, 204, 206
    Super Shad Rap 48, 82, 83, **153**, 154, 179, 185,
        199, 201, 208, 209
    Tail Dancer 114, 115, 172, 178, 182, 185, 199, 201,
        203, 205, 207
    Team Esko 86, 87, 175, 198, 201, 202, 204, 206
Fritts, David 183

Glad-Staf, Sirpa 107
Gowans, Ally 146
Greer, Steve **155**, 156
Grey, Zane 173
Guigo, Constant 68, 189
Guigo Marine 189
Guigo, Philippe 189, 190
Gustafsson, Kosti 72
Heddon, Jim 26
Hunt, Rex 172

Rapala/Normark distribution companies worldwide

BRAZIL
RAPALA VMC DO BRASIL LTDA.
Rua Dona Ana Pimentel No. 218
Agua Branca - Sao Paulo
BRAZIL

CEP 05002-040

CANADA
NORMARK INC.
1350 Phillip Murray Avenue
OSHAWA Ontario L1J 6Z9
CANADA

CZECH REPUBLIC
Normark s.r.o.
K.Konrada 6
190 00 Praha 9
CZECH REPUBLIC

DENMARK
NORMARK DENMARK A/S
Endelavevej 1
DK-8900 Randers
DENMARK

ESTONIA
NORMARK EESTI OÜ
Instituudi tee 2
EE-76 902 Harku
ESTONIA

FINLAND
NORMARK SUOMI OY
Box 17
FIN-41801 Korpilahti
FINLAND

FRANCE
RAGOT NORMARK FRANCE S.A.S.
B.P. 482
F-22 604 Loudeac Cédex
FRANCE

JAPAN
RAPALA JAPAN LTD.
1011 Sakusai-Cho
Kishiwada-shi
Osaka 596-0826
JAPAN

LATVIA
Normark Latvia SIA
Mukusalas str. 72b
Riga LV1004
LATVIA

LITHUANIA
NORMARK UAB LITHUANIA
Elektrenu 1E
LT-3031 Kaunas
LITHUANIA

MALAYSIA
RAPALA VMC (Asia Pacific)
Sdn Bhd
45, PSN Bayan Indah
Taman Bayan Bay, Bayan Lepas
11900 Penang
MALAYSIA

NORWAY
ELBE NORMARK A/S
Grini Naeringspark 3,
P.O.Box 113
NO-1332 Österås
NORWAY

POLAND
NORMARK POLSKA SP. Z.O.O.
Ul. Dluga 30
05 092 Lomianki
POLAND

PORTUGAL
NORMARK PORTUGAL LDA
Rua Escultor Barata Feyo, 70
2750-020 Aldeia de Juso
Cascais
PORTUGAL

RUSSIA
NORMARK RUSSIA
5/10 Gostinichnaya Street,
127106 Moscow
RUSSIA

SPAIN
NORMARK SPAIN S.A.
Camino Monte de Valdeoliva,
14 Nave L1
Poligono Industrial Norte el Raso
28750 San Agustin de Guadalix
Madrid
SPAIN

SWEDEN
NORMARK SCANDINAVIA AB
Hamnplan 11
S-753 19 Uppsala
SWEDEN

SWITZERLAND
RAPALA-FISHCO AG
Werkstrasse 43
CH-8630 Rüti/zh
SWITZERLAND

UKRAINE
VMC WATERQUEEN UKRAINA
68 Rue Sosury
02 090 Kiev
UKRAINA

USA
NORMARK CORPORATION
10395 Yellow Circle Drive
Minnetonka, MN 55343
USA